Critical Studies of the Asia Pacific Series

Series Editor: **Mark Beeson**, Winthrop Professor of Political Science and International Studies at the University of Western Australia

Critical Studies of the Asia Pacific showcases new research and scholarship on what is arguably the most important region in the world in the twenty-first century. The rise of China and the continuing strategic importance of this dynamic economic area to the United States mean that the Asia Pacific will remain crucially important to policymakers and scholars alike. The unifying theme of the series is a desire to publish the best theoretically-informed, original research on the region. Titles in the series cover the politics, economics and security of the region, as well as focussing on its institutional processes, individual countries, issues and leaders.

Titles include:

Stephen Aris
EURASIAN REGIONALISM
The Shanghai Cooperation Organisation

Toby Carroll
DELUSIONS OF DEVELOPMENT
The World Bank and the Post-Washington Consensus in Southeast Asia

Aurel Croissant and Marco Bunte (*editors*)
THE CRISIS OF DEMOCRATIC GOVERNANCE IN SOUTHEAST ASIA

Shahar Hameiri
REGULATING STATEHOOD
State Building and the Transformation of the Global Order

Lee Jones
ASEAN, SOVEREIGNTY AND INTERVENTION IN SOUTHEAST ASIA

Hiro Katsumata
ASEAN'S COOPERATIVE SECURITY ENTERPRISE
Norms and Interests in a Regional Forum

Jikon Lai
FINANCIAL CRISIS AND INSTITUTIONAL CHANGE IN EAST ASIA

Erik Paul
OBSTACLES TO DEMOCRATIZATION IN SOUTHEAST ASIA
A Study of the Nation-State, Regional and Global Order

Joel Rathus
JAPAN, CHINA AND NETWORKED REGIONALISM IN EAST ASIA

Barry Wain
MALAYSIAN MAVERICK
Mahathir Mohamad in Turbulent Times

Mikael Weissmann
THE EAST ASIAN PEACE

Robert G. Wirsing and Ehsan Ahrari (*editors*)
FIXING FRACTURED NATIONS
The Challenge of Ethnic Separatism in the Asia-Pacific

Critical Studies of the Asia Pacific Series
Series Standing Order ISBN 978–0–230–22896–2 (Hardback) 978–0–230–22897–9 (Paperback)
(outside North America only)

You can receive future titles in this series as they are published by placing a standing order. Please contact your bookseller or, in case of difficulty, write to us at the address below with your name and address, the title of the series and one of the ISBNs quoted above.

Customer Services Department, Macmillan Distribution Ltd, Houndmills, Basingstoke, Hampshire RG21 6XS, England

---

Financial Crisis and Institutional Change in East Asia

Jikon Lai
Visiting Fellow at the School of Politics and International Relations, College of Arts and Social Sciences, The Australian National University

palgrave
macmillan

First published 2012 by
PALGRAVE MACMILLAN

Palgrave Macmillan in the UK is an imprint of Macmillan Publishers Limited, registered in England, company number 785998, of Houndmills, Basingstoke, Hampshire RG21 6XS.

Palgrave Macmillan in the US is a division of St Martin's Press LLC, 175 Fifth Avenue, New York, NY 10010.

Palgrave Macmillan is the global academic imprint of the above companies and has companies and representatives throughout the world.

ISBN: 978–0–230–36063–1

This book is printed on paper suitable for recycling and made from fully managed and sustained forest sources. Logging, pulping and manufacturing processes are expected to conform to the environmental regulations of the country of origin.

A catalogue record for this book is available from the British Library.

A catalog record for this book is available from the Library of Congress.

10 9 8 7 6 5 4 3 2 1
21 20 19 18 17 16 15 14 13 12

Printed and bound in Great Britain by
CPI Antony Rowe, Chippenham and Eastbourne

To Mark

Contents

Tables

Figures

Abbreviations and Acronyms

AFC	Asian Financial Crisis
AMC	asset management company
ASB	Amanah Saham Bumiputera (Malaysia)
ASN	Amanah Saham Nasional (Malaysia)
ATM	automated teller machine
BAFIA	Banking and Financial Institutions Act (Malaysia)
BBC	Bangkok Bank of Commerce
BEX	Bond Electronic Exchange (Thailand)
BIBF	Bangkok International Banking Facilities (Thailand)
BIS	Bank for International Settlements
BLR	base lending rate
BNM	Bank Negara Malaysia (Central Bank of Malaysia)
BOK	Bank of Korea
BOT	Bank of Thailand
CDRC	Corporate Debt Restructuring Committee (Malaysia)
CME	coordinated market economy
CMP	Capital market master plan (Malaysia)
DTC	deposit-taking cooperatives
EPF	Employees' Provident Fund (Malaysia)
FDI	foreign direct investment
FIBA	Financial Institutions Business Act (Thailand)
FIC	financial investment company (Korea)
FIDF	Financial Institutions Development Fund (Thailand)
FISCMA	Financial Investment Services and Capital Market Act
FRA	Financial Sector Restructuring Authority (Thailand)
FSC	Financial Supervisory Commission, later Financial Services Commission (Korea)
FSF	Financial Stability Forum
FSMP	Financial Sector Master Plan
FSS	Financial Supervisory Service (Korea)
GATS	General Agreement on Trade in Services
GDP	gross domestic product
GFC	global financial crisis (of 2007–9)
HCI	heavy and chemical industries
IBF	International Banking Facilities (Thailand)

ICT	information, communications and technology
IMF	International Monetary Fund
ISB	Insurance Supervisory Board (Korea)
ITC	investment trust company
KAMCO	Korean Asset Management Corporation
KDIC	Korea Deposit Insurance Corporation
KEB	Korea Exchange Bank
KIC	Korea Investment Corporation
KLSE	Kuala Lumpur Stock Exchange
KOSDAQ	Korean Securities Dealers Automated Quotations
KRW	Korean won
KRX	Korea Exchange
KSE	Korea Stock Exchange
LME	liberal market economy
MAI	Market for Alternative Investment (Thailand)
MGS	Malaysian Government Securities
MIFC	Malaysia International Islamic Financial Centre
MOF	Ministry of Finance
MOFE	Ministry of Finance and Economy (Korea)
MYR	Malaysian ringgit
NASDAQ	National Association of Securities Dealers Automated Quotations (United States)
NBFI	non-bank financial institution
NDP	National Development Policy (Malaysia)
NEAC	National Economic Action Council (Malaysia)
NEP	New Economic Policy (Malaysia)
NPL	non-performing loan
OBS	Office of Bank Supervision (Korea)
OECD	Organisation for Economic Co-operation and Development
PIBF	Provincial International Banking Facilities (Thailand)
SC	Securities Commission (Malaysia)
SEC	Securities and Exchange Commission (Thailand)
SET	Securities Exchange of Thailand
SFC	Securities and Futures Commission (Korea)
SFI	state-owned financial institutions
SiME	State-influenced Market Economy
SME	small- and medium- enterprises
SSB	Securities Supervisory Board (Korea)
TAMC	Thai Asset Management Company
THB	Thai baht
TTRS	Two-tier Regulatory System (Malaysia)

UK	United Kingdom
UNCTAD	United Nations Conference on Trade and Development
US	United States of America
USD	US dollars
VoC	Varieties of Capitalism
WTO	World Trade Organization

Acknowledgements

This book would not have materialised without the encouragement and support of John Ravenhill in his many roles as supervisor, mentor and friend. I have drawn both moral and intellectual strength from our many conversations, and I look forward to many more.

Funding from a number of sources contributed to various aspects of the research that led to this book. I would like to acknowledge the generosity of the Australian Endeavour scholarship programme, the Institute of Humane Studies and the Australian National University.

During the course of my research for this book, I made several visits to Korea, Malaysia, Singapore and Thailand. I would like to acknowledge the kind hospitality extended to me by the following institutions during these trips: in Korea, the Graduate School of International Studies in Yonsei University and the Korea Development Institute (KDI); in Malaysia, the Malaysian Institute of Economic Research (MIER) and the Institute for Strategic and International Studies (ISIS); and in Bangkok, the Department of International Relations at Thammasat University. I am also grateful to the many individuals who took time off to educate me about their countries of residence and shared with me their knowledge in their respective areas of expertise.

I wish to thank Andrew Filardo for permission to reproduce Table I.2 from Andrew Filardo, Jason George, Mico Loretan, Guonan Ma, Anella Munro, Ilhyock Shim, Philip Wooldridge, James Yetman and Haibin Zhu (2010), 'The International Financial Crisis: Timeline, Impact and Policy Responses in Asia and the Pacific', in *The International Financial Crisis and Policy Challenges in Asia and the Pacific*, Vol. 52, ed. Bank for International Settlements (Basel: Bank for International Settlements). I am also grateful to the International Bank for Reconstruction and Development (The World Bank) for permission to use data extracted from *A New Database on Financial Development and Structure* (updated November 2010) authored by Thorsten Beck, Asli Demirgüç-Kunt and Ross Levine and available at http://go.worldbank.org/X23UD9QUX0. The World Bank also granted permission to reproduce Table 4.4 from Swati R. Ghosh (2006), *East Asian Finance: The Road to Robust Markets* (Washington, D.C.: World Bank).

Last but not least, I would like to thank Delphine Rabet, Kristina Rai Scott, Mark Tindale and two anonymous reviewers for comments and criticisms of earlier versions of this manuscript. I am also indebted to an anonymous reviewer for suggesting the title of the book. As is the usual case, all errors and omissions remain mine alone.

1
Whither the Asian Financial Systems Post-Crisis?

When key international financial institutions, such as Lehman Brothers and Merrill Lynch, spectacularly collapsed during the global financial crisis of 2008–9, regulators began to review the role of the state in the financial system and to reconsider the continued viability of the 'unfettered market' approach to governing the financial sector, and the economy more generally.[1] While the need to better regulate the market and to give financial authorities more power to oversee the activities of market actors was quite quickly identified, not many analysts and policy makers in the US and UK seriously advocated the type of interventionist policies that are commonly associated with the 'developmental states' of East Asia and the corporatist economies of continental Europe.[2] Instead, policy makers were warned that they would 'add to the damage [of the financial crisis], not only by over-regulating finance but by attacking markets right across the economy' (The Economist 2008). Thus, despite

1 Following Schmidt (1999), the term 'financial sector' will be used to refer to those specialised institutions such as banks, pension funds, securities markets and so on that provide financial services to the economy, and to the ways in which these institutions are shaped and managed, and how they operate and are regulated. The term 'financial system', on the other hand, encompasses not only the financial sector, but also the real sectors of the economy in so far as they are 'implicated' through their demand of financial services from the financial sector, as well as the interaction between the demand for and the supply of the services of the financial sector. The financial system, therefore, includes the financial sector as the provider of financial services as well as the real sectors of the economy in so far as they demand or, as the case my be, fail to demand, these services, and the complex relationships between the financial and the non-financial sectors.

2 See for instance Beddoes (2008); The Economist (2009).

concerns with problems embodied in the market, many observers ultimately advised caution in enlarging the role of the state and were keen to preserve key features of the liberal market economy that had previously worked so well to advance economic wealth and welfare.

This debate mirrors an earlier one conducted in the aftermath of the Asian financial crisis of 1997–8. Then, as now, instability in the financial system prompted a series of questions and analyses as to the cause or causes of the phenomenon, as well as generating heated debate on the desirable balance between the roles of the state and market that would help mitigate similar phenomena. As with the global crisis of 2008–9, the Asian financial crisis was said to have exposed weaknesses in the governance, management and institutions of the financial sectors of the East Asian economies. It also led to a reconsideration of not just the nature of their domestic financial systems but also the nature of their engagement with the global market. The Asian financial crisis also raised significant doubts about the effectiveness of financial systems in the region in sustaining further economic development.

While the crisis of 2008–9 led to calls for a (marginally) greater role for governments in regulating and supervising financial markets, the crisis of 1997–8 was, on the other hand, seen as a critical opportunity to retrench the role of the state and bring many of the East Asian economies in line with more market-friendly forms of economic governance. While this did not imply a complete rejection of the state's role in the market, the *activist* or *developmental* role played by states in the economies of East Asia did become the focus of criticism, as it was perceived to have been a key factor in engendering weaknesses in the financial systems. In its place, there was an expectation that governments would *transform* their role into one that was relatively 'passive' and that merely enabled, as opposed to enhanced or directed, market forces. It is this expectation, where governments have a key, but relatively minimal, role to play in regulating and supervising financial markets that unite both crises, underlying which is a broad acceptance of the longer-term viability of the liberal market model, particularly within the context of the contemporary globalised economy (a fuller discussion can be found in Chapter 2).

There has, however, long been a general resistance to the increasing liberalisation of economies in East Asia to the extent that it undermines state control of the economy. Aside from obvious self-interested reasons, policy makers were also concerned about the possible negative impact on economic growth given the historical experience of economies in the region in which it has long been argued that the state played a key role in economic growth. Some would even equate the process of market liberalisation, in particular the neoliberal variant, as a form of neo-imperialism: a device that foreign, usually western and liberal, powers were using to extract economic rents from poor, defenceless developing countries. The colourful views of the former Prime Minister of Malaysia, Mahathir Mohamed, come to mind here. This resistance to market liberalisation does not imply that the market played no role in the development of the East Asian economies. If anything, the converse was true. Korea could not have developed without the participation of private sector owned and managed large manufacturing firms and conglomerates.[3] Similarly, Malaysia's economy thrived as a result of foreign direct investment in export enclaves as well as the growth of SMEs in largely market-driven sectors. Family-owned firms and holding companies were the engines of economic growth in Thailand. However, the 'miraculous' economic growth of East Asia had been accompanied by significant state intervention (World Bank 1993). Whether the state was heavily 'directive' as in Korea, or provided a selectively enhanced environment for sub-sectors in the economy as with the manufacturing export zones in Malaysia, or formed a 'developmental social contract' based on a close state–business nexus as in Thailand (Hewison 1996), the fact is that the state had played an active and significant role in the growth of these economies. Admittedly, government interventions did not always result in positive outcomes for the economy or society. Corruption, cronyism, nepotism and mismanagement have surfaced at one point or another in all the economies that were highlighted in the World Bank's now infamous study of the 'miracle' of East Asian growth. Nevertheless, there is some consensus that state intervention has also had some positive impact in facilitating economic growth in these same economies. So, when it was suggested by a variety of policy analysts and international organisations such as the IMF that victims of the Asian financial crisis should further liberalise their financial sectors, strengthen market dynamics and retrench state intervention, the reception was understandably not unanimously positive.

The debates that ensued following the two financial crises, both the one in East Asia in 1997–8 and the more recent global crisis of 2008–9, ultimately point us in the direction of the literature on state–market relationships and their effect on the economy. Whether one subscribes

---

[3] In this book, Korea refers to the Republic of Korea, more popularly known as South Korea.

to the neoliberal economic model or to the Asian developmental one, there is common agreement that the nature of the state–market nexus has implications for economic development and growth. As such, it seems sensible that we pay attention to how these relations change particularly when prompted by significant events such as financial crises. While the effects of the 2008–9 global financial crisis continue to play out, it would be instructive to look back at developments in the East Asian economies since the crisis of 1997–8, as they can offer us insights into the nature of economic reform and the dynamics of change beyond the period immediately following a systemic financial crisis. This book helps with this exercise by offering an in-depth empirical analysis into how state–market dynamics have evolved in the financial sectors of Korea, Malaysia and Thailand since the Asian financial crisis. Before going any further, I will contextualise this study by briefly reviewing the debate on the causes of the Asian financial crisis.

The causes of the Asian financial crisis of 1997–8

The Asian financial crisis of 1997–8 had a significant impact on a number of countries in the region. The crisis severely blighted at least four economies and indirectly contributed to the change of governments in at least three.[4] It impoverished countless individuals many of whom were already living under difficult economic conditions in countries that were still considered to be developing, in particular in Indonesia and rural parts of Thailand. Social unrest and protests emerged in several of the affected economies in reaction to the social, economic and political dislocations inflicted by the Asian crisis. The financial systems of several economies in the region were brought to the brink of collapse and the IMF became intimately involved in three countries' attempts at resolving the crisis that included what was then considered to be the biggest IMF 'bail out' ever.[5]

What triggered the Asian financial crisis that resulted in such calamitous events?

[4] The four were Indonesia, Korea, Malaysia and Thailand. The abrupt end of Suharto's dominance over Indonesian politics is attributed to the financial crisis while eventual changes in government in Thailand and Korea can also be traced, in parts, to the crisis.

[5] Under the IMF financial assistance package, Thailand was allowed to borrow up to USD17.2 billion, Indonesia USD43.0 billion and Korea USD58.4 billion.

First, there was undoubtedly an international dimension to the crisis. Without the flow of capital across borders, or the difference in interest rates between countries, or the regime of heavily managed exchange rates that engendered a false sense of stability, some or all aspects of the financial crisis might not have occurred. Domestic banks might not have borrowed from abroad. International financial speculators might not have attacked the Thai Baht in reaction to slowing economic activity and political instability, thus igniting the crisis. Foreign capital might not have felt compelled to invest in or lend to developing countries in the first place or to leave so precipitously once confidence in the local economy was lost.

These observations suggest that there were issues, if not problems, with the way the international financial system operated and that it required attention.[6] This conclusion is reinforced by, and the argument repeated practically verbatim in, the debate about the 2008–9 global financial crisis. For instance, Simon Johnson (2009) recently pointed out, in relation to the 2008–9 crisis, that the global financial system was permissive in allowing 'bubbles to feed on money raised from anywhere in the world, exacerbating global risks'. Ann Pettifor (2008) suggested the 'taming of financial markets' and 'downsizing the single global market'. Jayati Ghosh (2008) went further and proclaimed that the current international financial architecture had failed in some very important ways and should therefore be abandoned for a 'better model'. In late 2008, world leaders such as French President Nicolas Sarkozy and British Prime Minister Gordon Brown called for a 'new Bretton Woods'. These more recent pronouncements are not at all new when juxtaposed against the debates of the Asian financial crisis of 1997–8.

The persistence of such views across two different crises over the past decade points to the continuing relevance and importance of these arguments. However, the fact that the same criticisms are being made about the international financial system in 2008–9 as they were a decade earlier reflects the poor progress made at the international level on these

---

[6] The international financial system, as it stands, is understood to be inherently unstable and prone to crisis, see Arestis, Nissanke and Stein (2005). The liberalisation of domestic financial and asset markets and the continued integration with the international system exposed domestic economies to the fragilities of this very system. Currency and financial crises have become more frequent in the past two decades, precisely the period during which more and more economies increasingly opened up and participated in the global economic system, see Demirgüç-Kunt and Detragiache (1999); Eichengreen and Bordo (2002).

issues since the late-1990s. This – the absence of significant changes in the international financial system since 1997 – can be attributed to the lack of consensus or political will among major industrialised countries on requisite changes.[7] The experience of the 2008–9 crisis might well alter this dynamic although the weak outcomes of various meetings at the international level throughout 2009 and 2010 do not provide cause for much optimism.[8] Additionally, the fragmented nature of existing sites of global governance poses a challenge to proposals for more comprehensive solutions. With little improvement in the global financial architecture after the Asian crisis (Bird and Rajan 2002; Grenville 2007, p.14 ff),[9] and criticisms directed at those that did materialise (Griffith-Jones and Ocampo 2003; Wade 2007), critics of the international system had to concede that in order to prevent, or mitigate the effects, of future financial crises, the best that could be achieved would be to accommodate the perceived excesses of the international financial system by implementing changes at the domestic level.[10] Indeed, Robert Wade (2007, p.128) went so far as to argue that the onus laid with developing countries to prevent future crises.

Notwithstanding the existing difficulty with resolving issues in the international financial system, there were also good reasons to focus on domestic reform since domestic factors were equally important as sources of financial instability (Goldstein 1998; Krugman 1998; Noland 1998). These included poor financial and corporate governance, connected lending, asset price bubbles, fiscal mismanagement, inappropriate exchange rate policies, and poor practices of public disclosure and transparency.

---

[7] See for instance Eichengreen (2003). For a more recent argument, see Kettle (2008).

[8] See for instance Walker (2009).

[9] Stephen Grenville (2006) suggested that the 'Asian Crisis impinged rather lightly on the world stage' and that it is hard to see 'much direct connection' between developments at the Bank for International Settlements (BIS) and the Financial Stability Forum (FSF) and the Asian crisis. He suggested instead that changes at the BIS and FSF were motivated more by crises that were closer to home in the US.

[10] Amidst the despair for progress at the international level, some observers saw the possibility of regional financial arrangements, see for instance Bird and Rajan (2002). However, regional arrangements have also proven to be rather limited in nature and largely subordinate to international ones, for example advance drawings from the Chiang Mai currency swap initiative are conditional on the existence of an IMF-supported programme.

Fixing the East Asian financial systems

In identifying 'flaws' in the affected economies and suggesting ways in which financial sectors could be further strengthened, many analysts worked on the assumption, either implicitly or explicitly, that there was a particular ideal type that should be emulated by those countries that sought to participate fruitfully in the modern international economic system. Thus, when deficiencies in the Asian economies were identified, features that were more closely linked with perceived 'Asian' forms of economic management, for example close government–business nexus and relationship banking, were singled out whereas features that were more closely identified with market-driven dynamics, such as greater competition and transparency, were recommended as a panacea. The main critique of the East Asian financial systems was the 'distortion of market forces' by the state, this being the key factor that unpinned various other issues such as the problem of 'moral hazard', poor governance, the lack of transparency, over-reliance on banks and crony capitalism, among others.

These criticisms of the East Asian financial systems, and the accompanying responses, effectively revived the earlier debate on the 'East Asian model' of economic governance or East Asian variants of capitalism. This is a debate that had begun in the early 1980s when many observers started to acknowledge that there was something distinctive about the forms of economic governance in many East Asian economies and suggested that this had contributed to their impressive economic growth since the 1960s. This argument was given particular prominence when the World Bank (1993) published its *East Asian Miracle* report and commended many of the policies that had been put in place. In the aftermath of the Asian crisis, critics of the 'Asian developmental state' interpreted events as having disproved the long run legitimacy of this model and consequently suggested that the East Asian economies adopt policies that conformed more to the dominant neoliberal paradigm. In fact, many such policies were enforced via IMF programmes with Indonesia, Korea and Thailand.[11] More importantly, supporters of the neoliberal economic model argued that such changes were unavoidable and that in a modern globalised economy, convergence, in particular

[11] Such policies were not necessarily imposed by the IMF. The governments of Kim Young-sam and Kim Dae-jung in Korea had a prior interest in some of the institutional changes and the IMF proved to be a useful ally, see chapter on Korea.

convergence onto the neoliberal model, was inevitable (Roche 2000). Some of these themes have, as noted earlier, been revisited in light of the 2008–9 global financial crisis. While there is recognition that there are serious issues with the market, by and large, the focus on corrective measures so far has been on improving regulatory oversight and finding ways to make the market function better, not changing it.[12] In other words, the onus is still on domestic economies to reform in order to better accommodate the dynamics of the contemporary global financial system.

Returning to the financial crisis of the late-1990s, it was expected that the governments of the affected economies in East Asia would reform their financial systems and converge towards a more market-based model, one that was at least a variant of what has come to be understood as the neoliberal model that is frequently associated with the US and UK.[13] The extent of the devastation inflicted by the crisis left very little room for mere tweaks and while it would have been convenient to shift blame elsewhere, policy makers had to be pragmatic and realise that defence against future similar crises would be best provided, even if imperfectly, by domestic reform. The answer had to be a transformation of the East Asian bank-based financial systems into what was considered the 'better' market-based model. This is reinforced by the perception that a market-based financial system, akin to the ones found in the US and UK, was understood as a sign of development and progress.

While the push towards a market-based model could be and was read as a political agenda, one designed to undermine the economic trajectory of the East Asian economies in favour of Anglo-American commercial interests, the debate was also a technocratic one, in so far as proposed reforms were attempts at making financial systems function more efficiently and effectively given accepted mainstream understandings in the field of Economics. Furthermore, although sources of weakness in the East Asian financial systems can be differentiated between 'sins of omission' and 'sins of commission' where the former can be solved by increasing bureaucratic capacity while the latter required more fundamental institutional and even political reform, in

---

[12] See for instance Goldstein (2008) and remarks by Tarullo (2009) of the US Federal Reserve Board.

[13] Indeed the programme agreed between Korea and the IMF could be seen as a comprehensive plan to change the Korean economy in the direction of a more robust market economy.

practice the two types of problems shaded into each other as bureaucratic ineptitude and weaknesses frequently interacted with the political context and dynamics within which they reside, as Haggard (2000, pp.32–8) has so vividly described. Consequently, whether it was 'sins of omission' or 'sins of commission', or both as Haggard would argue, or whether it was to advance Anglo-American financial interests, the solution proffered appeared to point in the same broad direction: less government intervention; greater transparency; strengthened regulation and supervision; and more market dynamics. There is therefore an overlap between the technocratic understanding of a modern financial system in a globalised market place and the more politicised argument about the 'Americanisation' of East Asian economies. Thus, whether it was through policy recommendations as a result of interaction with international organisations such as the IMF, or through voluntary policy initiatives, it seemed to many then that, in the medium to longer term, the financial systems of the East Asian economies would, and indeed should, converge on a market-based system.

Which brings us to the focus of this book. In this study, I identify and analyse changes in the financial systems of East Asia, in particular on the changing role of the state in its evolution and operation. Given the intense debate on the nature of economic governance and its implications for the economy that followed the Asian crisis of 1997–8, and indeed also the global crisis of 2008–9, it is important that we trace how state–market dynamics have evolved in East Asia and analyse whether they have indeed been transformed in such a manner that the economies affected by the Asian crisis could now be said to have converged onto the 'liberal market economy' or neoliberal model.

The book's main contribution is thus both empirical and analytical. Of the four economies that were most critically affected during the Asian financial crisis of 1997–8, the book focuses on three: Korea, Malaysia and Thailand.[14] Since the notion of economic convergence and ideal typical models of economic governance are important aspects of the book's argument, these key issues are discussed in the following chapter in which I also propose an analytical framework that can be employed to understand the nature and processes of change in the financial sectors of East Asia. This framework is built on and adapted from the work of Vivien Schmidt and forms a conceptual contribution

[14] The fourth being Indonesia. Resource constraints prevent a fuller investigation.

of the book, which can be developed further and employed in similar analytical work. This is followed with three detailed empirical chapters that analyse changes in the financial sectors of Korea, Malaysia and Thailand.

The book concludes with a comparative discussion of the evolution of the financial sectors of all three countries. Contrary to the expectations of critics of the Asian model, the book argues that the state in Korea, Malaysia and Thailand continue to play an active and interventionist role in their respective financial systems. What are interesting are the changes in the nature of these roles. In both Korea and Malaysia, the state now intervenes in the financial sector in order to develop it as an engine of growth in its own right, as opposed to subordinating its development to the real, that is manufacturing, sector. This can be seen in the adoption of the financial hub strategy in Korea and the development of the Islamic finance sub-sector in Malaysia. More modest developmental aspirations also motivate the Thai state's policies. Of course, more 'traditional' forms of state intervention in the financial sector, including those motivated by private interests, persist and these are all detailed in the following chapters. It is also worth pointing out in advance that although state intervention persists, the financial sectors of Korea, Malaysia and Thailand have also become more liberalised and diversified, as recommended by a range of analysts following the Asian financial crisis. The participation of foreign actors has also increased across the board. Many of these changes were suggested as key features that would improve market dynamics, systemic stability and overall economic efficiency (Claessens and Glaessner 1998; Eichengreen 1999; Ghosh 2006). The expansion of market forces was also expected to help retrench state influence and nudge these economies towards a liberal market model. Ironically, as the empirical chapters of this book demonstrate, these developments, that is the liberalisation and diversification of the financial sectors, have emerged largely as a result of state actions, motivated by a range of factors other than, but also including, belief in the superiority of the liberal market model.

Finally, as the analysis in this book goes beyond discussions and debates that arose in the period immediately after the Asian financial crisis, it can help us infer broader lessons about the impact of systemic crises on economic governance over the medium- and long-term. This is relevant to contemporary concerns over the longer-term consequences of the global financial crisis of 2007–8. The analysis in this book suggests the need to pay attention to the influence of institutions on the evolution of financial reform and how it is played out in the areas of policy, 'polity' and politics. It also cautions any expectations of revolutionary changes. Even though a financial crisis might leave an indelible mark on a country's economy, polity and society, institutional structures act as constraints, thus suggesting much more evolutionary changes. This, and other observations, is discussed in greater detail in what follows.

2
Analysing Economic Models

For many, the failure of the East Asian model of economic management was a primary contributing factor to the Asian financial crisis of the late-1990s. The crisis itself presented an opportunity to address these very weaknesses and the financial systems in East Asia were expected to converge onto a global norm, one that was underpinned by market dynamics, following a retrenchment of government intervention. The remarks made by Alan Greenspan (1997), then Governor of the Federal Reserve, at the Economic Club of New York are representative of these views:

> The current crisis is likely to accelerate the dismantling in many Asian countries of the remnants of a system with large elements of government-directed investment, in which finance played a key role in carrying out the state's objectives.... Government-directed production, financed with directed bank loans, cannot readily adjust to the continuously changing patterns of market demand for domestically consumed goods or export...the ability of these systems to handle their increasingly sophisticated economies declines markedly [as they develop].[1]

In this chapter, I set out the analytical framework that will be employed to assess the evolution of the financial systems of the East Asian economies. I first consider the notion of economic convergence before proceeding

---

[1] This is in sharp contrast to the remarks Greenspan made in October 2008 at the US House Committee on Oversight and Government Reform where he expressed 'shocked disbelief' at the failure of the 'self-interest of lending institutions to protect shareholders' equity'. See the report in the New York Times by Andrews (2008).

to discuss how economic and financial systems have been modelled or conceptualised, in other words, the ideal types that frame this debate. This discussion is followed with two sections on how I propose to observe the key dimensions or variables that characterise these ideal types, first quantitatively and then qualitatively. The chapter concludes with some comments and clarifications on relevant methodological issues.

Economic convergence and divergence

While scholars have long recognised that capitalist economies take different forms, it was probably not until the 1960s and 1970s that different iterations of capitalism were seen to be coherent, alternative forms of capitalism rather than as detours of a common trajectory.[2] The literature on 'Asian capitalisms', of which Chalmers Johnson's groundbreaking book *MITI and the Japanese Miracle* was an early example, was consistent with the view that there were many paths to industrial success. Nevertheless, the expectation that economic structures are in some sense evolutionary in nature and should therefore be converging did not disappear from the literature but persists until the present day.

Contemporary expectations of economic convergence focus on the impact of a diverse range of dynamics on national economic structures, in particular international competition, globalisation, regional integration and the deregulation of domestic economies. The common theme among these arguments is the expectation that the global mobility of factors of production, in particular finance, will tear down borders and create a world market with dynamics that national interventions will find difficult to resist.[3] The claim is that, since the 1970s, there has been a radical change in the *magnitude* and *character* of the flows of investment, services and goods across national boundaries and in the scope of the loss, or renunciation, of control by national actors over these flows. Market dynamics, according to Thomas Friedman (1999), would 'force' states to put on the 'golden straightjacket' – a set of 'neoliberal' policies that expand international openness, limit the role of government in managing the economy and cede full rein to private initiative and investment.[4]

---

[2] See, for instance, Dore (1973); Goldthorpe (1984); Womack and Jones (1990); Albert (1993).

[3] The key text here is Ohmae (1990).

[4] For a contrarian argument, Rogowski (2003) demonstrated, using formal modelling, that internationally mobile capital often implies greater diversity of policy among states.

In the specific case of the financial system, it is argued that technology and globalisation have facilitated the integration of financial markets and engendered new character in the dynamics of competition, trade and diffusion of innovation and capital mobility such that domestic transformations are inevitable. While capital market openness provides governments with greater access to capital, it also subjects them to external market discipline (Armijo 1999; Obstfeld and Taylor 2004). For instance, then General Manager of the Bank for International Settlements (BIS), Malcolm Knight (2004), stated that 'the forces of financial liberalisation, technological advances...and breakthroughs in financial risk management have made themselves felt across financial institutions and markets, across different types of financial institution and across national jurisdictions' such that 'the pressure to adopt similar arrangements across countries has grown' and the ability to pursue country-specific solutions to prudential frameworks has become more difficult.

From this perspective, the effects of globalisation therefore call into question the long-term sustainability of particular forms of capitalism such as those that have been identified in the East Asian economies. Beeson and Robison (2000, p.17), for example, observed that the growth of disintermediated credit in the Japanese system has led to a shift in the control of credit away from the government and this subsequently threatened the 'traditional' role that the state and banking sector have played in the allocation of credit in the growth of the Japanese economy. For Li (2003), the financial crisis of 1997–8 is an obvious manifestation of the functional breakdown of these Asian forms of capitalism, as it demonstrated the ill-fated destiny of the state–business relations that girdle these economies and the futility of resisting the rationality of the market, particularly as these economies become increasingly integrated into the global market place. The dynamics of the market will force the hand of governments that stray from the norm, where the norm in this case is a mode of economic governance that is most consistent with the current globalised economy.

Is convergence inevitable?

While there is little dispute that the level and perhaps even the nature of economic activity at the global level has changed dramatically in the past three decades, opinions differ on whether this represents a break with the past and, more importantly, on the effects these changes have on domestic practices and institutions.[5] Contemporary arguments in

[5] See, for instance, the volume edited by Berger and Dore (1996).

support of convergence identify several contributing dynamics including the absence of political will to sustain institutions and of values that transcend and restrain market-oriented outcomes, a condition that is accompanied by a kind of competitive race to the bottom (Dore 1996; Streeten 1996), or a quasi-Darwinian competition of different ways of dealing with contemporary issues and problems leading to either wholesale or partial adoption of 'best practices and methods' (Kester 1996; Kosai 1996). Others point to the 'contagion effect' on governments of competitive considerations and exposure to foreign ideas and models (Simmons and Elkins 2003). While these observers believe that convergence will eventually occur, they differ from their predecessors in that, from their point of view, exogenous pressures in the form of either global market forces or international political pressures are not sufficient in themselves to bring about change. They argue that domestic political and economic forces have as much an influence as exogenous factors in not only accommodating but also shaping how convergence occurs.

Defenders of national variances in economic structures seize on this observation – that domestic political and economic forces can influence the evolution of economic systems – to argue that market pressures have indeterminate effect. Consequently, convergence is more an anomaly than the rule. While market pressures may signal problems and provide general impetus for change, they do not provide unequivocal clues as to which policies or institutions need to be altered nor how it should be done. There may be functional equivalents in the way that economic activities are organised that are similarly competitive in world markets, thus suggesting a variety of sustainable models of economic governance (Hall and Soskice 2001b). Domestic politics or different resource considerations may explain the choices that are made. 'Path dependence' may limit the range of options that are possible (Bianco, Gerali and Massaro 1997; Monnet and Quintin 2007). More importantly, domestic politics are not necessarily always, if ever, benign processes that result in technocratic solutions to economic problems and challenges. Often economically 'suboptimal' outcomes result from the process of domestic politics, a point that is amply demonstrated by the extensive literature on the politics of interest groups.

The role of politics in mediating dynamics that contribute to pressures for convergence is observed at not just the domestic level but also at the international level. There has been, for instance, an increasingly important and overt political dimension to the process of globalisation. Key transnational authorities and actors have tried to encourage the process of convergence by persuading, negotiating or coercing governments into adopting structures and practices that conform to particular ideal types (Dumez and Jeunemaître 1996; Kahler 1996; Ostry 1996). The nature of the IMF's involvement in the East Asian economies during the crisis, for instance, was perceived as being politically motivated with the intention of making specific, profound and long-term changes to the organisation of economic and political structures in these economies (Yoon 2005). An evaluation report also concluded that the World Bank had 'proselytised on behalf of Bank policy' and had failed to adequately separate advocacy and research (Banerjee et al. 2006).

In short, despite persistent suggestions that economic convergence is inevitable, the process is ultimately indeterminate and can be influenced by both domestic and international institutions and politics. This highlights the importance of paying attention to the political dimension of the process of economic evolution. Whether one adopts the view that economic convergence is inevitable or otherwise, we need some conception of what is appropriate or possible in order to sustain this debate. In other words, what are the ideal types or different models of economic governance that have framed the debate? It is to this topic that the discussion will now turn.

Economic models and financial systems

Probably the most systematic and conceptually developed approach to modelling and analysing economic systems in the contemporary literature, and certainly one of the most widely cited, is the set of work that has come to be known as the *Varieties of Capitalism* (VoC), after the title of an edited volume by Peter Hall and David Soskice (2001b).[6] The basic premise of this perspective is that firms engage in strategic interactions with other actors in the economy with results that are conditioned by complementary institutional structures. In order to facilitate this analysis, most writers adopt a binary approach and construct two primary ideal types – a liberal market economy (LME) and a coordinated market economy (CME) – that form the poles of a spectrum. Attempts are then made to allocate every developed capitalist economy to one or other of these categories. In the following sections, I will discuss both these ideal types, paying particular attention to the liberal market model because

[6] Hall and Soskice's 'varieties of capitalism' is one of several major analytical frameworks that can be grouped under the umbrella of 'comparative capitalisms' that has a common concern in understanding the institutional foundations of diverse national 'varieties' of business organisation and in comparing how institutional diversity impacts economic outcomes.

it is a key concept that has structured the discussion of the evolution of financial systems in East Asia post-1997–8 crisis, and indeed discussions of the contemporary global economy. I will then argue that this binary approach to conceptualising economic systems is deficient on both empirical and conceptual grounds and that an alternative ideal type, a state-influenced market economy, is necessary in order to restore greater analytic validity to the idea of comparative capitalism.

Liberal Market Economies (LME)

In the LME ideal type, most closely identified with the Anglophone countries (Australia, Canada, Ireland, New Zealand, the United Kingdom, but primarily the US), firms coordinate their activities primarily via competitive market arrangements that are characterised by the arms-length exchange of goods or services in a context of competition and formal contracting. Actors adjust their willingness to supply and demand goods or services in response to price signals generated by such markets, thus providing the means to coordinate the endeavours of economic actors. It is this ideal type that became the dominant articulation of the economic model best suited to a modern, globalised economy since the 1990s.

The LME ideal type is closely associated with 'neoliberal' economic policies, which owe much of their intellectual roots to the 'Washington Consensus', a phrase initially coined by John Williamson (1990) to describe a specific set of economic policy reforms that the sluggish state-directed economies of Latin America could adopt in order to attract private capital back to that region following the crippling debt crisis of the 1980s. Although this policy package was originally understood as a reform agenda for Latin America, it was quickly seen as a model for the wider developing world and eventually also the transitional economies. The economic discourse embodied by the 'Washington Consensus' – at the core of which were macroeconomic discipline, a market economy and openness to the world economy (at least with respect to trade and FDI) – helped fill the need for an economic policy framework after central planning and import-substitution trade strategies were discredited, and served to reunite development economics and mainstream economics (Naim 2000).[7]

[7] For a detailed argument of the intellectual 'shift' that occurred in development economics with the emergence of the 'Washington Consensus', see Gore (2000).

These days the term 'Washington Consensus' is often understood as synonymous with 'neoliberalism', or market-oriented policies more broadly and has developed a life of its own.[8] While the core elements remained constant, a range of other policies that Williamson did not consider was added. These include: a minimalist welfare state, decentralised labour relations and a weakening of unions, fiscal discipline taking precedence over social policies, and a reduction of barriers to trade. Underlying these various specific policies is the key 'philosophy' or policy orientation of 'neoliberalism' in which the 'unfettered market' is the driver of economic development. States in LMEs do not seek to structure firms' strategies or behaviour, but operate remotely and allow 'market forces' to determine outcomes.

Financial systems in LMEs reflect these broader principles and dynamics. They are 'liberalised', as opposed to 'repressed',[9] with the market given the primary role to determine who gets and grants credit and at what price. Full market liberalisation involves governments also allowing entry into the financial-services industry to any company that can satisfy objectively specified criteria based on prudential considerations alone, giving banks the autonomy to run their own affairs, and abandoning control over international capital movements.

LMEs have also been associated with market-based financial systems, as opposed to bank-based ones (e.g. Germany, Japan). This is an alternate way of differentiating financial systems in the literature that is based on different forms of formal institutional structure, where the principal–agent problem is resolved differently in different systems (Zysman 1983; Allen and Gale 2000; Rajan and Zingales 2003).[10] A bank-based system monitors firms and reduces post-lending moral hazard or asset

---

[8] For Williamson's own defence, see Williamson (2000). For a wonderful survey of the 'life' of the term, see Naim (2000).

[9] Differentiating financial systems as being either 'repressed' or 'liberalised' was made by Ronald McKinnon (1973) and Edward Shaw (1973) in what has now come to be understood as seminal works.

[10] A narrow definition of a bank-based system is one in which the most important source of external financing for non-financial companies is bank loans. The key distinctions between bank- and market-based financial systems are between direct and indirect finance and between debt and equity financing. The difference between the two types of systems is of the relative importance of the types of financing rather than their absolute levels. Some have argued that there are hardly any systemic differences between national patterns of corporate financing, or that if differences exist, they are inconsistent with what one would expect on the basis of theory or casual observation, see Mayer (1988), (1990); Corbett and Jenkinson (1996) and Byrne and Davis (2002).

substitution through the development of close relationships between financial institutions and borrowers while competitive capital markets do so by aggregating diffuse market signals and transmitting them to investors. Although this approach to differentiating financial systems points to differences in types of institutions, those working with this typology also frequently suggest that bank-based systems are 'repressed' or certainly less 'liberalised' than market-based ones. As such, they demonstrate a normative preference, however slight, for market-based systems. There is similarity here to the arguments advanced by those working in the VoC literature, such as Hall and Soskice (2003), who, while arguing that different models of capitalism can co-exist, conceded that there is a 'long term historical bias leaning in the direction of liberalisation' as a result of the logic conceived for the other of their two primary varieties of capitalism, the coordinated market economy (CME).[11]

More recent work on financial systems has extended our understanding of 'liberalised' financial systems while also refining the way in which distinctions are made between bank- and market-based systems. While financial repression would be less likely in a market-based system, there is no reason why financial liberalisation could not emerge in both bank- and market-based systems. Thus, more recent studies have demonstrated that 'well-developed' financial systems exert positive influences on economic growth *independently* of whether they are dominated by banks and other financial intermediaries or financial markets (Demirgüç-Kunt and Levine 2001; Levine 2002), and this therefore mitigates the normative preference

---

[11] Volmer, Jörg, and Zimmermann (2007) suggested that this is attributable to the current reliance on markets and that the LME model has a strong comparative advantage under such conditions. In his reading of the literature, Goodin (2003) concluded that 'CMEs are naturally doomed to extinction, and LMEs ultimately to prevail' based on the premise that relations of trust are crucial to the operation of a CME and easier to abrogate than construct. Although Hall and Soskice (2003, p.245) acknowledged that economic efficiency alone is insufficient to dictate patterns of institutional change and that governments respond to many considerations beyond those of economic efficiency (such as political pressures), they nevertheless cannot help but point out that 'firms must be attentive to the efficiency of their operations and responsive to pressures to improve it' and that governments or politicians 'confront electoral pressure to enhance the performance of the economy'. In other words, despite suggesting that different forms of capitalisms can exist side-by-side as coherent alternatives, the argument advanced by Hall and Soskice nevertheless incorporated a certain element of convergence towards LMEs, albeit in a passive form.

for market-based financial systems, assuming that it is concerns for efficiency that motivate policy makers.[12] Nevertheless, such studies continue to reinforce the argument that greater market-dynamics, and thus liberalisation, is one of the key components of 'well-developed financial systems'. This is furthermore to be complemented by various institutions that contribute to financial systems functioning more efficiently and effectively. This emergent perspective, also known as the 'financial services view', argues that the institutional setting – which embraces areas such as regulation, competition policy, as well as the legal system – determines the performance of financial systems by, for instance, promoting transparency and greater flow of information that facilitate the ability of market actors to make better market judgements, or protecting the rights of minority shareholders in order that greater competition arises in the governance of firms (Merton and Bodie 1995; Levine 1997; La Porta et al. 1998, 2000; Levine 2002).[13] Critics argue that this systemic reordering of the institutional structures of economic governance will also 'promote the commodification of every aspect of social life' by extending the reach of market disciplines (Pirie 2008, p.14), thus not just reinforcing but also institutionalising market dynamics of the LME kind (Vestergaard 2004; Walter 2008).

Finally, although 'neoliberalism' and the liberal market economy have been criticised following a series of major financial crises from the mid- to late-1990s, there has so far been little to suggest that in practice much of the economic orthodoxy that has guided policy makers since the 1980s is being seriously challenged.[14] As noted in the previous chapter, while there is recognition that there are serious issues with the 'efficient markets' hypothesis, by and large, the focus has been on corrective measures aimed at improving regulatory oversight and finding ways to

[12] For a more comprehensive literature review on the impact of financial development on economic growth, see Dolar and Meh (2002); Ahn, Hahm, and Kim (2008, pp.30–2).

[13] These are also known as 'second generation' reforms in the literature. See also Lena Rethel's (2010b) discussion of the 'new financial system development paradigm'.

[14] See, among others, Fine, Lapavitsas and Pincus (2001); Cooper and Savage (2008). The President of the US and the Prime Minister of the UK have also publicly criticised the 'Washington Consensus' following the global financial crisis of 2007–8, see Weisman and Macdonald (2009); Brown (2009). For an earlier reading that the 'Washington Consensus' did not fail or die, see Purcell (2003).

make the market work better.[15] A panel at the World Economic Forum in February 2009 concluded that talk of the death of the '[Washington] Consensus', and by extension the LME model, was exaggerated and that its core principles – good economic governance, trade liberalisation, fiscal discipline and market principles – remained valid, if requiring revision in parts (The Nation 2009). The LME thus continues to be viewed as a desirable ideal type for many policy makers.

Coordinated Market Economies (CME)

Despite the dominance of the neoliberal discourse and ideology, alternative models of economies continued to exist both empirically as well as conceptually. Germany was often held up in the 1980s and 1990s as a form of 'divergent capitalism' and is considered the prime example of one of the key alternative ideal types to the LME, that is a coordinated market economy (CME). In the CME ideal type, firms depend more heavily on non-market relationships to coordinate their activities with other actors. These non-market modes of coordination generally entail more extensive relational or incomplete contracting, network monitoring based on the exchange of private information inside networks and more reliance on collaborative, as opposed to competitive, relationships to build the competencies of the firm. In contrast to LMEs, where the equilibrium outcomes of firm behaviour are usually given by demand and supply conditions in competitive markets, firms and various social and political institutions and actors engage directly in shaping economic action in CMEs.

As CMEs rely more heavily on forms of coordination secured through strategic interaction, institutions that reduce the uncertainty actors have about the behaviour of others and that allow them to make credible commitments to each other will be more prominent. These include powerful business or employer associations, strong trade unions, extensive networks of cross-shareholding and legal or regulatory systems designed to facilitate information sharing and collaboration. Where membership in a network has continuing value, reputation is also a key factor and participants will be deterred from providing false information. CMEs are thus characterised by extensive systems with 'network

---

[15] Even though renowned economist, Barry Eichengreen (2008, p. 2) felt that the 2008 crisis had 'cast considerable doubt' on the idea of emerging markets emulating financial arrangements in the advanced economies, he nevertheless did not explore the viability of alternative financial systems but rather pointed to the importance of strengthening regulation and supervision.

reputational monitoring' (Vitols 1997). In the realm of finance, we would expect to find 'patient capital' in CMEs, where investors are more willing to supply capital to firms on terms that are not entirely dependent on publicly available financial data or current returns. Investors would only do so if they are able to monitor the firms' behaviour; and this can be facilitated by dense networks in CMEs that permit access to information about the internal operations of firms. In particular, financial institutions in bank-based systems develop closer relationships with borrowers than atomistic investors in market-based systems, hence the dominance of banking institutions in the financial systems of CMEs.

State-influenced Market Economies (SiME)

Although many comparative political economists who work in the VoC literature have largely accepted the division of capitalism into only two ideal-typical varieties, the LME and the CME,[16] they frequently had to deal with countries that do not meet this dichotomous categorisation, resulting in the consideration of these 'anomalies' as 'mid-spectrum' economies (Hall and Soskice 2001b), or 'mixed market economies' (Hall and Gingerich 2006; Molina and Rhodes 2007), among others. While this shortcoming of the binary approach can easily be rectified by expanding the range of labels to better account for empirical cases, it is important to note that the binary approach in the VoC literature suffers from key conceptual weaknesses.

First, the VoC approach in general, and that of Hall and Soskice (2001b) in particular, focuses on firms as key agents of change and tends to downplay the role of the state in resolving coordination problems.[17] While they do not discount governments' contribution towards economic performance, the role of governments in the VoC literature comes across as being somewhat passive, if not residual, in nature. Hall and Soskice (2001a), for instance, viewed the economy as being 'firm-centred' in which the 'principal problem' facing policy makers is one of creating an environment in which market actors can better coordinate

---

[16] It should be noted that a number of scholars have also argued that there are anywhere from three to five varieties of capitalism, including national, sectoral and regional varieties. See, for instance Hollingsworth, Schmitter and Streeck (1994); Schmidt (2002); Amable (2003).

[17] The VoC approach has also been criticised for overlooking the role of labour, see Kang (2006).

and cooperate between themselves.[18] In privileging the role of firms and the primacy of the market in solving 'coordination' problems, it is clear that the binary models could not account for the East Asian and a number of key European countries such as France, Spain and Italy where the relatively more activist role of the state in these economies meant that they are neither LMEs nor CMEs. There is therefore an insufficient specification in the ideal types of 'classical VoCs'. Second, there is a problem with the conceptual treatment of the 'mid-spectrum' economies. Given that the LMEs and CMEs were conceptualised as coherent institutional arrangements or national production systems that are best suited for particular types of economic activity, and that these form the only possible ideal types of economic arrangements, then it is merely logical that 'mid-spectrum' economies would necessarily underperform because, by definition, they necessarily lack the complementaries of the more coherent national production systems.

In short, it is difficult to view how distinct national forms of capitalist arrangements can be comprehensively identified without allocating a more important and independent role to the state in the analytical construction of ideal types. As Hancke et al. (2007, p.24) had pointed out, 'the diversity in state-economy relations that persist until today suggest that there is a benefit in establishing the state and the mode of business coordination as analytically independent properties of any given model of capitalism'.[19] Thus, following a number of other authors,[20] I argue that there is analytical utility, if not imperative, in explicitly accounting for a more participatory and active role of the state in our ideal types of models of capitalism. At a broad level, this ideal type can be called, following Vivien Schmidt (2009), a 'state-influenced market economy' (SiME), which can be understood as one in which the state – referring to

---

[18] In more recent writing, Hall and Thelen (2009) made it clearer that they see a key role for governments, in particular with regard to responses to international challenges. Elsewhere, Martin and Thelen (2007) argued for the importance of state action in understanding different trajectories of change in coordinated market economies.

[19] It should be noted that Hancke et al. also argued that the introduction of the state as a variable merely differentiates a 'mode of coordination' rather than a 'model of capitalism'. As such, they considered cases where the state has close direct influence over the economy as 'transitional'. This echoes the argument of Hall and Soskice, as noted earlier, in which the state acts as a facilitator of activity rather than a more active participant of market coordination.

[20] For example Schmidt (2002); Kohli (2004); Whitley (2005).

the range of public institutions and actors that can have a major impact on what happens in national political economies – intervenes in order to organise cooperation among autonomous economic actors to direct or influence their economic activities.

While it is true that all states intervene, there is a greater level, or importance, of intervention in SiMEs that results in business interactions and labour relations that differ both in character and in logic of coordination and interaction from LMEs and CMEs and, therefore, makes for very different mechanisms of adjustment (Schmidt 2002; Evans 1995). Evans (1995, pp.77–81) and Whitley (2005) have argued that 'arm's length states' (LMEs in this discussion) perform custodial, or regulatory, roles that concentrate on establishing and applying rules as remote policing agents, while more 'promotional states' (SiMEs in this discussion) take active steps to develop new industries and skills as direct producers, midwives and supporters. These often involve providing financial and other types of assistance and sanctioning failure of specific firms and groups, as well as organising markets to support entry into new industries. These actions go above and beyond merely creating an environment that is conducive to 'market dynamics' as in LMEs, or coordinating and facilitating activities as with the 'enabling' state in CMEs. While government policies in SiMEs can sometimes be responses to demands from the private sector through either (illegal) corruption or (legal) political lobbying, state 'activism' or 'influence' in SiMEs involves greater intent or strategy on the part of the state, and thus reflect a certain 'independence' from specific market actors as opposed to passively responding to private demands. While the business relationship tends to be state-organised in SiMEs, interaction between firms when not mediated by the state can be competitive and distant as in LMEs or characterised by ties through cross-shareholding as in CMEs (Schmidt 2002). A similar point is made by Linda Weiss (1998) who conceptualises these state–market arrangements as 'governed interdependence', which in its most evolved form involves negotiated public–private policy making under government sponsorship.[21] Similarly, for Peter Evans (1995), the state's relationship to the market is one of 'embedded autonomy' where there is close cooperation between the state and business but also a measure of insulation for the bureaucratic elite to exercise autonomous policy- and decision-making.

[21] In her most recent work, Weiss (2010) began to call these state–market arrangements 'governed market economies'.

The 'East Asian developmental model' can be considered a subset of the SiME. It shares the same key features: organisational capability of state institutions; their relatively more 'dirigiste' relations with social, especially producer, groups; and the existence of an ideological or normative element-driving policy goals. What is distinctive about the ideal-typical East Asian model, however, is the particular normative goal adopted by the state, that is economic growth through industrialisation and export. A further distinction is also made in the literature between the Northeast and the Southeast Asian economies due to their historically different economic outcomes attributable to the different quality of states, with the latter sometimes labelled 'ersatz capitalism' (Mackie 1988; Yoshihara 1988; Jomo 2001). Atul Kohli (2004) would differentiate the Northeast from their Southeast counterparts as the difference between 'cohesive-capitalist states' and 'fragmented-multiclass states'. As a result of the particular historical and social context of their societies, governments in Southeast Asia had to consider goals other than economic growth and industrialisation, in particular redistribution and rent capture. Since these states had to prioritise their responses to the demands of various social groups, they are more 'fragmented-multiclass states', though 'fragmented-multi*ethnic* states' or 'fragmented-society states' would be more appropriate labels. This difference aside, industrial policy has been crucial to economic growth and development in both Northeast and the Southeast Asian economies, with less of an impact in the latter group of countries (Jomo and Ch'en 1997). We can therefore legitimately still speak of an (ideal-typical) East Asian model where the state intervened and influenced the market through its decision and policies, even if these interventions sometimes and in some cases led to poor economic outcomes.

Finally, what about financial systems in SiMEs? What would they look like?

While bank-based financial systems can be autonomous of the government, as in Germany (an example of a CME), government intervention or influence over financial systems is more likely to be stronger and more effective in bank-based rather than market-based systems as governments are more likely to influence or control a smaller number of important institutions. This was one of the main criticisms made during the Asian financial crisis in 1997–8 where many attributed the failings of the East Asian financial systems to undue government intervention which could be mitigated by, among other measures, a change from bank-based to market-based financial systems. In SiMEs, the government set financial prices (through, for example, the control of interest rates) or influenced the allocation of credit (through, for example, the control of sources of financing) and thus exercised influence over the pattern of investment in the economy (in order to achieve their policy/political goals) (Zysman 1983). Governments can also socialise the risk that accompany the extension of credit (by, for instance, acting as lender of last resort, or more generally, guaranteeing credit) in order to promote higher rates of investment. Finally, governments might have outright ownership of financial institutions (as was widely the case in Korea until the 1980s) and thus achieve any, or all, of the previous objectives in a much more direct fashion. As high rates of investment were argued to be one of the crucial variables that explained high rates of economic growth in East Asia, state control of finance, or more generally, the capacity of the state to manage a relatively closed national financial system in collusion with private sector insiders, was critical in facilitating these high rates of investment (Zysman 1983; Papanek 1988; Amsden 1989; Woo 1991).

At this point, it is worth noting that state intervention or influence can either 'enhance' or 'hinder' the market and/or market outcomes depending on how its behaviour impacts economic actors' interactions and productive capabilities, and this is distinct from a value judgement of state intervention itself. For instance, policy makers in Korea intervened in the market and 'changed prices' that led to macroeconomic outcomes that many would consider as desirable (Amsden 1989). On the other hand in Malaysia, state economic policies that favoured the majority *bumiputera* community were frequently judged as having negative economic outcomes although there is some agreement that these same policies did serve useful and sometimes desirable socio-political goals (see chapter on Malaysia). It is also possible that state intervention can, at a macroeconomic level, have a 'neutral' outcome when distributional differences at the microeconomic level outweigh each other. The point I wish to make here is that it is important to make a distinction in our analysis between a normative judgement of the outcome and of state intervention. There is heuristic and analytical value in the identification of state intervention that should not be conflated with a normative judgement thereof.

To recap, while the VoC literature made an important and distinctive contribution in systematically modelling and analysing economic systems, the dominant binary categorisation of ideal types resulted in an insufficient ability to account for many empirical cases of capitalisms. The SiME ideal type mitigates this weakness and confers greater analytic validity to the VoC approach by explicitly accounting for the role

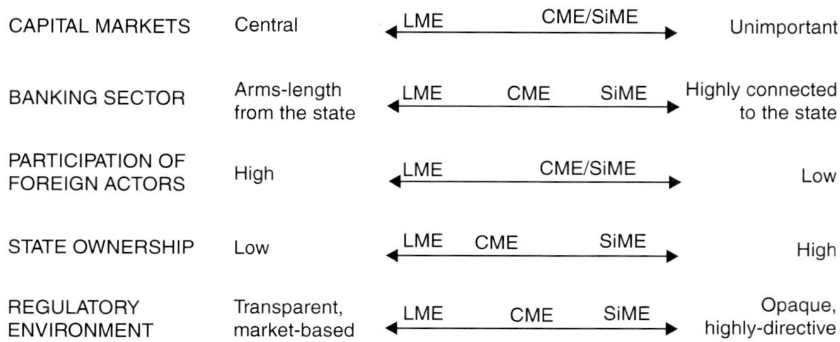

Figure 2.1 Key features of different varieties of financial systems

of the state. Bringing the state back into the VoC literature also enables us to better explain institutional change across countries, something at which the binary approach to varieties of capitalism was not very successful given their more static firm-centred perspective – this point will be developed in a later section of this chapter. Finally, different distinct features of financial systems were identified in the above discussion and associated with the different ideal types of capitalism. These are summarised and presented in a stylised form in Figure 2.1.[22]

Having discussed the ideal types that frame this research project, I would now like to turn to our discussion to the observation and measurement of the models of financial systems that we have just identified.

Observing the characteristics of different financial systems

Now that I have identified the key characteristics that are associated with various types of financial systems, how should I measure or observe them? Rendering these characteristics into measurable or observable variables for analytical purposes is not an easy task. For instance, while it is argued that a diversified financial system is highly desirable, particularly within an LME model, it is not at all clear from the existing literature at what point the balance between the banking sector and the capital market within a domestic economy would result in a financial system being categorised as an LME, CME or SiME variant. Does the capital market have to reach a threshold of 30 per cent, 50 per cent or

[22] I do not mean to imply with the figure that the ideal types rest on a continuum where economies transition smoothly from one to the other.

80 per cent of GDP before a particular financial system is considered to have met the requirements of an LME financial system? Furthermore, an examination of quantitative indicators alone could lead to misleading conclusions. For instance, Malaysia has long had a large active stock market that dwarfed those in the UK and US when measured in terms of size relative to GDP;[23] however prior to the Asian financial crisis few observers would classify the Malaysian financial sector as 'liberal' or market-based when compared to those in the UK and US, pointing to the institutional setting and practices in the Malaysian financial system as critical factors in this assessment.

The classification of financial systems, and its comparison across economies, must therefore be based on more than just quantifiable indicators and must include other forms of assessments – such as institutional settings, local practices/politics and government policies – that are more qualitative in nature. Moreover, the way in which the ideal types of different financial systems have been conceptualised in the preceding section demand that we investigate non-quantitative variables (in addition to quantitative ones). For instance, in the earlier discussion on LME financial systems, I noted that the institutional setting is now understood to be a very important factor in determining the efficient and effective operation of a liberal market system. Similarly, in the ideal type of an SiME financial system, it is institutional variables and the nature of government policies and actions that characterise and distinguish this model from its LME and CME counterparts. Furthermore, since gaps can exist between formal rules and actual practice, as we will see in the later chapters, it is important that we analyse these more qualitative institutional practices in order to uncover a more complete understanding of the nature of economic governance structures. In short, we need to go beyond quantitative assessments and conduct qualitative investigations of institutional features, policies and practices (this is discussed further in the following section).

Despite these issues with quantifiable variables, they nevertheless still provide useful information with which we can make some judgements and conclusions. While it may be difficult, if not impossible, to say for certain whether a particular financial system has crossed a quantifiable 'threshold' and thus should automatically be categorised as a different kind of system, we can at least conclude by looking at time series of

[23] See, for instance, Ghosh (2006, pp.26–7).

quantitative data whether financial systems are evolving in particular directions. For example, if over time, the size of the assets in the capital market of a particular economy (when measured in terms of percentage of GDP) is growing while the size of the assets in the banking sector is diminishing over the same period, we can conclude that the financial system is becoming more diversified, and thus converging towards an LME financial system from a formal institutional perspective (without concluding that it has become one). Similarly, we can measure and quantitatively observe whether foreign ownership of financial institutions has increased or declined over time, thus allowing to us to make tentative inferences about whether governments have become more or less constrained in their behaviour as a result of having to take into account the interests of increasingly important foreign actors. These quantifiable indicators however, as noted, can take us only so far. In order to provide more robust conclusions, we also need to take into account more qualitative observations.

Institutional analysis

How should an analysis of more qualitative variables be conducted in order to discern varieties of economic models and changes in financial systems? One of the dominant, if not the dominant, methodological approaches to analysing institutional change and discerning varieties of capitalism in the literature on contemporary comparative politics is the set of approaches known as 'new institutionalism', which typically comprises rational-choice, historical and sociological institutionalisms.[24] Of the different frameworks within this set of literature, I will concentrate on the approach developed by Vivien Schmidt as I believe it best responds to criticisms directed at 'new institutionalisms' difficulties in explaining change while also incorporating more recent developments in the theoretical literature on the importance of considering and analysing ideational variables. It is also a framework that was developed with research goals that are similar to this project, that is to analyse and assess institutional changes in types of capitalisms.

In her analysis of the impact of globalisation and Europeanisation on the capitalisms of Britain, France and Germany, Vivien Schmidt (2002) employed a framework that emphasised three main variables

---

[24] For overviews of 'new institutionalism', see Hall and Taylor (1996); Schmidt (2006b).

or dimensions: policy, 'polity' and politics.[25] By 'policy', Schmidt had in mind the substantive (government) policies affecting business and labour; 'polity' referred to how such policies as well as the interactions among political and economic actors are shaped by political institutional contexts; and finally, 'politics' pointed not just to strategic interactions among political actors but also to political actors' substantive ideas and discursive interactions (Schmidt 2006a). Underlying her framework was a methodologically diverse approach that combined historical and sociological institutional analyses with a 'new' form of institutionalism that she named 'discursive institutionalism'.[26] Discourse was broadly defined as consisting of whatever policy actors say to one another and to the public about a given policy programme; and in Schmidt's discursive institutionalist approach, focus was given not only to the ideational content of the discourse but also to the interactive processes by which the discourse facilitates policy making (Schmidt 2002, p.6). She therefore combined in her framework soft rational-choice institutionalist assumptions about the interest-motivated basis of policies and practices, sociological institutionalist references to the differing cultural norms informing those policies and practices, and perceptions of interest with a focus on the discursive bases of action.

Schmidt's policy, 'polity' and politics are in some sense a 'repackaging' of the 'conventional three-fold classification of independent variables as relating either to ideas, interests or institutions' within an institutional framework (Hay 2004),[27] since underlying Schmidt's policy, 'polity' and politics are these primary variables. In other words, Schmidt's three P's can be seen as arenas or dimensions in which the three I's (referring to ideas, interests or institutions) play out. The utility of re-configuring the three I's in this form lies in its heuristic value in clarifying where we might investigate in order to identify the nature of and variations in capitalisms or forms of economic governance. For

[25] Hancke, Rhodes and Thatcher (2007) made a similar case for the consideration of 'interests, coalitions, and institutional frameworks' as a response to criticisms of 'classical' VoC. These correspond to Schmidt's polity and politics but not policy. Schmidt's inclusion of 'policy' permits the additional consideration of ideational factors.

[26] Schmidt would also have been happy with a number of other labels for 'discursive institutionalism', including 'ideational institutionalism', 'constructivist institutionalism', and 'economic constructivism', see Schmidt (2006b).

[27] For earlier research that adopted combinations of the three I's in their approaches, see, among others, Bhagwati (1989); Varshney (1989); Garrett and Weingast (1993); Milner and Rosendorff (1997); Irwin and Kroszner (1999).

instance, although proponents of convergence have argued that state policies in recent years seem very similar in content since all countries have liberalised their financial markets, deregulated their businesses and increased the flexibility of their labour markets, in actual fact countries show subtle differences in the kind and degree of adoption of such policies which we will discover once we focus our analysis on the three P's.[28]

Schmidt's three P's were also conceptualised to serve a second purpose, that is to introduce 'discursive institutionalism', within a methodologically diverse framework, in order to provide a dynamic account of change and thus respond to some of the limits identified in the 'new institutionalisms'.[29] While the reason for combining the variables of policy, 'polity' and politics with the methodological approach of institutional analysis might not be immediately clear, in Schmidt's mind the two are intricately linked in the analysis of institutional change as suggested by the following quotation (2002, p.9):

> policies without politics may impute an interest-based rationality and path-dependency to decisions that obscures the paths not taken and the culturally embedded reasons for action or non-action; practices without policies or politics may make change appear economically determined and path-dependent; and politics without policies or practices may bring in ideas and discourse without acknowledging the economic factors that act as an impetus to or brake on change, the institutional contexts that constrain or enable actors, and the 'objective' interests that may motivate actors, regardless of the ideas or discourse.

Thus, in Schmidt's framework, 'discursive institutionalism' is deeply connected with rational-choice, historical and sociological institutionalisms. What distinguishes 'discursive institutionalism' from the other variants of 'new institutionalism' is the focus on ideas as explanans of change, often with a demonstration that such ideas do not fit predictable 'rationalist' interests, are undermined by structural factors and/or represent a break with historical paths (Schmidt 2006b, pp.109–14). Ideas here are seen as constitutive of, even if they are shaped by, institutions; unlike with historical institutionalists who

---

[28] See, among others, King and Wood (1999); Lütz (2000); Thatcher (2002); Westrup (2007); Hall and Thelen (2009).

[29] See, for instance, Hay and Wincott (1998); Blyth (2003).

continue to see institutions as being prior to ideas. While actors act on the basis of interests, in 'discursive institutionalism', and unlike 'rational-choice institutionalism', ideas about interests can encompass much more than strictly utilitarian concerns and are much more than simple reflections of interests or positions. 'Discursive institutionalism' is differentiated from its 'sociological' cousin as it is interested *only* in the dynamic use of ideas that facilitate how actors not only conceptualise but also reconceptualise the world thus serving as a resource to promote change; whereas 'sociological institutionalism' is interested in *both* this and the more static conceptualisation of ideational variables as constituted by culture. However, it is not just the focus on a dynamic concept of ideas that sets 'discursive institutionalism' apart but also its turn to the interactive processes of idea generation, acceptance and legitimisation, that is discourse, that are used as resources to produce and legitimate ideas, and consequently channel action. Schmidt is thus able to account for some dynamic change and avoid the economic, historical or cultural determinisms that have been attributed to the other 'new institutionalisms'. Schmidt (2006b, p.114) admits that there is the risk of 'discursive institutionalism' ignoring material interests *qua* material interests or appearing highly voluntaristic. While this risk of omission, or an exaggeration of the importance of selected variables, is present in all theoretical approaches since they necessarily prioritise certain variables above others, Schmidt attempted to guard against this risk through her methodologically diverse approach thus casting structural constraints on her discursive analysis.

Schmidt's approach to analysing ideational factors has the same epistemological status as rational-choice, historical, or sociological institutionalism, that is, as 'a descriptive language or analytic framework that allows one to identify, describe, and analyse important phenomena when they occur' (Schmidt 2002, p.8). As such, she does not go beyond an instrumental handling of ideational variables and probe their 'deeper' constitutive or inter-subjective dimensions. Her approach is therefore open to the criticism of being no more than an ad hoc modification of rationalist perspectives rather than a turn from it (Blyth 1997). It is however worth noting that whilst 'thicker' forms of constructivism may well offer deeper insights into particular forms of social action, even those who accept the theoretical foundations of this perspective have encountered practical difficulties in developing methodological tools that meet the requirements of their epistemological orientation

(Checkel 2004).[30] Indeed, they may be insurmountable when engaged in full comparative research where process tracing, the preferred strategy, may be impractical given time and other resource constraints.[31] That said, Schmidt's approach to analysing discourse would be consistent with the epistemology, and perhaps even ontology, of those who adhere to 'thinner' variants of constructivism and have developed and applied empirical hypotheses on social interaction that emphasise arguing, persuasion, social influence and rhetorical action.[32] As such, this analytical framework engages with some aspects of the more recent theorising on ideational approaches.

To summarise, in order to analyse variety and change in economic models, we should focus on the three dimensions of policy, 'polity' and politics coupled with a methodologically diverse approach that combines the three 'new institutionalisms', that is rational-choice, historical and sociological, with discursive institutionalism. This analytical framework will facilitate the identification of the details and micro-foundations of particular policies and institutions, and consequently permit the discrimination of varieties in a globalised system of capitalism. The framework will also help correct the theoretical weaknesses of earlier VoCs as well as better address the issues of change and convergence.

For this particular study on institutional changes within financial systems in East Asia, the methodological approach of my analysis will in the first instance involve an investigation of time-series of quantitative

---

[30] For example, while Culpepper (2005) made the important point that explaining institutional change should include an analysis of 'cognitive maps' and shifts in 'joint beliefs', this was not followed with the detailed process-tracing analysis that is required in his empirical argument in order to best substantiate his ontological perspective. Instead, Culpepper resorted to passing rhetoric as well as inferences from other observed behaviour that did not do full justice to a social constructivist approach. Interestingly, the 'deeper' social constructivist ontology disappeared in a later work, see Culpepper (2008), although he retained the focus on ideational variables. However, the ontological basis of Culpepper's explanations in this later work rested on rationalist accounts and is therefore no different to Schmidt's approach to discourse analysis.

[31] Checkel (2004, p.242), for instance, acknowledged that he and his colleagues chose not to include the work of 'interpretative constructivists' in a research project on European integration 'out of a practical concern to finish within a reasonable time frame'.

[32] See for instance Price (1998); Risse (2000); Johnston (2001); Checkel (2003); Schimmelfennig (2003).

data that relate to some of the key aspects that differentiate between types of financial systems: changes in relative importance of banking sector v. capital markets, participation/ownership levels of foreign actors and levels of state-ownership in financial institutions. This exercise will provide us with an initial impression of the nature of the evolution and changes within these financial systems. However, as argued earlier, I need to go beyond quantitative analyses in order to better discern and explain differences in the varieties of financial systems. This will be facilitated with an institutional analysis that pays particular attention to the three dimensions of policy, 'polity' and politics. In operationalising the analytical framework of the three P's, I will investigate (1) how the state interacts with other actors in defining and constituting the institutional setting that structures the actions of public and private actors in financial systems; (2) how the state conceptualises, introduces and implements financial sector policies that may alter the incentive structure for actors' behaviour and consequently affect the nature of capitalism; and (3) in terms of politics, I will investigate the strategic interactions among actors as well as the discursive behaviour employed within historically conditioned contexts. In the process of this analysis, I will simultaneously uncover the 'conventional' independent variables of the three I's: (1) the interest-based coalitions and power resources that are mobilised to influence economic outcomes within financial systems; (2) the rules and regularities that shape the development of institutions within financial systems, and that consequently influence and constrain economic actors' rational choices; and (3) the ideational elements and discursive processes adopted to justify policy moves.

Some methodological clarifications

Before moving onto the more substantive analysis in the following chapters, I would like to clarify remaining methodological issues that are important to this study.

Ideal type v. empirical cases

We need to be careful about the use of ideal types and not conflate them with empirical cases. Unless by design, it is difficult to imagine empirical cases matching perfectly with ideal types, since the latter are necessarily abstractions of reality constructed for specific heuristic value. Consequently, it is possible, and indeed expected, that we will observe characteristics of more than one ideal type within specific empirical cases, or alternatively that we cannot fully account for an empirical case with only one ideal type. Ideal types should be seen as constituents of cases, rather than the latter as exemplifiers of the former (Crouch 2005). Otherwise, the analyst runs the risk of reifying ideal types as describing the entirety of political economies rather than as idealised representations of particular dynamics, features or tendencies.[33]

We also need to avoid the tendency to focus on 'labelling' empirical cases and instead pay more attention to 'analysing' them (Crouch 2005). In other words, while our models are logical constructions about how 'things' (in this case, institutions) fit together, our research should be about how things actually do or do not fit together in a messy empirical reality (Morgan 2005, p.4). However, just because empirical cases are 'messy' does not render the distinctions we make with ideal types useless, both conceptually and empirically. As analysts, we can, and often do, exercise judgement as to which ideal type(s) is/are reflected in empirical cases, in which sectors/dimensions, and to what extent they are represented. This approach, I believe, will lead us to a more nuanced understanding of empirical cases. Although there is a subjective element in the exercise of our judgement, careful and methodical use of both quantitative indicators as well as qualitative observations will help us reach conclusions that are better substantiated and that can be improved through constructive critique.

In adopting this approach to the use of ideal types and their application to empirical cases, it is possible to recognise that even in the US, a country that is often cited as a prime example of an LME, a 'hidden' developmental state dimension exists in the research and commercialisation of new technologies (Block 2008), and in the defence industry, even while it displays (to varying degrees) characteristics of an LME in a range of economic sectors, in particular the financial sector.[34] Similarly, the British governments of Thatcher, Major and Blair have engaged in more direct government action in the process of regulatory reform than in the past, this even though the UK is frequently labelled as an LME (Moran 2003). That the UK and US exhibit aspects of both LMEs and SiMEs should not be problematic, nor perhaps even surprising. After all the LME is a heuristic abstraction, not a direct representation of the

---

[33] This criticism could be directed at the Hall and Soskice (2001b) approach to VoC.

[34] It has also been pointed out that the US, frequently cited as a prime example of an LME, has not always followed the diktats of the ideal type such as the prescriptions of the 'Washington Consensus'. See, for example, Hudson and Sommers (2008); The Nation (2009).

specific case of either the UK or the US. I suggest that recognising, and accepting, this complexity enriches our understanding of empirical reality.

Finally, given my understanding of the relationship between ideal types and empirical cases, my aim in this research project is not to ascertain whether empirical cases have morphed, or transformed, from one ideal type into another but more to analyse how the empirical cases have evolved and to what extent and in which way these paths of evolution or changes reflect one or more ideal types, if at all. Underpinning this approach is my understanding of both the nature of economic models and the nature of change. I see change being more often than not an incremental, rather than revolutionary, process that can lead to evolutionary paths that are 'crooked' or diverging as a result of exogenous and endogenous factors (Thelen 2004; Streeck and Thelen 2005). Institutional change can arise from a variety of processes that result from continuous interaction between key social actors engaging in discursive behaviour as well as the (strategic and rational) exercise of power (Höpner 2001; Crouch and Farrell 2004; Deeg 2005). As a consequence, I see capitalist systems constituted by loosely connected components that evolve historically and thus change at different rates in different ways through different processes. With this in mind, this study aims to assert no more than that empirical cases are becoming 'more (less) like', or moving towards (away from), a certain ideal type along some specific dimension as opposed to asserting that they 'have become' a certain model, lock, stock and barrel.

The focus of the study

In analysing economic change, the objects of study here are the state, as actor, and the financial system, as opposed to the economy more broadly. This selective focus is primarily motivated by the research question, which in turn is motivated by the debates that emerged during the 1997–8 Asian financial crisis that identified the role of the state as one of the key causes of the financial crisis and consequently the need to reform, if not retrench, its role in order to sustain these economies' continued engagement with the global economy. As such, the selective, if perhaps narrow, focus on the state and financial system is justified, in the first instance, on the grounds of the orientation of the research project.

More than that, given the nature of the questions that I am asking in this study, that is how have economic systems/markets evolved, the focus on the state is also important since state action is understood to be crucial in influencing and structuring market economies. Many of the key institutions that govern the constitution and behaviour of economic actors have been nationally specified (Whitley 2005), as such it is important to understand the role of the state if we wish to understand the nature of the market. I am, however, not ignoring non-state actors. Their role in shaping the nature of capitalist markets is also important. Furthermore, I am obliged to consider the roles of non-state actors given the three P's framework that I have adopted. It would be meaningless to discuss 'polity' or politics if I considered only one actor, that is the state.

Finally, the focus on one economic sector, that is the financial, may be seen as too narrow with questionable implications for broader generalisations. While I agree that it is difficult, if not sometimes impossible, to extrapolate the implications derived from one sector to the broader economy, this research on the financial sector can still serve a wider utility on at least two grounds. First, if one subscribes, as do the VoC approaches, to the notion of complementarity as an underlying dynamic of capitalist systems, and argue that changes in one part of the system will be reflected in changes elsewhere, then the results of this research into financial systems can be used to complement discussions about broader changes in models of capitalist systems. Second, if we do not subscribe to this notion of complementarity but believe that there can be disaggregation in different components within capitalist systems, then understanding the changes that have taken place in financial systems alone is still an important exercise since the financial system is understood to play a critical role in the functioning and growth of a modern capitalist economy and is therefore central to economic change (Mishkin 2001), particularly in a globalised world. Changes in financial systems will have wide implications although it is beyond the scope of this research project to test or make assertions about the nature and extent of its impact on the broader economy.[35] While it would be desirable to conduct a wider multi-sectoral study, such an endeavour is not possible given the resource and time constraints available. This broader investigation will have to be picked up on another occasion.

---

[35] Many, like Hall and Soskice (2001a) and Culpepper (2005), have argued that 'financial deregulation could be the string that unravels coordinated market economies', and for that matter SiMEs, thus asserting the central role that financial systems can play in institutional change.

3
Korea

Historical control of the financial system by the Korean government was considered by many as one of the most important, if not the most important, instrument employed in the country's path to economic development (Nam and Lee 1995; Choi 1993). In regulating businesses' access to credit, the government was able to direct and influence their decisions over resource allocation and thus the pattern of industrial development. However, as the 1990s dawned, the Korean government began to liberalise its financial system. This was motivated in part by its aspiration to accede to the OECD and in part to address the 'developmental blockage' that had emerged as a result of the nature of the evolution of the Korean state–business nexus (Weiss 2003). As this process of liberalisation was partial and arguably ill conceived, it rendered the financial system vulnerable to financial turmoil and consequently contributed to Korea falling victim to the financial crisis that spread through East Asia in 1997. The experience of the crisis led to calls to address the perceived weaknesses in Korea's form of economic governance: the dominant role of the state in the economy, the close state–business nexus, and the inability or absence of market dynamics to rein in poor business practices. A programme of financial reform and restructuring in the period post-crisis was expected to address these issues.

I begin this chapter with a brief historical account of the evolution and development of the Korean financial system, highlighting the interest-based, institutional and ideational factors that explain the evolution of the state–market dynamic in the financial sector. This is followed with an examination of developments in the Korean financial system since the crisis of the late-1990s. First, I assess the nature of changes in the structure of the market through the use of quantitative indicators. Since these quantitative indicators only provide us with a partial view of the evolution of the Korean financial sector, the discussion continues with an institutional analysis of financial sector reform since the crisis. This analysis will be structured along the lines of three broad but important institutional developments of the last decade: the expansion of financial markets, the attempt by the Korean state to develop a 'financial hub', and changes in regulatory and supervisory arrangements. The chapter will conclude with an assessment of the changing state–market dynamic in the Korean financial sector and evaluate how this has fared against the LME ideal type.

History

Korea's financial sector has traditionally been characterised as a 'repressed' regime in which the state wielded great influence, if not outright control, over interest rates, entry and exit, and policy guidance.[1] As finance was seen as a major instrument of industrial policy, the goal of which was the economic development and growth of the country, a wide range of credit allocation requirements on banks and on central bank lending were imposed in order to influence the distribution of credit,[2] facilitated by government control over the financial system through the establishment of various specialised banks, the nationalisation of commercial banks, and the subordination of the central bank (Maxfield 1994; Nam and Lee 1995, pp.47–8; Cho 1997).[3] These practices began in the 1960s under the regime of Park Chung-hee when export promotion and 'outward orientation' strategies were adopted with the aim of achieving economic development and growth.

The state's extensive influence was also observed in other aspects of the monetary and financial system. In the mid-1960s, the local currency was devalued to encourage exports and interest rates were raised

---

[1] For a detailed discussion of the development of Korea's financial system and government policies from 1945 to 1978, see Cole and Park (1983).

[2] According to Woo-Cumings (1997, p.63), banks had no voice in the allocation of policy loans and had to accommodate these loans irrespective of their portfolio strategies.

[3] The entire Korean banking system came under government ownership in 1961 when the new military regime of Park Chung-hee nationalised commercial banks as a way of confiscating 'illicit' wealth accumulated under the previous regime. The government remained the major stockholder of nationwide city banks until the early-1980s, generally holding more than 20 per cent of total shares. For details, see Nam and Lee (1995, p.33); Choi (1993).

in order to mobilise domestic savings for investment and support the export credit programme. The state-owned Korea Development Bank was authorised to borrow funds from abroad and guarantee foreign commercial loans as a major source of financing for economic development.[4] Domestic banks also became facilitators and guarantors of external finance when the Law of Guaranteeing Foreign Loans was promulgated in July 1962, although they did not actually intermediate between foreign lenders and domestic borrowers (Cole and Park 1983, p.62). Foreign loan negotiations were instead managed by the Economic Planning Board with the banks issuing guarantees on instruction from the government (Choi 1993, p.28). Finance was, in turn, almost automatically extended to the export industries by commercial banks and the Bank of Korea (BOK) at heavily subsidised interest rates. The export credit programmes were designed and implemented in close consultation with major exporters and were explicitly linked to export performance (Hahm 2001).

State action was therefore instrumental in cultivating this institutionalised 'partnership' between the government and business in order to promote the economic development of the country. The government was understood to be the 'senior partner' in this relationship and state control of the financial system in the 1960s was seen as part of a social bargain to achieve economic industrialisation and development. The effect of the state's policies resulted in an institutionalised set of incentives that channelled business actors into export-based economic activities. Even when the degree of government repression was reduced through the liberalisation of interest rates in the late-1960s, the effect of this reform was to divert funds from the informal money, or curb, market to the formal banking sector over which government had tight control (Cho 1997).

Government intervention became more 'acute, direct and specific' in the 1970s when its policy focus in terms of economic development shifted from light manufacturing to heavy and chemical industries (HCI) in response to rising real wages in the broader economy and increasing competition from other developing countries (Ahn 2001, p.15). As private firms were reluctant to invest in HCI because of their long gestation period and uncertain rates of return, Korean policy makers had to tighten their control over finance in order to allocate resources to the

---

[4] The Korea Development Bank was founded in 1954 to finance and manage major industrial projects in order to expedite industrial development.

HCI. A massive investment programme for these industries, financed largely by foreign loans and central bank credit, was put into effect in 1973 and pursued vigorously until 1979 (Haggard 1990; Cho and Kim 1995). Government authorities had to keep nominal bank lending rates below market levels and to intensify credit rationing which resulted in negative real interest rates. The government also became more actively involved in the allocation of economic activities and assigned the *chaebol* to pre-selected industries in order to minimise inefficient competition and duplication. The government used both carrot and stick approaches to encourage business firms to engage in HCI. Those that were considered to have performed poorly and inconsistently were punished by being cut off from lines of credit whilst those that appeared to perform well were assured of continuous funding. Woo-Cumings (1997, p.62) contended that the Korean banking system of the 1970s exhibited 'the most extreme case of dependence on the state' and that Korean banks 'did not enjoy even limited autonomy with respect to the criteria of lending and response to non-performing loans'.

Credit rationing in the official sector and negative interest rates in the 1970s effectively reversed the earlier effects of interest rate reform in the late-1960s. As a result, the unorganised money market, or the curb market, re-emerged and became an important source of short-term financing for smaller Korean firms and individuals neglected by official policy. By one estimate, over one quarter of total domestic credit to the private sector in 1972 came from the unorganised money market, this despite the fact that the interest rates charged were fairly high (Nam and Lee 1995, p.34). An opportunity to bring this market under control became available when a number of large firms suffered financial distress.[5] The government responded by enacting the Presidential Emergency Decree of August 1972 that placed a moratorium on debt services to curb market lenders and rescheduled bank loans at substantially reduced interest rates, which effectively froze the curb market. With nowhere else to go, investors returned to the formal organised market. In order to help absorb funds from the curb market and mobilise financial resources through organised markets, a new legal form of financial organisation, non-bank financial institutions (NBFIs), was introduced through the enactment of the *Short-Term Financing Business Act* in 1972 (Choi 1993;

[5] The failure of these large firms followed a burst of investment in the second half of the 1960s and the tight monetary policy and devaluation adopted to cope with a large current account deficit.

Nam and Lee 1995; Hahm 2001). A favourable environment was created for the growth of NBFIs with lower entry barriers, the introduction of new financial instruments and more attractive interest rates offered to depositors (often circumventing interest rate controls). While these policies contributed to the expansion and diversification of Korea's financial sector, they were ultimately motivated by the desire of the government to reassert control and regulate the market. More importantly, as the corporate sector was effectively bailed out at the expense of private curb lenders and bank depositors as a result of the Emergency Decree, the move was read as a signal to the market that the government was willing to share major risks in the corporate sector (Cho and Kim 1997). This implicit insurance, as a result of state intervention in the market, significantly aggravated moral hazard and was to become an important factor in repeated problems and crises experienced within the Korean financial sector.

In summary, throughout the 1960s and 1970s, in both financing and general economic matters, the government played an extensive role in the nation's development. The state in these early decades did not just influence but also controlled large segments of the market. Government policies and actions created an institutional structure with incentives that steered investment into priority sectors within a framework of a 'governed market' (Wade 2004). While there were efforts to reform the supply side of the financial system to develop money and capital markets, they were prompted more by government attempts to further control and command the financial system. The expansion of the financial sector led to the emergence of a second-tier financial market, dominated by the NBFIs, in which there was greater market competition. However the main financial system was still largely state owned, controlled and guided. The financial system had therefore bifurcated. The financial needs of individuals and smaller Korean firms were met initially by an unregulated curb market and then later by the growth of NBFIs, while the needs of large manufacturing and export firms were serviced by commercial banks that were effectively controlled by the government.

The 1980s

The Korean economy experienced a crisis in 1979–80 due to the combined effects of soaring inflation fuelled by rising wage levels and massive infusion of foreign capital; a global economic slowdown induced by rising oil prices and interest rates; and excess capacity in some of the heavy industries established in the 1970s (Woo-Cumings 1997). Rising exchange rates were also affecting some export industries, in particular the textile sector. This contributed to a significant increase in the amount of non-performing loans (NPLs) from earlier lending to the *chaebol*. The continued availability of external finance needed to support the government's growth-first policy also became doubtful as Korea's credit standing in the international financial markets eroded with the deterioration of its current account (Park 1994), while rising interest rates raised the cost of borrowing. These developments threatened the legitimacy of the Korean state and its modernisation strategy.[6]

The government's response came in the form of the Fifth Five-Year Economic and Social Development Plan formulated in 1981 in which it was argued that Korea's poor economic performance had to be remedied with price stability followed by economic liberalisation. The policy decision to liberalise the economy and put in place a more market-oriented system was in part a recognition of the debilitating effects of the interventionist regime institutionalised in the earlier decades, as much as it was driven by the government's desire to maintain its political legitimacy. Liberalisation in this period was also partially driven by American economic interests, with the help of US trained technocrats in ministries or research outfits such as the Korean Development Institute (Woo-Cumings 1997).

In the financial sector, market liberalisation and privatisation took place throughout the 1980s. Restrictions on bank management were lifted and government equity shares in all five nationwide city banks were divested (Choi 2002). Along with the changing ownership structure, the state also addressed the disparity in interest rates that existed between policy and other types of loans in order to scale down the extent of policy loans. However, despite privatisation and greater managerial autonomy by commercial banks, the banking system was still subjected to heavy government intervention in its lending decisions and appointments of top managers and members of the boards of directors (Nam and Lee 1995, pp.50–1). Similarly, although the gap in interest rates was almost completely eliminated in 1982 (Ahn 2001, p.15), they were nevertheless still regulated. More importantly, despite liberalisation, in practice, regulated interest rates had been maintained well below the market rate and have not been adequately flexible (Nam and

[6] This was complicated by the social and political problems that arose with the death of President Park Chung-hee in October 1979, preceded by the failure of the ruling party, for the first time, to win more popular votes than the opposition in the 1978 National Assembly election, despite the less than perfectly free and fair electoral environment.

Lee 1995, Table 1.2), which suggested that the Korean financial market was still far from being fully integrated and operating on a purely competitive basis. The absence of greater liberalisation represented a continuance of the state's effort to deploy the banking sector as an instrument of economic growth, leading Choi (2002) to suggest that the process of financial liberalisation during the 1970s–80s was more one of 'regulated deregulation'.

The government nevertheless attempted to bolster market dynamics by substantially lowering entry barriers into the financial market and diversifying the types of financial services that different intermediaries could permissibly provide. These deregulatory measures triggered competition between the commercial banks and the NBFIs, although the playing field was not level. The NBFIs were much less constrained than the banks in their ability to expand sectoral allocation of credit especially after the enactment of the revised *Banking Act* in 1982 that was in part designed to stem the loan concentration of bank, but not NBFI, credits among the *chaebol* and to ensure SMEs access to bank credits (Hahm 2001). As a result, the NBFIs emerged as an important alternative source of financing for *chaebol* (see Hahm 2003). The regulatory bias in favour of the NBFIs was also evident in the range of financial activities that they were permitted to undertake as well as in the extension of special tax treatment. The NBFIs were often also allowed to circumvent interest rate ceilings, which were already set at levels that were more generous than those on bank deposits and loans.

The variance in the level of government control over banks and NBFIs appeared to be the result of perceived differences in the externalities associated with the failure of different types of financial institutions as well as the desire to maximise the mobilisation of financial resources through organised markets, as opposed to the unregulated curb market, while simultaneously retaining control over certain institutions, namely commercial banks, that can be used to provide low-cost funds to industry. It was also suggested that such special dispensation reflected the interests of *chaebol* that had by then acquired a lion's share of NBFI-ownership (Choi 2002).[7] Certainly, by the 1980s, if not earlier,

---

[7] In contrast to the banking sector, no outright ownership regulation was applied to the NBFIs. In the absence of transparent entry requirements, discretionary issuance of licenses resulted in the increasing ownership of NBFIs by *chaebol*. Ownership of commercial banks, however, was limited up to 8 per cent of voting shares under the *Banking Act* amendment of December 1982. The ownership limit was strengthened to 4 per cent in 1994.

clientelistic relationships had developed between the government and the *chaebol*. Credit policies had become politicised and the *chaebol* saw financial liberalisation as a means of limiting the government's intervention in their economic affairs (Haggard and Moon 1990, p.227; Choi 1993, p.42).

From the perspective of prudential regulation, the government's policies and responses in the 1980s undermined market stability since deregulation took place without due consideration to the issues of transparency, credit analysis, risk management, and lending practices. On the other hand, the liberalisation of the financial sector in this period was, as outlined, uneven, and it could therefore be argued that further market liberalisation might well have addressed financial sector weaknesses and inadequacies. However, the legacy of the government's earlier heavy intervention in resource allocation during the 1970s hindered further financial liberalisation. Although the government exercised substantial power over business from 1961 through to the mid-1970s, with the institution of the policy on heavy industrialisation in the early-1970s, business groups grew larger in size, became more powerful, and consequently wielded more leverage in negotiations. Thus, as the Korean economy became more industrialised, the relationship between government and business shifted from the 'supremacy' of the state over business to a 'strategic interdependence' (Choi 1993), or a 'mutual hostage' situation (Kang 2002), between the two. This altered the politics of the financial sector in which the government could no longer fully decide, on an independent basis, how credit was to be allocated or how the financial sector would evolve, but was caught in a situation where it could no longer ignore the economic power held by the *chaebol*.[8] The growing strength of the *chaebol* had altered the 'polity' in which policies were made and the state had to accommodate their interests.

Other aspects of the government's earlier intervention in the economy also posed obstacles to further financial liberalisation. The significant volume of policy loans, accounting for almost half of all domestic credit, made it difficult to remove credit ceilings and other direct monetary controls. The heavy burden of NPLs, in part the result of government intervention in bank lending in the 1970s, also supported the need for continued interest rate regulation. Finally, the government felt it had to continue regulating most of the interest rates in order to prevent major

---

[8] By 1980, the chaebol accounted for 49 per cent of GDP, 24 per cent of total sales, 18 per cent of manufacturing employment and over half of Korea's total exports. See Haggard and Moon (1990) for details.

financial crises that would otherwise result from the bankruptcies of highly leveraged firms. This concern was starkly substantiated in the crisis of 1997–8.

Socio-cultural factors were also important in explaining the difficulty encountered in transforming the state-led model into a free-market one. Both Choi (1993) and Park (2001) argued that the traditional Korean state–society relations in which the bureaucrats and power-holders believed that the government was more adept than the market was a powerful influence on the nature of policies adopted and may explain why, despite privatisation and liberalisation in the 1980s, the underlying financial structure and the way in which business was conducted remained very much unchanged. According to this view, the government's liberalisation of the financial sector was historically and culturally conditioned, even if it was also influenced by the vested interests of *chaebol*, their affiliated NBFIs and state actors themselves.

Thus, if the Korea of the 1960s and 1970s was a 'quasi-internal organisation' led by a 'strong developmental state' and supported by an efficient bureaucracy that was instrumental in bringing about rapid structural changes and economic development (Lee 1992), the introduction of numerous liberalisation measures from the 1980s onwards and the growing economic and political influence of *chaebol* have brought the effectiveness of this quasi-internal organisation as a development institution into question (Nam and Lee 1995; Park 1994). At the dawn of the 1990s, the Korean economy began to display features of a mixed economy in which the state's considerable influence had become increasingly attenuated. The state's ability to solve coordination problems began to weaken while market dynamics, albeit perverted by the nature of the historical evolution of Korea's economy in which the *chaebol* dominated, made inroads into the Korean financial system.

The early 1990s

Significant financial deregulation began to emerge from 1993 as a result of three key dynamics. First, from the perspective of polity and politics, competition among domestic financial and corporate institutions over declining rents led to demands for greater freedom in decision making (Chang, Park and Yoo 1998). Financial liberalisation was also seen as a means to facilitate the international expansion of *chaebol* businesses (Kalinowski and Cho 2009), and thus, Korean economic growth. Second, foreign financial service providers sought to enter the lucrative Korean financial market (Noland 2005, p.3). Finally, the Korean state in the 1990s saw financial reform as the price to be paid for admittance to the OECD to which its leadership aspired, as a result of a policy decision to validate the country's level of development (Mann 1998).[9]

This led to the introduction of a five-year blueprint for financial reform in 1993 that focussed on liberalising interest rates, reducing the scope of government intervention in the financial sector and giving banks more independence in allocating credit as well as greater operational freedom (Mann 1998). However, the banks' degree of independence remained constrained by government 'encouraged lending' (as opposed to 'directed lending') and ties with the *chaebol* remained tight. Furthermore, the state retained control of the financial market through its influence over decisions regarding the appointment of bank directors and senior executives (Choi 2002; Park 2006, pp.186–7). Even in privately owned banks, any personnel decisions involving top executives still had to be approved by the government and most of these positions were filled with retired bureaucrats, particularly from the Ministry of Finance and Economy (MOFE) (Choi 2002). This practice of so-called parachute appointment (*nakhasan insa*) encouraged rent-seeking behaviour. While the introduction of a more transparent system for nominating bank presidents in 1993 helped impart some managerial autonomy to the banks, state interference continued to be legitimised as a counterbalance to the influence of *chaebol* stockholders (Woo-Cumings 1997).

Notwithstanding the persistence of these constraints on bank operations, Korea's financial system was significantly liberalised and brought closer to a market-led system in the early- to mid-1990s due in part to conditions imposed on the country as it sought membership of the OECD. There were however inconsistencies in the nature of financial sector reforms. Domestic concerns – political, nationalistic and economic – stymied forward movement on greater foreign participation in the delivery of financial services and the independence of domestic intermediaries that might have introduced greater competition and market dynamics. There were restricted liberalisation of foreign investment in the stock market and the continuation of 'encouraged' lending by the government and 'relationship' lending by the *chaebol*. What market deregulation and reform that did emerge were accompanied with fragmented and inappropriate supervision, in part because reform to banking supervision was not consistent with *chaebol* or government needs. For example, while banks were required to meet global financial

[9] Korea was admitted into the OECD in 1996.

standards such as BIS capital adequacy guidelines and CAMEL-based reporting procedures, these systems were undermined by the liberal interpretation of 'bad loans' (Walter 2008, p.130). Furthermore, although the *chaebol* were not permitted to own commercial banks, they were permitted to own and manage NBFIs, a market segment in which regulations were relatively lax compared with those of commercial banks. The inconsistency of policy measures that were introduced during this period, and the consequent effect on market stability, can in large part be explained by the intricate and deep relationships among the state, the *chaebol* and the banks that have developed over the previous decades. The contradictory tensions resulting from the close relationship of the government, the corporate sector and the market led Hahm (2004) to suggest that the Korean financial system at the onset of the crisis in 1997 was not a 'normal' market but rather a 'pseudo-market and quasi-bank-based system'.

One key effect of financial liberalisation during the early 1990s was the continued structural weakening of the traditional risk partnership between the state and the *chaebol*. Furthermore, although financial liberalisation in the 1990s was meant to address the 'developmental blockage' that had emerged by the end of the 1980s (Weiss 2003, p.251), this attempt ultimately failed given the nature of liberalisation efforts. The deregulation of interest rates on non-bank financial products while leaving deposit rates of commercial banks effectively unchanged contributed to the rapid expansion of NBFIs throughout the 1980s and 1990s (Shin and Park 2001). As a result, in the 1990s, the share of NBFI loans has been consistently larger than the share of bank loans (Hahm 2001). Given the differentiated ownership regulation of NBFIs and commercial banks, growth in the NBFIs ended up in the hands of the *chaebol* with the 70 largest *chaebol* owning 140 NBFIs at the onset of the financial crisis in 1997–8. This dominance of *chaebol*-ownership in the NBFIs, coupled with a more liberal operating environment as compared with commercial banks, and the absence of effective supervision and monitoring systems, resulted in serious conflict of interests that contributed to the emergence of the financial crisis in the late-1990s (Kim 2000). In the process, the state's grip over the market became increasingly weak even though it attempted to continue intervening and influencing the market. Although liberalisation in the early-1990s put the Korean financial system on the path towards an LME model, at least in the formal institutionalised sense, it did not yet function like one. More importantly, it was proceeding on dynamics that ultimately undermined its stability and threatened the broader economy's developmental trajectory.[10]

The Financial Reform Bill

The varied difficulties of Korea's economy were clear when Vice-Prime Minister Kang Kyung Sik took over the economic portfolio in March 1997. His approach to these challenges was to persist with reforming the country's economic institutions to render the economy more market-oriented. In the financial sector, the government introduced a bill proposing key institutional reform including the creation of a consolidated supervisory agency that would supervise all financial institutions. The bill was however delayed due to differences of opinion between the MOFE and the BOK over which of the two would have jurisdiction of the new supervisory agency (Heo and Kim 2000, p.504).[11] The presidential election scheduled for 18 December 1997 further complicated the process of arriving at a political compromise.[12] The financial reform bill was only finally passed by the National Assembly on 29 December 1997, after Korea had succumbed to the Asian financial crisis.

The presence of the IMF in the midst of the crisis proved to be a catalyst that rendered financial sector reform politically acceptable in the face of domestic resistance from the *chaebol*, the MOFE and the large banks. Although the external influence of the IMF was important – for instance, the acceptance of the financial reform legislation by the National Assembly was one of the conditions of the financial assistance programme entered by Korea with the IMF – economic reform in Korea in the late-1990s was also an extension of Kim Young-sam's government's efforts to roll back the developmental state and to liberalise its economy. As discussed in the preceding section, the process of financial reform in Korea in the 1990s began well before the outbreak of the crisis with the impetus coming initially from within Korean

---

[10] For a more vivid account of how policy changes in this period contributed to destabilisation in the financial system, see Sharma (2003, pp.180–7).

[11] Both the BOK and the MOFE previously shared responsibility for financial supervision.

[12] For more details, see Hahm (1999).

political and economic elites rather than external actors.[13] A draft of the financial reform bill of 1997, based largely on the recommendations of a 31-member Presidential Commission for Financial Reform established by President Kim Young-sam, was submitted to the National Assembly on 23 August before the outbreak of the financial crisis in Korea. Thus, even before the experience of the crisis, policy makers had already intended to introduce better market regulation, further liberalisation and greater competition in the financial sector. However, with the onset of the financial crisis, the government's immediate objective was to stabilise the financial sector.[14] It is to this that the discussion will now turn.

Managing the crisis

The government's initial focus, from early-1998 until early-2000, was on stabilising the economy and restoring the financial sector's intermediary function by injecting public funds into financial institutions that faced severe liquidity crunches. Bad assets were cleaned up and weak financial institutions were restructured through mergers and acquisitions (M&As) or purchase and assumptions (P&As).[15] In order to mitigate moral hazard, assistance to distressed financial institutions was provided on the condition that the institutions made effort to reduce costs, recapitalise themselves by attracting foreign investments, and write down the capital of existing shareholders. This first stage of stabilising the financial system quickly eased the credit crunch and, to some extent, restored the financial intermediary system. However, when the Daewoo Group collapsed and the Hyundai Group suffered liquidity problems, financial institutions found themselves even

---

[13] Mathews (2001) suggested, on the basis of interviews with officials in the Korean Ministry of Finance, that most of the structural reforms in the December 1997 agreement with the IMF were incorporated at the instigation of the Korean side.

[14] More detailed review and analyses of Korea's recovery from the crisis have been conducted elsewhere and are beyond the scope of this project. For fuller account of the financial crisis and policies taken immediately thereafter, see, among others, Hahm (1999); Shin and Hahm (1999); Park (2006); Ito and Hashimoto (2007a); Kang (2009b). For a recent account of the causes of the Asian financial crisis in Korea, see Gu (2008).

[15] For detailed accounts of the restructuring of financial institutions during this period, see, among others, Shin and Hahm (1999); Kim and Park (2001); Kim, Kim and Ryoo (2006); Park (2006).

further distressed, incurring losses to the tune of KRW31.2 trillion (J-y Lee 2008; B-y Kim 2008).[16] Thus a second round of restructuring began in September 2000 where the primary goal was to strengthen the competitiveness of financial institutions which the government attempted to achieve by not only removing financial and corporate distress from the market, but also promoting the consolidation of institutions and universal banking services (Park 2006, p.175).

One policy 'innovation' that emerged at this stage was the introduction of the legal entity of 'financial holding companies' as an alternative to M&As and P&As in resolving unviable financial institutions. The Woori Financial Holding Company established in April 2001 was the first of these that consolidated a range of institutions under one corporate umbrella. Aside from financially depressed banks, healthy banks were also strongly encouraged to consolidate and develop universal banking services in order to become 'leading' banks, which in turn sparked a competitive pressure on other institutions to follow suit (Park 2006, p.176). These developments met with the approval of policy makers who by this stage saw consolidation as not only a means to increase stability to the financial system but also to improve the competitiveness of the financial sector and the potential for overall economic growth. The process of consolidation however led to a large reduction in the number of institutions and while this arguably helped produce a more sustainable profit base for the industry as a whole, it simultaneously raised questions as to the changing dynamics of competition in the market and of the power of the banking units that survived. Nevertheless, by latching on to the idea of the 'financial holding company' as a means to resolve some of the issues that emerged from the crisis, the state began to shape the evolution of the market as well as seized on the further possibility of developing or upgrading the financial sector, a point that will be elaborated later in this chapter.

Another notable development during this period was the substantial increase in the issuance of bonds by the government, inadvertently contributing to the expansion and diversification of the financial sector. In the course of resolving NPLs and restructuring the banking system, a total of KRW167.6 trillion (including recycled funds) of public funds were injected into financial institutions from November 1997 to July

---

[16] The difficulties encountered by Daewoo and Hyundai in this period also implicated the state through its policies of regulatory forbearance and state-sponsored credit. For details, see Walter (2008, pp.134–5).

2005 through two main government agencies: Korea Deposit Insurance Corporation (KDIC) and the Korean Asset Management Corporation (KAMCO).[17] These funds were raised mainly by issuing bonds of the Deposit Insurance Fund run by KDIC and of the Non-Performing Loans Management Fund run by KAMCO, from government fiscal sources, and recycled funds. Although these bonds were all quasi-fiscal,[18] they were not included in official budget deficit figures, thus muddying the actual fiscal position of the government (Lee and Rhee 2007). The issuance of these bonds did however have a positive effect as the bond market began to expand, thus addressing the 'spare tyre' argument that emerged during the crisis.

A final key policy measure adopted during this period that had significant consequences for the subsequent evolution of the financial sector was the relegation of the restructuring of NBFIs until after the commercial banks had been stabilised. The absence of controlling shareholders at commercial banks, and the greater involvement and influence of the government in the management of banks, rendered the large-scale restructuring of the banking sector more politically acceptable as compared with the NBFIs where there was significant control by the *chaebol* (Lim and Hahm 2006, p.101). While the government was focussed on restructuring the banks, it allowed *chaebol* access to bond financing through investment trust companies (ITCs) in order to avoid a severe credit crunch. A large volume of funds consequently flowed through the capital market into the *chaebol*, which not only postponed the resolution of insolvent corporate firms, but also magnified the scale of the problem when they eventually defaulted on their loans. Before the Daewoo Group collapsed, it had issued a significant amount of corporate bonds and commercial paper in 1998 – made possible by the government's 'bank first, NBFI second' approach – only to dishonour them in July 1999. This helped push the share of NPLs of non-depository institutions to 23.2 per cent in December 1999, up from 9.6 per cent in March 1998 (Kim and Park 2001).

With such large-scale failures, depositors and investors began to consider the financial products of NBFIs as being risky and redirected much

[17] For more detailed information of sources of and uses for government funds, see Ito and Hashimoto (2007a, pp.41–4).

[18] Bonds of both the Deposit Insurance Fund and the Non-performing Loans Management Fund were guaranteed by the government.

of their deposits to commercial banks, particularly since the latter were able to restore their capital adequacy ratios, and thus their credibility, with the help of the government's recapitalisation programme. The shift of funds away from the capital markets and ITCs toward commercial banks contributed to the eventual failure of and large reduction in NBFIs. Given public dismay in the role of the *chaebol* in the development of the financial crisis and the latter's stake in the NBFIs, this was, for many, not an unwelcome development (Weiss and Hobson 2000; Graham 2003). However, the failure of NBFIs had consequences for competitive dynamics. With the process of consolidation that was taking place in the banking sector, these developments contributed to strengthening the commercial banks' power and role in the financial sector. Commercial banks thus again became important as a source of corporate financing (Hahm 2005, p.391).

Many of these banks came under government control in the process of addressing issues raised by the financial crisis (Park 2006). Most of these were subsequently re-privatised although the government still retained major equity ownership in the Woori Financial Holding Company at the end of 2010. State intervention in the financial sector during the crisis has however changed the dynamics of the market as well as the nature of the state's involvement. First the 'bank first, NBFI second' approach contributed to the eventual collapse of a large number of NBFIs. While this outcome might have been politically welcome, it was not orchestrated, or at least not well orchestrated since the authorities' initial decision to allow *chaebol* access to funds via the ITCs while the banks were being restructured led to the collapse of a number of *chaebol* and subsequently the NBFIs, which further destabilised the market. The reduction in the number of NBFIs contributed to a weakening of competitive dynamics in the market, and eventually, in the course of developments in the post-crisis period, to the increased market power of the commercial banks. Second, underpinned by the strong commitment of the Kim Dae-jung government together with popular and electoral support, the state began to mould the financial sector in an attempt to transform the industry into one that was globally competitive in contrast to earlier efforts at liberalisation where the financial sector was still seen as hand-maiden to the real sector (Hahm 1999; Kim 2005). This point will be elaborated in the remainder of this chapter but initial signs of this development was already evident in the financial reform bill and the use of the 'financial holding company' entity to consolidate financial institutions.

Post-Crisis evolution of the financial system

The rest of this chapter investigates the extent and nature of changes in the Korean financial sector since the Asian financial crisis. In particular, the discussion seeks to ascertain whether the Korean financial sector has indeed become more market-oriented since the crisis and to determine what has become of the state–market relationship in the course of the evolution of the financial sector. In the next section, I evaluate changes in the Korean financial sector by analysing quantitative indicators. This will be followed with a fuller discussion of some of the more important institutional developments of the last decade in the financial sector: the expansion and diversification of the sector, the Financial Hub Strategy and regulatory and supervisory developments.

Quantitative indicators of change

Let us first consider whether the Korean financial sector has taken on aspects of an LME by analysing quantitative indicators.

There have undoubtedly been significant changes in the financial sector of Korea in the decade since the crisis given that the response involved wide-ranging reforms in restructuring financial institutions and efforts to address the structural weaknesses that left Korea vulnerable to a financial crisis. The number of financial institutions decreased from 2,103 in 1997 to 1,315 by the end of 2006, and a total of 899 insolvent financial institutions were closed or merged (Hahm 2007). Most of those institutions that have disappeared were NBFIs although the number of nationwide banks has also declined from 16 to 7.

Even though there was, in a sense, a contraction of the banking sector as a result of the reduction in the number of banking institutions in the market, the banking sector continues to dominate the Korean financial system a decade after the financial crisis. Bank assets amounted to 107 per cent of GDP in 2007 as compared with 101 per cent of GDP for the capitalisation of the stock market and 107 per cent of GDP for bonds outstanding (see Table 3.1). At the end of 2007, domestic bank credit still represented a significant source of private funding (101 per cent of GDP) compared with private bonds (where outstanding volume represented 59 per cent of GDP) and the stock market (where capitalisation stood at 121 per cent of GDP) – see Table 3.1 and Figure 3.1. Furthermore, as a result of consolidation and conglomeration, coupled with the reduction in competition from NBFIs,

Table 3.1 Korea: structure of financial systems (per cent of GDP)

	1996	1997	2002	2005	2006	2007
Deposit Money Bank Assets	50.75	55.26	87.78	94.88	101.46	107.61
Private Credit Extended by Deposit Money Banks and Other Financial Institutions	112.42	121.00	129.15	125.18	112.40	100.89
Stock Market Capitalisation	28.98	18.05	43.17	72.81	88.38	101.52
Bonds Outstanding	50.25	42.53	89.39	98.36	102.32	106.93

Source: Compiled from data extracted from The World Bank: Thorsten Beck et al.'s World Bank Database on Financial Development and Structure available from http://go.worldbank.org/X23UD9QUX0.

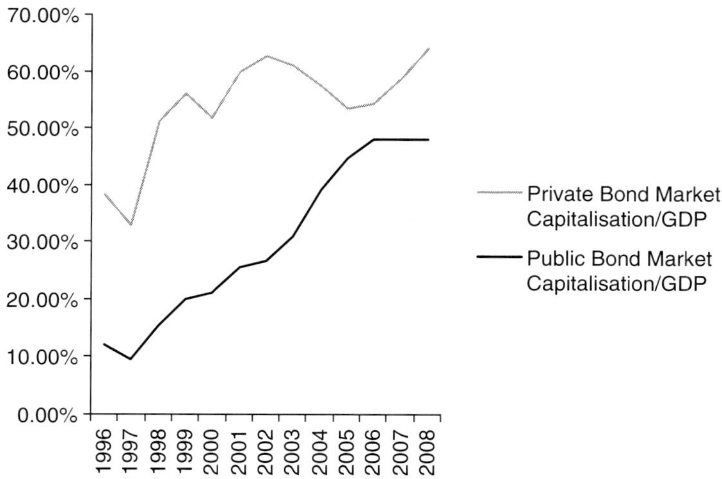

Figure 3.1 Korea: bond market capitalisation (per cent of GDP)

Source: Constructed from data that was extracted from The World Bank: Thorsten Beck et al.'s World Bank Database on Financial Development and Structure available from http://go.worldbank.org/X23UD9QUX0.

the share of financial institution assets that belong to financial conglomerates in general has grown substantially from 56.4 per cent in 1996 to 87.8 per cent in 2006 (Hahm 2007, Table 2). In other words, the banking sector has become more concentrated in a smaller number of players. This development is also reflected in a bank concentration indicator compiled by Beck and Demirgüç-Kunt (2009) for the World Bank. The indicator computes the ratio of the three largest banks' assets to total banking sector assets and this rose from 0.2425 in 1997 to 0.5268 in 2008.[19]

In contrast to the increasing concentration of the market in the banking sector, the wider financial sector as a whole has become more diversified and deep with the expansion of the capital markets. The combined market capitalisation of the Korea Stock Exchange (KSE) and KOSDAQ, the Korean variant of the American NASDAQ, has increased over 13 times in the last decade (from KRW77.9 trillion at the end of 1997 to KRW1051.8 trillion at the end of 2007). Bond market capitalisation in Korea rose from just over 50 per cent of GDP in 1996 to over 100 per cent of GDP in 2007 (see Table 3.1). While the banking sector might still constitute the largest component of the financial sector, the size of the equity market now rivals the banking sector (see Table 3.1). The drawback to the growth in the bond market from an LME perspective however is that a considerable component of this development is attributable to government rather than private sector activity (see Table 3.2 and Figure 3.1).

Foreign participation in the financial sector has also increased with foreigners' total share in commercial banks in Korea rising from 12.3 per cent in 1998 to more than 70 per cent in 2006 (Kang 2009b). Foreigners' share of every bank except Woori Bank and Jeonbuk Bank was over 50 per cent as of February 2007 (Kim and Lee 2008). Considering the miniscule equity stakes held by foreigners in the period before the crisis, this is a significant development. In the KSE, the share of foreign investors in Korean capital markets, when measured by trading value, has increased substantially in the post-crisis period from 5.2 per cent in 1999 to 26.9 per cent in 2008 (see Figure 3.2). The foreign share of market capitalisation in the KSE has also doubled (Hahm 2007). The increased participation of foreign actors in the Korean financial sector has certainly been significant and indirectly addressed some of the concerns raised during the crisis about the dynamics of market competition.

---

[19] This indicator is based on bank-level data from BankScope and needs to be used with some caution as bank coverage is not complete in BankScope and therefore variation across countries and time may be the result of differences in coverage rather than differences in market structure.

Table 3.2 Korea: bond issuance trend (in KRW trillion)

	1998	2000	2002	2004	2006	2007
Treasuries	61	72	99	178	258	274 (4.5)
Monetary Stabilisation Bonds	51	67	83	143	158	150 (2.9)
Corporate Bonds	123	145	156	133	158	190 (1.5)
Financial Bonds [1]	44	49	83	112	169	210 (4.8)
Others [2]	127	135	179	145	199	158 (1.2)
TOTAL	**406**	**468**	**600**	**711**	**942**	**982 (2.4)**[3]
% of GDP	**86.82**	**92.74**	**99.46**	**98.68**	**113.92**	**113.49**

1) Bank-issued bond.
2) Special bonds (issued by non-private, public-purpose companies established by law), Municipal bonds.
3) Figures in parentheses denote growth factor between 1998 and 2007.

Source: Data extracted from Financial Hub Korea's website at http://www.fnhubkorea.kr/.

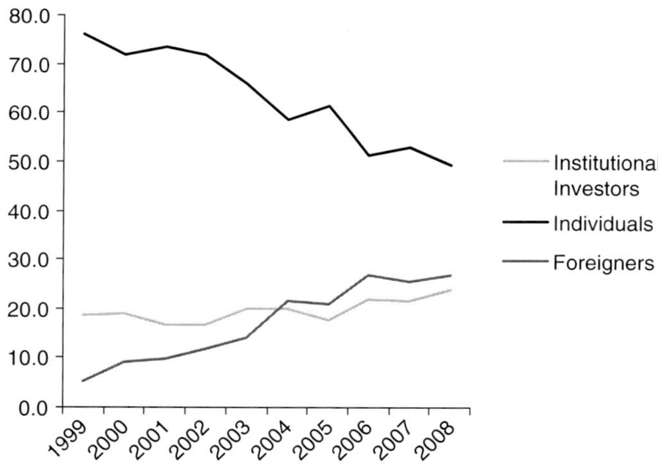

Figure 3.2 Korea: stock market trading value by investor group (in per cent)
Source: Constructed from data that was extracted from KRX Fact Book (various issues).

In summary, there has certainly been an apparent move towards the liberal market model in the Korean financial sector. The capital markets have grown contributing to market diversification, and foreign participation has risen thus contributing to improved market dynamics. Two indicators of financial structure – Structure-Size and

Table 3.3 Korea: indicators of financial structure

	1996	1997	2002	2005	2006	2007
Structure-Size	0.5844	0.3334	0.5121	0.8149	0.9335	1.0062
Structure-Activity	0.6410	0.6156	1.7180	1.7012	1.5936	2.0176

Note: *Higher values indicate a more market-based financial system.*

Source: Compiled from data extracted from The World Bank: Thorsten Beck et al.'s World Bank Database on Financial Development and Structure available from http://go.worldbank.org/X23UD9QUX0.

Structure-Activity – support the conclusion that the Korean financial system has become more market-based (see Table 3.3).[20] Various productivity indices in the financial sector have also since substantially improved and approached the levels of industrially advanced countries like the US (Kang 2003, pp.3–4). However, do these changes necessarily imply a convergence towards the LME model? Specifically, has the historically interventionist role of the state, outlined earlier, been retrenched and have market norms taken its place? How have these developments affected what has previously oft been cited as one of the quintessential 'governed' economies in the literature on the Asian 'developmental state'?

The significant role of government activity in the expansion of the bond market suggests a need to pay greater attention to how the market has evolved before we can conclude that the Korean financial sector is moving towards the LME model. Thus, in order to provide a more complete picture of the nature of the changes that have taken place in Korea since the crisis of 1997–8, it is instructive to investigate in more detail some of the more important institutional developments in the last decade in the financial sector that have led to the changes described above. I will begin by focussing on the nature of the expansion and diversification of the financial sector in the last decade, followed with the Korean state's attempt to develop a 'financial hub', before concluding with changes in regulatory and supervisory arrangements.

[20] Structure-Size is the ratio of Stock Market Capitalization to GDP divided by Bank Credit to GDP, while Structure-Activity is the ratio of Stock Market Value Traded to GDP divided by Bank Credit to GDP. The difference between these two indicators is that Structure-Size focuses on the total shares outstanding in the economy's stock exchanges, while Structure-Activity focuses on the liquidity of the exchanges. See Beck and Levine (2002).

Expansion and diversification of the financial markets

As discussed in the introductory chapter, the expansion and diversification of the financial sector was seen as a panacea to the shortcomings of the bank-based financial system of not just Korea but also the other crisis-hit economies. In Korea, the first development in this regard, the growth of the bond market, was a by-product of the government's need to raise a large volume of funds for financial restructuring as well as fiscal expenditure. Growth of the bond market post-crisis was also the result of corporate companies being pushed to raise funds from the bond market when commercial banks adopted a very cautious approach to corporate lending as they struggled to meet Basel capital adequacy ratios (Lee and Rhee 2007). The bond market therefore acted as a 'spare tyre' while the banking sector was being restructured.

While the financial crisis might have inadvertently contributed to the growth of the bond market, active state-led initiatives were also important. The state facilitated the expansion of the bond market by raising the ceiling on an individual firm's corporate bond issuance from two to four times its equity capital and eliminated all remaining restrictions on foreigners' investment in domestic bonds in December 1997. As market liquidity and efficiency were important for the expansion of a secondary market, a primary dealer system and a 'reopening' system were introduced in 1999 and 2000 respectively to address these issues (IMF 2003a; Kang, Kim, and Rhee 2006, pp.95–6).[21] The government then mandated the primary dealers to use the more modern and efficient electronic trading platform of the KSE in order to boost the liquidity of government bond trading in the market. This subsequently attracted the interest of a greater number of traders and increased trading in the exchange (Kang, Kim and Rhee 2006). Compulsory regular issuance of a variety of government bonds were made from 1999 in order to address the absence of benchmark government bonds that had previously limited the market's ability to price risk and further develop the money and bond markets (IMF 2003a), this despite the fact that the government no longer had a fiscal need to raise this volume of funds from the market.

---

[21] Primary Dealers have exclusive rights to participate in government bond auctions, access to securities financing facilities for secondary market trading, and regular consultation directly with the MOFE. However, they also have an obligation to act as a market maker and follow certain operational and performance guidelines. The 'reopening' system streamlines the issuance of bonds and expands the volume of benchmark issues.

Similar state-led efforts in shaping and promoting the market were also observed in the Korean Securities Dealers Automated Quotations (KOSDAQ) market. The KOSDAQ is a trading board of the Korea Exchange (KRX) that was initially set up as an independently operated stock market in 1996 with the goal of developing a venture business oriented stock market similar to the NASDAQ in the US. To encourage its development, the Korean government not only offered tax incentives to both companies listing on the market and investors of venture businesses (Shin 2002), but it also 'flexibly' enforced the legal standards for due diligence and the penalties for failure to comply with regulation in order to encourage greater participation in the market. Significantly, the government also employed public funds and publicly funded loan programmes to develop the market, thus effectively acting as an investor. The government was therefore seen as an essential factor in creating and fostering the growth of the KOSDAQ market through 'strong intervention' (Shin 2002). Furthermore, in promoting the growth of the KOSDAQ market, the state was not just developing venture capitalism, that is the market to finance venture businesses, but also the venture businesses as well (Weiss 2003, p.257).

Finally, the government also shaped the nature of the evolution of the capital markets when it permitted greater foreign liberalisation. When measured by market capitalisation in the KSE, the share of foreign investors has increased substantially during the post-crisis period from 14.6 per cent at the end of 1997 to 40.1 per cent at the end of 2003, decreasing slightly to 32.4 per cent in 2007 (Hahm 2007 and KRX Fact Book 2008). In part, this increase was facilitated by changes in legislation immediately following the crisis that harmonised the Korean regime on equity purchases with the OECD countries while various limits on foreign ownership of Korean shares and bonds were also removed in 1997 and 1998 (Lee 1998). This was a reversal of the Korean government's previous position whereby the government had stated that it would only remove restrictions on foreign ownership of bonds when the differential between domestic and international interest rates was reduced to at least 2 per cent, which was then expected to occur at the beginning of the twenty-first century (Joo 1998, p.34). At that time, they were afraid of a potential surge in capital inflows induced by large interest rate differentials, followed by excessive liquidity. The huge surge of capital out of the country during the crisis proffered a different perspective on the issue and the need to attract capital back into the economy in the midst of the financial crisis motivated these changes.

In short, while the initial burst of growth in the bond market was an inadvertent by-product of the financial crisis, the subsequent expansion of the capital markets was facilitated by conscious changes in government policies, such as the liberalisation of foreign ownership, as well as government initiatives to both shape and promote the growth of these markets. Government commitment to diversifying the capital markets is also reflected in the use of public funds to both invest in the KOSDAQ and issue government bonds in order to catalyse market growth. Since the crisis, the total volume of bonds issued has increased over four-fold from KRW222 trillion at the end of 1997 to just over KRW980 trillion at the end of 2009 (see Table 3.2). Similarly the growth of the KOSDAQ market post-crisis has been described as 'dazzling' with the number of listed companies doubling between 1999 and 2001 (Shin 2002).

Despite market expansion and diversification, the financial sector is still riddled with potential issues and weaknesses. In the bond market, the flow of funds was highly concentrated with the largest firms obtaining disproportionately more funds from the issue of bonds. When the Daewoo Group collapsed in July 1999, after a period of expansionary strategies financed by bond issues, it undermined confidence in the corporate bond market. An accounting scandal involving the SK Group and insolvencies among credit card companies in March 2003 prompted further crises in the corporate bond market. The number of listed issues declined from 8,170 in 1997 to 2,139 in September 2007. Compared to the government bond market, the secondary market for corporate bonds has nearly vanished: listed amounts and trading volumes for corporate bonds are 15.0 per cent and 0.4 per cent respectively of government bonds (Park 2008). Government bonds therefore ended up growing relatively faster than corporate bonds and accounted for the bulk of bonds issued in the last ten years (see Table 3.2 and Figure 3.1), which raises questions as to the nature of diversification in the financial market.

As a result of the instability in the capital markets, money began to flow back into the banking sector, which together with the consolidation and conglomeration that was encouraged in the midst of managing the crisis, contributed to banks becoming arguably stronger players in the financial sector than before the crisis. Commercial banks have, however, shifted the focus of its lending from the corporate sector to the household sector as firms became more dependent on internal funds or the equity market (Kim, Kim and Ryoo 2006). Consequently, the Korean financial sector's contribution to economic growth since the crisis has become relatively more attenuated, and finance has become 'separated' from real productive activities (Ahn, Hahm and Kim 2008).[22]

Despite the increased market concentration in the banking sector, market competition was not seen as an issue as nationwide commercial banks appeared to struggle for market leadership (Kim, Kim and Ryoo 2006). However, as a result of this process of consolidation, and its impact on the political institutional context of policy making (that is 'polity'), the potential for systemic risk may have become greater and the 'too big to fail' argument so often cited during the crisis has become even more pertinent. The top four banks/financial groups control three-quarters of the market by most measures (Hahm 2007). Although diversification may have increased within individual institutions as a result of conglomeration, both direct and indirect interdependencies among large financial groups have also increased substantially in the post-crisis period as their business portfolio and asset structure have become increasingly similar. Differentiation among banks is limited, especially among the larger banks that are similar in size and resources (Byrne 2005), and this is reinforced with institutions pursuing similar activities.[23] Furthermore, financial conglomerates have become more vulnerable to contagion risks from non-bank and non-financial sectors as financial conglomerates have expanded their activities into those areas previously dominated by non-bank financial firms and capital markets.

In other words, while there have been superficial changes towards the liberal market model in terms of market diversification, attributable in part to government policies and initiatives, this development has not necessarily addressed the underlying issues that were criticised in light of the crisis of 1997–8 since government initiatives have contributed to developments that have a greater potential of destabilising the market.

Financial hub strategy

In 2003, the government became more systematically involved in developing the financial sector when it launched a two-pillar strategy to promote Korea as a (Northeast Asian) financial hub by 2011 as part

---

[22] This development owes much to the rise in foreign ownership in commercial banks in Korea as foreign-owned banks have tended to focus more on retail banking than loans to the corporate sector. See Kang (2009b, pp.260–2) for details.

[23] Similar comments were also expressed by a couple of financial industry professionals during interviews conducted in Seoul in October 2007.

of a broader vision of establishing Korea as an important trade and economic centre in Northeast Asia (Semblat 2006). As the manufacturing sector was then performing poorly, the financial sector was meant to serve as an alternative driving force for economic growth in contrast to its historical role of supporting the real sector (Korea Times 2005). Although this strategy was announced at the end of 2003, its genesis was in an earlier report published in November 2002 by the Seoul Financial Forum, a non-profit organisation that drew together a group of leading scholars, policy makers and industry professionals with a strong interest and expertise in finance. The report entitled *Korea as an International Financial Center in Asia: Vision and Strategy* contained key recommendations intended to extend the reforms and liberalisation introduced in the wake of the Asian crisis. It was taken into consideration by a government–private sector commission established by President Roh Moo-hyun to map out strategies to shape Korea into both a financial and a major business hub for all of Northeast Asia and eventually fed into the 'Northeast Asia Financial Hub Road Map' that was adopted as official government policy in December 2003.

Although the government's adoption of the roadmap was significant, members of the Seoul Financial Forum felt that there were at least three major shortcomings in the government's strategy. First, the government's approach was seen as far too gradualist and failed to take into account the fact that many other countries or cities in Asia were also simultaneously competing to become financial centres. Second, in the early phase of development, the government had intended to focus only on becoming an asset management centre (Kwon 2006). Members of the Forum felt that this did not sufficiently exploit many of the other competitive advantages that Korea had already enjoyed in many other financial markets or products such as private equity and derivative markets. Third, it was felt that the roadmap did not clearly designate the government department or agency that was to be primarily responsible for its implementation. The Seoul Financial Forum, therefore, released a follow-up report in September 2004 that not only stressed the need to rectify what they felt were major weaknesses in the government's original policies but also suggested ways in which these weaknesses could be overcome.[24] At a major policy meeting of the First National Economic Advisory Council on the Financial Hub chaired by President Roh on 03

---

[24] This second report was entitled *Korea as an International Financial Hub: Policy Recommendations for Strengthening and Implementing the Government's Roadmap*.

June 2005, the Korean government officially adopted a second roadmap incorporating most, if not all, of the key recommendations of the Forum's report.

This represented, to some extent, a consultative exercise between the private sector and the state in formulating development strategies for the economy. While the financial hub strategy was initiated by the private sector, it found appeal among policy makers in search of alternative development strategies in light of the then ailing manufacturing industry. The government felt that Korea's 'large' equity and bond markets would provide the country with a natural comparative advantage in developing an advanced financial industry, in particular in asset management (Kim 2002; Seoul Financial Forum 2003). Furthermore, the demand for financial services was expected to increase with an aging population and rising GDP per capita. If the approach and policies adopted to develop the financial sector can be read as 'developmental', then the financial hub strategy is notable as it reflected a more bottom-up approach that differed from earlier developmental processes in the manufacturing and industrial sectors in Korea. However, the development of the financial sector could not succeed on private-sector initiatives alone as it also required government cooperation in at least reforming and liberalising the sector through policy and legislative changes. That said, the role of the government went much further as the strategy marked a form of state influence, if not interference, in the financial sector that was different from the past, in that the financial sector was now viewed as an instrument for economic growth on its own right rather than as a handmaiden to the real sector of the economy.

The financial hub strategy was presented as standing on two 'pillars': one was the deregulation of the capital markets; and the other the liberalisation of the capital account framework and the foreign exchange system. These were seen as connected issues as there would not be much cross-border transactions as long as domestic capital markets remain underdeveloped and illiquid, and conversely, the capital markets could not develop quickly without active involvement of non-residents. Thus, unlike the previous scepticism shown towards foreign actors, the government now accepted the potential benefits of leveraging on foreign participation in order to achieve national development goals. This change in perspective is motivated by the government's and the financial industry's new found interest in the benefits of a globally competitive financial sector, which in turn is the result of a change in ideas of the perceived best way forward for the Korean financial sector specifically, and the Korean economy more generally.

With the Financial Hub Strategy, there was a return to and renewed effort in reforming, liberalising and developing the financial sector. In order to expand the liquidity and depth of the capital market, the stock exchange, futures exchange and KOSDAQ were consolidated into the KRX in 2005. Longer-term securities were also issued in the bond market in order to further develop the benchmark yield curve. The government also established the Korea Investment Corporation (KIC) in July 2005 to act as a catalyst to spark the growth of the capital market industry and help realise the vision of a financial hub more quickly. The KIC is a government-owned investment management company mandated to manage part of Korea's foreign exchange reserves, initially about USD20 billion, and other public funds by investing in a variety of financial assets in the international financial markets (Kwon 2006). Through the activities of the KIC, the government hoped to attract foreign financial institutions to Korea and accelerate the transfer of financial knowledge and global best practices to local managers. In the midst of the global financial crisis, the Korea Exchange, the Korea Exchange Financial Investment Association and the Korea Securities Depository jointly created a KRW515 billion fund to invest in the stock market for three years beginning in November 2008 in order to alleviate anxiety among investors during the crisis. While the size of the fund was small and unlikely to have had much impact on the stock market, it was a further reflection of the Korean government's interventionist approach to the financial market in order to support its existence and development.

The government also pursued a range of initiatives to liberalise the capital account framework and the foreign exchange system in order to increase the depth and liquidity of the domestic foreign exchange market as well as to support the international business of financial institutions. Remaining capital transactions requiring prior approval under the *Foreign Exchange Transaction Act* were fully liberalised in 2006 and the government undertook to achieve complete liberalisation of foreign exchange transactions by 2009 under the 'Foreign Exchange Master Development Plan'.[25] The Korean government also abolished the capital transaction 'licensing system' and transformed it into a more 'favourable' 'ex-post reporting system' in January 2006.

The cornerstone of the governments' vision of establishing a financial hub however was the new *Financial Investment Services and Capital Market Act* (FISCMA) that will be discussed in the next sub-section. For

[25] This was brought forward from the initial target of 2011.

now, it suffices to note for the argument that the Korean government's approach to the financial sector under the Financial Hub Strategy consisted of more than just mere market liberalisation as it also embodied aspects of development. In creating markets, promoting market activity and introducing liberalisation measures, government policies and actions did not just establish an enabling environment for the market but were also influential in shaping the latter.

Not all observers were convinced about the viability of the governments' vision to produce a regional financial hub (H-s Lee 2008; Yoon 2008).[26] In a survey conducted by the Korea Trade-Investment Promotion Agency, non-Korean executives felt that high regulatory barriers, bureaucratic procedures, labour flexibility, credit regulations and English language skills were key issues (Y-m Kim 2008).[27] Seoul was consistently seen as lagging far behind Tokyo, Hong Kong and Singapore (H-s Kim 2008). Also stacked against the government's vision were the comparatively small size of the economy and the low international status of the Won. Foreign firms with more experience in providing a broader spectrum of products were expected to be formidable competitors to local firms. It was also felt that the investment patterns of pension plans and household assets would hinder the pace of change in the capital market (Walker 2008). Nevertheless, the government's financial hub strategy served as a useful discourse under which further liberalisation and restructuring of the non-bank financial sector could take place. Given that the aspiration of becoming financial hubs had become popular and had also been adopted by regional competitors, the financial hub strategy appealed to nationalistic passions and mobilised popular support for the government's actions. Thus, while it may be difficult for Korea to achieve the goal of becoming a regional hub, few objected to the need to develop the financial services industry and provide a boost to the national economy (Korea.net 2005). The financial hub strategy can thus be read, at the very least, as a useful discursive mechanism that fell in line with the government's desire to achieve broader policy goals. With the government committed to the financial hub strategy, the FISCMA was passed in 2007.

---

[26] During interviews conducted in October 2007, none of the financial industry professionals provided enthusiastic responses when asked about the Korean government's aspirations to create a regional financial hub.

[27] Their views were not very different in the preceding three years' surveys. For a report on the results of an older survey, see Kim (2003).

Financial Investment Services and Capital Market Act

While it was felt that Korea could have a comparative advantage in the trade of financial services, it was also widely recognised that Korean securities firms were not yet sufficiently competitive and that this was attributable to the historical effects of the country's legal and regulatory environment. First, the range of investment products and services that could be offered in the market was extremely circumscribed under the law due to a 'positive listing system' to the regulation of the introduction of financial products whereby securities firms could only deal with products that were explicitly listed in the *Securities Exchange Act*. As a consequence, securities firms had little incentive to develop the capability for designing innovative financial products, which is seen as a key factor in a successful modern investment banking business. Second, Korean securities firms were also very strictly limited under various laws on the range of activities in which they could participate (Cho 2007). Consequently, the business portfolios of competing firms became rather similar regardless of the differences in other firm characteristics, such as size. The existing laws prevented Korean firms from transforming themselves into comprehensive financial service providers in the mould of modern investment banks, which was the aspiration of policy makers (Asia Pulse 2001). Furthermore, until 2005, securities companies did not have competitive advantages against banks (Jeon 2005). This was largely the result of government policy that had favoured the banking system as the main channel for the intermediation of savings during the high growth period from the 1960s until the mid-1990s (Semblat 2006). Banking activities and capital market activities were kept separate and as a result, the development of non-bank financial firms has lagged that of banks.

It was therefore the government's intention with the FISCMA, popularly seen as a 'big bang' development in the Korean securities market, to remove restrictions that separated securities, futures, asset management, trust services and other financial services businesses (excluding banking) and transform the Korean financial system into a three-pillar system divided into banks, insurance and investment banks by 2008 (Hahm 2007). The first important provision of the FISCMA was the liberalisation of the types of financial products that may be sold in the market through a change in the definition of an 'investment product'. This more liberal approach to the ability of financial institutions to introduce financial products was further bolstered by a 'negative list' principle in the regulation of products and services in the market. Both these policy changes widened the frontiers of product innovation for securities firms. Complementing this liberalisation in the product market is a significant deregulation in the institutional structure of firms whereby firewalls among investment service businesses were abolished thus allowing a single firm, classified as a 'financial investment company' (FIC), to carry out various capital market and investment service businesses under one roof.[28] This mirrored the 'financial holding company' concept that was introduced in 2004 in the banking sector. These two changes in the regulatory framework gave Korean securities firms the freedom to evolve into 'true' investment banks with the scope and functions that are comparable with global players such as Goldman Sachs and Morgan Stanley. The government ultimately hoped that at least one domestic firm would turn into an investment bank that could compete at the regional level (Walker 2008).

Of the liberalisation measures, the decision to grant FICs the permission to participate in retail payment and settlement services – once the preserve only of banks – in 2005 was particularly contentious. This policy change gave FICs access to new customers as well as reduce their funding costs and allowed former brokerages and securities firms to effectively act like banks in attracting deposits. It was intended to facilitate the growth and specialisation of Korean securities firms, however, given that brokerages and securities firms have traditionally been able to offer higher interest rates, there was real concern that this would cannibalise the banking sector through a mass migration from bank deposits to cash management accounts (CMAs) in securities firms through which customers' funds could be invested into many different types of investment products such as commercial paper, certificates of deposit and government bonds.[29] This ultimately led to fears that securities companies participating in the retail payment system would threaten the stability of the entire financial system (D-h Kim 2008), especially given significant *chaebol* participation in the securities market, and their earlier role in destabilising the financial sector prior to the crisis. In other words, many feared that as with the experience of the 1980s and 1990s, liberalisation would undermine market stability.

---

[28] As long as it installs 'Chinese walls' which are in-company barriers, in the form of physical walls with different entry ways erected between different departments or divisions. These are meant to prevent conflicts of interests within financial institutions arising from the sharing of privileged information.

[29] Fitch Ratings, for instance, thinks that CMAs would provide tougher competition to commercial banks. See Forbes (2007). See also, Asia Pulse (2007).

These measures were nevertheless welcomed for the effect of introducing greater competitive dynamics in the financial sector as a whole.

On the whole, the FISCMA introduced some fundamental changes to the legal environment of the capital markets and investment services industry of Korea (Cho 2007). As part of the Financial Hub Strategy, it was driven by the desire to rebalance the Korean financial system that had heretofore been dependent on the banking sector and to 'sharpen Korean capital markets' competitive edge in the global market' (Financial Services Commission 2009). The consolidation of financial institutions was seen as a route to global competitiveness with the aim of developing 'national financial champions', in the form of Korean variants of global investment banks, while the expansion of scopes of business was aimed at improving market dynamics. The government was so keen to drive the emergence of investment banking groups that it removed the embargo on the establishment of new brokerage houses in order to facilitate banks making inroads into the securities business when existing brokerage houses made it difficult for banks to acquire the former by raising their prices (Korea Times 2007). More recently, reiterating its desire to produce, or at least nurture, Korean investment banks that are global in scale, Finance Minister Kwon O-kyu encouraged local banks to expand their operations overseas and to move into more 'high-risk, high-returns' activities, promising that the government would overhaul banking regulations and help revive investment banking operations (Jung 2007). While there were sceptical views about emulating American-style investment banks, there was nevertheless a recognition that the change in the financial landscape was a desirable result of economic growth (The Hankyoreh 2008; Kim 2009b).

The government's current approach to developing the financial services sector bears some resemblance to the approach taken earlier in developing the manufacturing sector.[30] The FISCMA, and the Financial Hub Strategy more generally, can be viewed as development strategies adopted by the state, in collaboration with the private sector, to ensure future economic growth. While many of the measures are in line with aspects of the liberal market model, they were introduced through state initiatives. The state's commitment to the developmental strategy is seen in changes in legislation, the introduction of policies supporting the promotion of 'national financial champions' and the investment of public funds through vehicles such as the KIC. As such, although the

---

[30] See also Weiss (2003).

Korean financial sector has acquired features of the LME model, this has been through state involvement and leadership. Given the level and nature of state interference, the Korean financial sector can hardly be seen as an example of the LME model despite outward appearance.

Regulation and supervision

Since regulatory failure was considered a critical factor that contributed to weaknesses in the Korean financial sector, I will discuss in this section how regulation and supervision have evolved in light of not just the crisis but also these recent development plans.

Prior to the crisis, financial regulation was heavily concentrated in the MOFE, which was legally entitled to supervise most financial intermediaries except for commercial banks. The latter came under the jurisdiction of the Office of Bank Supervision (OBS) in the BOK. Limited organisational resources made MOFE delegate some of its regulatory functions to other government agencies, including the OBS, the Securities Supervisory Board (SSB), the Insurance Supervisory Board (ISB), and the Board of Audit and Inspection. However, since the SSB and ISB were under the direct control of MOFE and the BOK was under the de facto influence of the MOFE, all the regulatory and supervisory powers ultimately belonged to the MOFE either directly or indirectly (Park 2006, p.197). As the ultimate blame for regulatory failure would fall on the ministry, the various regulatory agencies other than the MOFE had little incentive to perform their delegated responsibilities, a situation that was compounded by a lack of clarity in the division of labour and authority (Choi 2002). This complex regulatory structure and inadequate coordination among the supervisory agencies led to a lack of consistency and effectiveness in supervision. Furthermore, as the MOFE always had multiple policy goals with growth in the real sector being given top priority, the safety and soundness or competitiveness of the financial sector had been relatively neglected (Walter 2008, p.132). The 'polity' of financial regulation thus explains the poor state of financial regulation and supervision before the crisis of the late-1990s.

Post-crisis financial sector reform attempted to address some of these shortcomings. The fragmented supervisory arrangements were consolidated into a single body with the new *Act for Establishing Financial Supervisory Institutions*, passed by the National Assembly on 29 December 1997. The consolidation of the supervisory authorities was important for two main reasons. First, separating supervisory authority from the MOFE was a necessary condition for neutrality and independence in supervision. Second, financial deregulation, which led to the convergence of financial services and the blurring of distinctions between various financial sectors, had made distinction between financial institutions increasingly meaningless.

A 'policy making arm' of the consolidated supervisory structure was created in April 1998 in the form of the Financial Supervisory Commission (FSC). The agency reported to the Office of the Prime Minister and was designed to overcome problems of inter-agency communication and policy coordination experienced before and at the onset of the crisis and to play a more streamlined supervisory role in the face of rapidly changing financial markets. It was empowered to oversee all financial institutions and markets except for three specialised banks (the Korea Development Bank, the Industrial Bank of Korea, and the Export-Import Bank of Korea). The Financial Supervisory Service (FSS), established in January 1999, was the executive arm of the FSC and administered the latter's regulatory functions.[31] The FSS was the result of the consolidation of four supervisory bodies – OBS, SSB, ISB and Non-bank Supervisory Authority. The primary function of the FSS was examination and supervision of financial institutions but could be extended to other oversight and enforcement functions as charged by the FSC and the Securities and Futures Commission (SFC).

While the new system required the MOFE to reduce its direct supervisory role in the financial markets, the ministry nevertheless retained the responsibility of outlining bills related to financial supervision in consultation with the FSC. The BOK, on the other hand, lost most of its regulatory role in policing the banking industry and was reorganised as an independent central bank in charge of monetary policy.[32] However, the BOK, in its role as lender of last resort, did retain some of its previous supervision functions such as checking prudential requirements for

---

[31] Technically, the FSS is a private corporation in the form of a special legal entity operating in the public sector, and is formally separate and independent from the FSC. The FSS's major roles include (1) conducting examinations and inspections over financial institutions; (2) administering prompt corrective and disciplinary action; and (3) serving as an arbitrator of disputes between financial institutions and their customers.

[32] The Governor of the BOK, previously appointed by the MOFE, is now appointed by the President on the advice of the State Council. The governor of the BOK, instead of the minister of MOFE, now chairs the Monetary Policy Committee that is the supreme policy-making body of the BOK. The previous dual objectives of the central bank – maintaining the stability of currency value and the soundness of the banking and credit system – were replaced by the sole goal of maintaining price stability.

banks. The Monetary Policy Committee at the BOK also had the right to request reconsideration of any decision of the FSC that may affect monetary policy. In addition, the BOK and the Korea Deposit Insurance Corporation may ask the FSC and the FSS to examine financial institutions on a joint basis.

In line with the new regulatory structure, several new supervisory mechanisms were also introduced. As a first step, a prompt corrective action system, based largely on BIS ratios, was put in place in April 1998 to move aggressively against troubled financial institutions. Second, 'forward looking' criteria for loan classification and provisioning that reflected borrowers' capacity for future payments were introduced in December 1999. A range of supervisory criteria were tightened between 1998 and 1999 including the system of classifying NPLs; reducing the politicisation of bank credit allocation; the regulation of foreign currency transactions; and various limits on the extension of credit. There were also initiatives to strengthen the corporate governance of banks to help depoliticise the relationship between the government and the financial institutions (Park 2006).

Although the new regulatory structure defined clearer responsibilities and authority compared with the pre-crisis structure, and introduced supervisory and prudential mechanisms that conformed more closely to current international best practices, these did not address all existing weaknesses and concerns. First, the FSC, FSS and SFC did not necessarily have full operational independence. The FSC and FSS were formally embedded in the President's Office and were supervised by the Prime Minister. The government controlled the appointment of senior regulators through various provisions (Walter 2008, p.133). In addition, the rapid turnover of the FSC chairmanship, the occupant of which was simultaneously also the governor of the FSS, and the situation whereby FSC staff sometimes move to and from MOFE raised doubts as to the real independence of these new supervisory agencies (Ko 2008b). The role played by MOFE in interpreting laws and supervisory regulations also gave the FSC, FSS and SFC limited freedom in implementing supervision (IMF 2003a). The MOFE still retained the legislative authority to decide entry and exit of most financial firms and was responsible for drawing up billş on supervision. Finally, the relationship between the FSC and the FSS was not working nearly as efficiently as had been expected (Park 2008; Ko 2008b), and this could be attributed to differences in bureaucratic culture as personnel for the FSC came largely from the MOFE while that of the FSS came from the private sector (Ito and Hashimoto 2007a). On the operational front, insufficient legal protection for FSC,

FSS and SFC staff against lawsuits for supervisory actions carried out in good faith, as well as insufficient staffing resources, hampered supervisory effectiveness (IMF 2003b).

While the new supervisory structure and mechanisms were an improvement on the previous systems, and came closer towards approximating the LME model, it is clear that with these outstanding issues, the modus operandi of the regulatory system as a whole did not make a complete break from the administrative procedures and organisational culture of the past. A great deal of discretion was still exercised by the FSC in its regulatory operations as it made use of indirect means to control the management of financial institutions, harking back to pre-crisis regulatory systems (Choi 2002). Some regulations that have been introduced and interpreted were criticised for being opaque (IMF 2003a). There was also a perception in the market that violations of applicable regulations were often overlooked or weakly sanctioned. The IMF also voiced concern over the regulator's ability to keep abreast of the role of connected lending and cross ownership (IMF 2003a). Regulatory forbearance also persisted in that asset classification was, at times, not implemented properly while provisioning rates were questionable and ad-hoc relaxation of regulatory requirements continued (Walter 2008, pp.136–7). Finally, the FSC was still able to deploy traditional policy mechanisms of credit rationing and threaten financial institutions that made loans that were not sanctioned by the government, prompting Linda Weiss (2003, p.252) to suggest that the FSC was reminiscent of the now defunct pilot agency, the Economic Planning Bureau (EPB), that frequently intervened heavily in the industrial sector.

These concerns ultimately pointed to a disjuncture between formal institutions and policy practices and norms. This fed into scepticisms of the regulator's ability to supervise certain risks in an integrated and coherent manner or to respond to new challenges, despite notable progress in improving the supervisory structure. These views were further strengthened when a series of serious problems, notably the SK Global accounting fraud in March 2003 and the financial problems encountered by numerous credit card companies including LG Card, were not detected or prevented by the supervisory agencies (H-B Kim and C H Lee 2004). In some cases, the regulators were undermined by the government's own policy, thus suggesting diverging interests in policy coordination and formulation if not much more endemic institutional issues (Byrne 2004; Jeon 2004). This was most evident in the fallout arising from the boom in consumer credit, the emergence of which the government had a key role to play in so far as it encouraged banks to shift the focus of its lending from corporations to consumers. The government, hoping that private consumption would help boost economic activity, had stimulated the credit card market by loosening cardholder requirements and card issuing processes, and providing tax benefits to users of credit cards (Jeon 2004, p.2). These policy changes served as encouragement to financial institutions to issue credit cards without sufficient due diligence while reaping the gains from increased market share. When the delinquency ratio and the amount of rescheduled loans began to pose serious liquidity and capital problems to the financial system, the government encouraged related institutions to roll over the debt of the credit card companies (OECD 2004). Government owned banks, such as Korea Development Bank and Woori Bank, figured prominently in the rescue efforts. For many, the credit card debacle indicated that, despite the profound and significant institutional changes in the Korean financial sector, the cultural dimension of the supervisory and regulatory system, and the behaviour of market players, had not quite evolved (H-B Kim and C H Lee 2004). At its worse, it is possible to conclude that state institutions were still captured by business interests, a point that was made abundantly clear when an illegal-loan scandal, involving the FSS, a venture firm and two mutual savings and finance companies surfaced (Choi 2002).[33] The Korean regulatory system might well be on the path to looking more like liberal market ones but it did not appear to function in a corresponding manner, at least not yet.[34]

In order to address some of these shortcomings, the incoming government of Lee Myung-bak announced in January 2008 that it would consolidate further the financial policy making functions of the MOFE and the FSC. In February 2008, the Financial Policy Bureau was excised from the former MOFE (now renamed the Ministry of Strategy and Finance) and integrated with the FSC, with the new agency being renamed the Financial Services Commission (not to be confused with its previous

---

[33] The scandal disclosed that Young-jae Kim, deputy vice-governor of the FSS, received a bribe of KRW1.1 billion (about USD1 million) in exchange for allowing illegal loans totaling KRW63.7 billion (about USD56.4 million) to the once-promising venture firm, Korea Digital Line, from Dongbang and Daishin mutual savings and finance companies. See Daily Chosun, 9 and 11 November 2000.

[34] A similar disjuncture is observed in the corporate governance of banking institutions, see Park (2006).

name which was Financial Supervisory Commission).[35] The FSS continued to act as the executive arm of the FSC but now had a Governor who was a different individual from the FSC Chairman. The new FSC was given broad statutory mandate to carry out three key functions: the formulation of financial policies, the oversight of financial institutions and markets, and anti-money laundering. It has greater independence from the ministry as, unlike the old FSC, it has the authority to draft and amend financial laws and regulations as well as issue regulatory licenses to financial institutions. This further consolidation and empowerment of the regulatory authority ironically led to an almost diametrically opposing sort of criticism, that is that the new FSC wielded excessive power and that the consolidation of functions would impair the independence of the regulator while facilitating state intervention (Jin 2008). In practice however, the new FSC's negligence in regulating the sales of derivatives such as KIKO currency options which resulted in great losses to many SMEs in 2008 undermined the newly reformed regulator's credibility (Lim 2008),[36] suggesting that despite empowerment through legal changes in the regulatory framework, the transformation of its actual institutional, and perhaps also cultural, capacity in regulation is another matter altogether.

Conclusion

It is undoubtedly true that in the period since the financial crisis of 1997–8, the Korean financial sector has acquired features that are commonly associated with the LME model. It has become more diversified with an expanding capital market and greater foreign participation. Supervisory and regulatory systems have also been overhauled with features that conform more closely with current international best practices and thus, with a liberal market model. Although these changes suggest that the Korean financial sector has become more market-oriented, active state interference, both in the 'developmental' sense as well as in the 'state-capture' sense, has not disappeared. Even though the

---

[35] The Financial Policy Bureau directed financial policies and had the right to enact and revise financial regulations.

[36] KIKO (knock-in, knock-out) are currency-related financial derivatives used to hedge against foreign currency risks. The government estimated in August 2008 that 517 firms, including 471 SMEs, had exposures to KIKOs valued at USD7.9 billion, of which USD2.3 billion were deemed 'over-hedged', that is not backed by prospective foreign exchange revenues.

government might no longer be able to directly influence market participants in the manner that it did before the financial crisis, it has not shied away from attempting to influence and intervene in the financial sector. As the analysis in this chapter makes clear, the Korean state has not confined itself to just establishing and providing an enabling environment for the market to function, as one would expect from within the perspective of an LME ideal type, but has also attempted to actively influence the direction that the market should take.

The persistence of state interference in Korea can be explained using the three-dimensions of policy, politics and 'polity' discussed in the previous chapter. First, the Korean government made a conscious decision to intervene in the market in order to reform the financial sector such that it took on more of the features frequently associated with liberal market economies. This process of liberalisation, as discussed, began well before the crisis took hold and was enacted through a range of policy changes that was eventually consolidated when the state took substantial steps in 2003 to promote Korea as a financial hub. Of course, state intervention did not always yield developmental outcomes but could also have unintended negative consequences for the market. I discussed earlier the government's attempt to stimulate economic activity in the post-crisis period by encouraging the extension of consumer credit through the use of credit cards, which eventually resulted in a consumer credit bubble and insolvencies among credit card companies in early 2003.

Policy making is not often made in a vacuum and political considerations frequently factor in the process. In Korea interest groups continue to influence policy making and implementation, as reflected in the persistence of regulatory forbearance in the name of market development. The government's 'bank first, NBFI second' approach adopted during the financial crisis can be read in part as political manoeuvring against the *chaebol* that were, during the time of the crisis, seen in negative light by both the government and the broader public. The interests of the domestic financial sector as well as broader nationalist, or anti-foreigner, sentiments were also important factors in the persistence of discriminatory practices against foreign financial institutions, despite significant liberalisation of the financial sector to foreign actors.[37] Officials have been known to interpret and apply regulations more

[37] See OECD (2007, p.5); Office of the United States Trade Representative (2008); Office of the United States Trade Representative (2009). Similar comments were made by an expatriate employee of a foreign-owned financial institution operating in Seoul during interviews in 2007 and 2009.

strictly when it concerned foreign firms (Klingner 2006). Regulatory entities reportedly also hinder foreign providers in the market through the use of regulatory delays.[38]

The institutional context of policy making, or 'polity', can also account for the persistence and nature of state interference in the market. From an historical institutionalist perspective, the Korean state's ability to drive the process of liberalisation in the 1990s can in part be explained by its political structure wherein the President's office had great influence in policy making that allowed the state to stamp its mark on the rapid introduction of greater financial liberalisation and reform once the President had decided to adopt these goals as part of his political agenda (Kalinowski and Cho 2009). The importance of the preferences of the country's leader in this process also suggests the relevance of a rational-choice institutionalist perspective, in particular during the time of the crisis, as then President, Kim Dae-jung's personal commitment to greater liberalisation of the financial sector and the economy more generally is understood by many to have been a critical factor in explaining the policies adopted and implemented.[39] Similarly, as we saw in this chapter, the President's decision to develop Korea as a financial hub following the proposal put forth by a commission that he had earlier established. The state's discourse on the financial hub strategy also illustrates the pertinence of Vivien Schmidt's discursive institutionalism. The state justified and legitimised its interventionist role in developing Korea as a financial hub by adopting the argument that the financial sector can represent a new source of potential export earnings in the face of the then poor performance of the manufacturing industry. State intervention and interference were also facilitated by the persistence of institutional culture and the path dependence of historical practices. As Kim and Lee (2004) argued, the reforms that had been undertaken were mostly in formal institutions of financial supervision while 'informal institutions', such as supervisory culture, had barely changed and that this can explain the gap between policy implementation and compliance.

---

[38] During an interview in November 2007, an employee of a foreign-owned financial institution in Seoul voiced frustration over repeated rejections of applications to conduct business activities over seemingly trivial reasons, for example incorrect wording.

[39] We could of course adopt a constructivist or a critical-theory approach and further interrogate the source of these individual's preferences and interests but that is beyond the scope of this project.

The Korean financial sector currently consists of a mixture of elements from both the SiMe and LME ideal types, and could arguably be in a transition between the two varieties of capitalism given the progressive liberalisation introduced since the mid-1980s. Indeed, the deregulation of the financial sector, in terms of ease of entry and the ability to offer new products, looks set to continue (Ko 2008a). The FISCMA was enacted in the midst of, and despite, the development of the global 'credit crunch' crisis. Further deregulation would certainly be perceived to be consistent with Korea's level of economic development and might well be reinforced with the country's continued integration into the global economy. However, greater market-dynamics do not necessarily imply the absence of active state intervention. In fact, state influence and leadership appear to be compatible with greater market liberalisation, at least to a limited degree, as demonstrated in our discussion of the Financial Hub Strategy. While current measures are not as interventionist as those adopted during the heydays of HCI development in the 1970s, contemporary attempts by the state to mould the evolution of the financial system of Korea have some resemblance to previous efforts at developing the real sector of the economy in that the state still sets the macroeconomic direction under which market forces operate despite the emphasis on greater market dynamics post-crisis. Contemporary development of the financial sector has been identified as a route to economic growth as well as the modernisation of the economy; and the government has introduced a strategy with which it believed this can be achieved through selective intervention, fiscal incentives and the use of public funds. Even though the state's ability to govern the market, as it is understood in the literature on Asian 'developmental states', might have been weakened, the state continues to actively influence and intervene, except that its focus of development has now turned to the financial sector as an engine of growth in its own right.

4
Malaysia

Malaysia emerged from the financial crisis of 1997–8 relatively unscathed when compared with its regional neighbours Indonesia, Korea and Thailand.[1] This was because local banks and corporations had far more restricted access to foreign borrowings than their counterparts in the other crisis economies (Chin and Jomo 2003). Capital market flows, on the other hand, especially those into and out of the stock market, were a more important factor in the crisis but had a smaller impact on the financial sector (Radelet and Sachs 1998; Chin and Jomo 2001; Chin and Nordhaug 2002). Malaysia was reputed to have one of the better regulated financial sectors in the region and this contributed to its ability to emerge from the crisis in better shape. The fact that the country was able to avoid having to recourse to the IMF certainly attested to its capacity to mobilise resources to confront the crisis. While the regulatory grip of the authorities stretched from significant currency controls on capital account transactions to strict regulation on the activities of foreign participants, this level of relatively greater control coexisted with what was otherwise a generally vibrant market economy. At the time of the crisis, Malaysia had one of the three largest capital markets in East Asia and a banking system that was so fragmented in both number and types of players, including significant foreign presence, that the central bank felt that market consolidation was required to boost the efficiency of the overall market.

How did this mix of state and market dynamics evolve in the period after the crisis? How was control and regulation exercised in the face of

[1] Although Malaysia's GDP contracted by a greater percentage than Korea in 1998, it did not experience a change in government and did not have to turn to the IMF for financial assistance.

greater pressure for liberalisation emanating not just from the criticisms raised during the crisis but also the emerging regional competition in the financial services industry? The imposition of capital controls and the refusal of external help during the crisis suggested that the Malaysian state's capacity to control and regulate was still very much in the foreground. However, the period post-crisis also saw the Malaysian authorities welcoming liberalisation measures and allowing foreign actors greater access in a variety of areas. Did these developments result in a reduction in state involvement in the economy and concomitantly an improvement of competitive market dynamics? Or do these developments reflect an extension, and thus persistence, of the state not only enhancing but also interfering in the market and consequently suggesting that no convergence in forms of economic governance has taken place since the financial crisis of 1997–8?

This chapter begins with a brief historical review of Malaysia's financial system, paying particular attention to the roles of both the state and market in its evolution. This will be followed with a brief discussion of some of the measures adopted to manage the financial crisis of 1997–8. I then survey changes in the Malaysian financial sector in the last decade, first through the use of quantitative indicators and then with an institutional analysis of key reform measures implemented since the crisis. Three policy initiatives in particular stand out: the various master plans conceived in 1999–2000 for the financial sector; the 'aggressive' promotion of Islamic finance; and the greater but selective liberalisation of the financial sector for foreign players. The chapter concludes with an analysis of regulatory changes in the last decade.

History

When the Federation of Malaya gained independence in 1957, the financial system had 20 commercial banks of which only four were incorporated locally (Ong 1999, p.144). Three British banks, primarily involved in financing international trade, dominated the system. The securities market was then practically non-existent. A number of domestic banks began to develop rapidly only in the 1960s when they were given preferential treatment to expand a nation-wide network of branch offices. With independence and a new found 'sense of sovereignty', it was believed that the financial sector, as the 'commanding heights of the economy', should come under 'Malaysian control' (Ong 1999, p.145). In order to protect domestic banks and to offer them an advantage in the market, foreign banks were no longer allowed to establish new branches in Malaysia from 1974 onwards. Foreign banks were however free to establish representative offices in the country and this was the route taken by many from the second half of the 1970s.[2] As a result of policies that discriminated in favour of domestic actors, foreign banks' share in deposits, loans and Malaysian securities dropped from above 60 per cent in 1970 to between 20 and 30 per cent by 1985 where it has since largely stayed (Marashdeh 1994).

In its early days, Malaysia's central bank, Bank Negara Malaysia (BNM), focussed on developing the regulatory aspects of the financial sector (Hamilton-Hart 2002, pp.114–28). One of BNM's early moves was to impose substantial reserve ratios on banks and other financial institutions as well as require commercial banks to produce regular financial reports. It also placed an early priority on the development of the banking system and the mobilisation of savings, using, until the late-1960s, exhortation and material incentives to influence the geographical spread of commercial bank branches to these ends (Lee 1981, 1987; Singh 1984). BNM never made much use of interest-rate controls (Hamilton-Hart 2002, p.122), but it did manage a flexibly 'administered' interest rate regime until the rates were progressively liberalised from 1978 onwards (Hussein 1994, p.150). Until then, BNM would, in consultation with commercial banks, determine the minimum lending rate and the ceiling on deposit rates. The objective of this approach was more to prevent excessive competition among banks, in particular, to prevent foreign banks from outbidding local banks than to divert credit for the purposes of industrialisation (Lee 1981).

The development of a market-oriented system of determining interest rates was only encouraged at the end of the 1970s and was part of a package of measures designed to promote a more liberal and competitive financial system. These changes in policy were a partial response to the difficult economic conditions of the 1970s that were coloured by high inflation in 1973–4 and the recession of 1975 (Hussein 1994, pp.147–50). However, when liquidity became tight during the recession of the mid-1980s, the central bank returned to placing limits on the movement of interest rates out of fear that the competitive bidding of interest rates would jeopardise the recovery of the economy. However, instead of imposing direct controls, the central bank opted to use moral suasion to prevail on commercial banks and finance companies to peg

---

[2] There were 14 representative offices in 1974 before rising to a high of 34 in 1986.

their interest rates (Hussein 1994, p.151). This was eventually superseded in 1987 by the base lending rate (BLR) system that removed much of a bank's discretion in discriminating against some of their customers through prescribed restrictions on the BLR. The central bank thus exercised renewed control over the market through these policy changes, though it sought to induce a better market outcome, at least for consumers of financial products, through its actions.

Financial liberalisation in the 1980s

It was not until the country experienced severe fiscal and external debt problems from the early 1980s, followed by recession in the mid-1980s, that policy makers returned to and instituted major reforms in financial liberalisation. This followed the recognition that the private sector had to be one of the primary engines to bring the economy back onto the path of growth.[3] Local elites were also in favour of these policy changes as they accepted the argument that liberalisation and deregulation would lead to greater investment and increased trade flows (Shari 2003, p.113), in part emulating measures that had been adopted in advanced industrial economies. Given the country's reliance on exports, the role of greater investment and increased trade flows were very important.[4]

Aside from the difficulties encountered in the macroeconomic environment, part of the impetus for reform emerged from within the financial sector. In the 1980s, poorly regulated deposit-taking cooperatives (DTCs) with weak capital bases had mushroomed and engaged in speculative and unproductive investments as well as connected lending to, or investments in, subsidiaries and related companies. These small institutions, considered as fringe institutions operating outside the regulatory framework of the central bank, came to pose systemic risks as they began to attract a larger share of deposits even as a large number of them began to fail. By the mid-1980s, 24 ailing DTCs had collapsed, dragging with them over 522,000 depositors and total deposits of MYR1.5 billion (Sheng 1989, p.22). While a number of prudential measures were implemented in the wake of this financial distress (Sheng 1989, pp.17–19), a comprehensive package of reform measures covering different components and aspects of the financial sector was only introduced later in

[3] This change in orientation and focus was reiterated with the publication of the Second Outline Perspective Plan, 1991–2000.

[4] Malaysia is one of the most 'open' economies of the world. Exports and imports combined have exceeded GDP since 1980 and in more recent years have even doubled GDP.

1989. The package was designed to be implemented progressively over time as the Malaysian authorities wanted to avoid the costly mistakes made by countries that had adopted a financial 'big bang' approach to liberalisation while at the same time recognising the need to address the adverse consequences of financial repression.

One of the more important elements of this reform package was the enactment of the *Banking and Financial Institutions Act* (BAFIA) in 1989 to consolidate and replace the *Banking Act 1973*, the *Finance Companies Act 1969* and the *Islamic Banking Act 1983*. This conferred broad powers of supervision to BNM over all banking and licensed financial institutions as well as all fringe institutions involved in the provision of credit and finance. More importantly, it required that the 16 foreign banks then operating in Malaysia be incorporated locally, which brought them under the regulatory umbrella of BNM.[5] This meant that they had to maintain the same minimum capital requirements as Malaysian-owned banks, thus losing the advantage foreign banks previously enjoyed when they operated on a lower, unregulated, capital base. The playing field among the various types of financial institutions were also levelled through a range of other measures: a weighted risk asset approach to capital adequacy assessment was made uniform; the statutory reserve and minimum liquidity requirements were standardised for all financial institutions in order to eliminate artificial barriers to fair competition; and finance companies were allowed, in October 1987, to also participate in the domestic inter-bank money market along with commercial and merchant banks that had long enjoyed the privilege.[6] Finally, in February 1991, the BLRs of the banking institutions were completely freed from the administrative control of BNM, although the margin between lending rates and the BLR was fixed at 4 per cent, this being an extension of BNM's policy of the late-1980s to ensure that borrowers were not disadvantaged and subjected to exorbitantly high interest rates (Lin 1994, pp.119–20; Hussein 1994, p.151).

In summary, the regulatory role of the central bank has expanded over the years, conferring the BNM with more control even as the market was being progressively liberalised. These measures sought, in general, to improve market dynamics among the various financial institutions although domestic institutions were protected against greater competition from foreign-owned ones. However, even as BNM regulated the

---

5 They were still allowed to retain 100 per cent foreign ownership.

6 For a more detailed account, see Hussein (1994).

market, it did not 'govern' the market in the sense that is understood in the literature on Asian 'developmental states'. BNM did not control or direct credit other than for a small volume of policy lending. Instead, it sought to promote market outcomes through liberalisation measures. In this limited sense, the Malaysian state's role vis-à-vis the banking sector resembled that of a market enabler. However, state intervention in the financial sector was also coloured by the racial politics of the country (discussed in a later section) and private, rather than public, interests. This was far more apparent in the capital market and it is to this topic that we now turn.

Capital market

The government played a significant role in the early stages of the capital markets' development as the latter's initial expansion was mainly the result of servicing the needs of the public sector. About 75 per cent of the new funds raised in the capital market during the 1980s was through the issuance of Malaysian Government securities (Lin 1994). The first major deepening of the capital market occurred in 1987 with the introduction of mortgage-backed securities issued by Cagamas, the national mortage corporation jointly owned by the BNM, which remains its biggest shareholder with a share of 20 per cent, with a group of commercial banks, finance companies and merchant banks. Cagamas would purchase housing loans from, and thus provide liquidity to, the loan originators (essentially the banks, finance companies and the government) and 'repackage' them as the 'basis' against which bearer mortgage fixed- or floating-rate bonds could be issue. Through its various activities, Cagamas was instrumental in creating a market for private debt securities as well as helping to establish market-related yields for private mortgage-based paper (Ong 1999; Rethel 2010a). This was complemented by various tax incentives to encourage the growth of the private debt security market, which was a significant development as it added greater depth, breadth and sophistication to the money and capital markets, and offered investors a wider range of investments with which to structure their portfolio. At the same time, the expansion of the security market gave borrowers readily accessible alternative sources of financing in addition to bank borrowing and the issue of shares. However, the secondary market was underdeveloped as there were a captive demand for, and shortage of, Malaysian Government Securities (MGS), an illiquid cash market and an absence of a futures market in Malaysia. This curbed the level of issuing and trading activity. In addition, the bond market was also thought to be over-regulated (Lin 1994; Thillainathan 2003; Ibrahim and Wong 2006). A major transformation of the private debt security market did not occur until after the crisis (discussed later). The rapid growth of the equity market as an alternative source of funding to bank loans might have reduced the incentive for policy makers to focus on developing the security market.

While the state was a dominant player in the bond market, it played a more modest if no less significant and catalytic role in the rapid growth of the equity market. The privatisation policy of the government was a significant and steady source of new listings to the equity market in the late-1980s and early-1990s. In 1992, the privatisation of Proton (the producer of the national car) and Tenaga Nasional (the national electricity corporation) and the cash call by Malaysian Airline System Berhad (the national airline) accounted for 58 per cent of new funds raised on the stock market (Hussein 1994, p.163; Lin 1994, pp.124–5). Fourteen public corporations that were privatised in 1992 accounted for a third of total market capitalisation and 14 per cent of the aggregate value traded that year. Privatised public entities also figured prominently in the list of largest companies in terms of market capitalisation. Furthermore, government-controlled investment institutions such as the Employees' Provident Fund (EPF) were called upon to invest in stocks thus contributing to the expansion of the market.

Although the state was a critical and significant actor in catalysing the growth of the capital markets, in particular the bond market, the private sector too eventually developed an active presence, increasing their fund-raising through the capital market at a faster rate than the public sector. Public sector borrowings from the capital market have been in decline since 1990 as the government downsized its operations and shifted the emphasis in the economy to the role of the private sector, consistent with its reform orientation. While total net funds raised in the capital market reached almost MYR34 billion in 1997, the public sector redeemed a net total of MYR1.5 billion worth of securities (see Table 4.1). In other words, funds raised in the capital market that year went in effect entirely to the private sector. With capital market financing growing on average 16 per cent per annum between 1962 and 1992, double the growth rate for the economy as a whole, annual funds raised in the capital market slightly exceeded the amount of financing provided by the banking system for the first time in 1992 (Singh and Yusof 2002). Despite the expansion of the capital market, the banking system remained the main provider of funds for the private sector in both absolute and relative terms (see Figure 4.1).

Table 4.1 Malaysia: funds raised in the capital market (in MYR million)

	1997	1998	2001	2003	2005	2007	2008
Net Funds Raise by the Public Sector	–1,407.20	9,803.70	15,214.10	23,850.97	15,824.81	25,178.38	36,188.06
Net Funds Raised by Private Sector	35,142.30	7,963.10	23,700.80	26,502.08	25,894.06	20,299.80	21,114.26
– *Shares*	18,358.30	1,787.80	6,123.50	7,771.53	6,315.19	7,125.86	5,477.00
– *Net Debt Securities Raised*	16,784.00	6,175.30	17,577.30	18,730.55	19,578.87	13,173.94	15,637.26
Net Funds Raised by Both Public & Private Sectors	33,735.10	17766.80	38914.90	50,353.05	41,718.86	45,478.19	57,302.32
As % of GDP	117.93%	61.79%	110.37%	120.24%	79.85%	70.85%	77.36%

Source: Author's own calculations from data extracted from BNM's Monthly Statistical Bulletin (various issues).

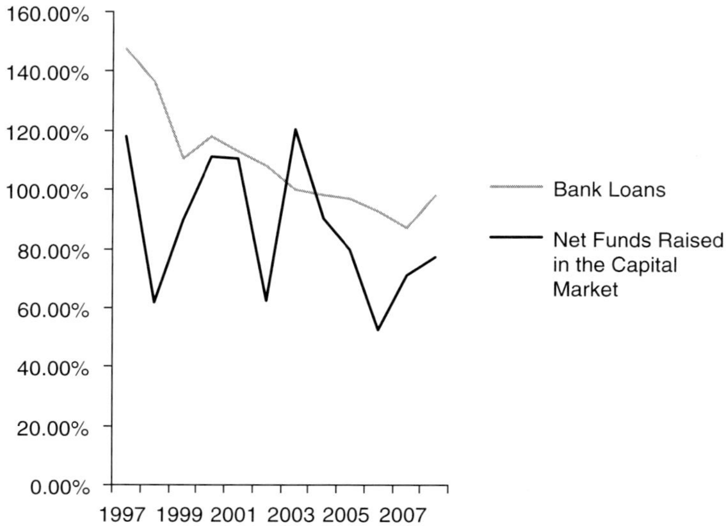

Figure 4.1 Malaysia: bank loans and funds raised in the capital market (per cent of GDP)

Source: Constructed from data that was extracted from BNM's Monthly Statistical Bulletin (various issues).

Nevertheless, on the eve of the crisis, the Malaysian financial system had become both much broader and deeper, especially when compared with those of Korea and Thailand (see Table 6.1). Bank assets as a percentage of GDP in Malaysia exceeded those of Thailand and were more than six times those of Korea. Similarly, equity market capitalisation as a percentage of GDP in Malaysia was more than 5.5 times that in Thailand and almost seven times that in Korea. Some of the growth in both the banking sector and capital market in Malaysia can of course be explained in functionalist terms: in order to meet the needs of a rapidly expanding economy and the changing needs of the market place, the financial sector had to transform itself from playing the role of mainly financing trade to one that could efficiently mobilise savings and channel resources for productive investments in a wide spectrum of activities.

However, government policy was also significant. In Korea, the banking sector was generally subordinated to development in the real sector and no significant effort was taken to develop a capital market. In Malaysia, however, the government attempted to develop both the banking sector and the equity market, which accounts for the difference in the state of development between Malaysia and Korea on the eve of the crisis. In Malaysia, the state influenced the development of the capital market in several ways. First, the government intervened to create markets as we saw in the role played by Cagamas in private debt securities (Rethel 2010a). The government, through its agencies ASN and ASB,[7] was also influential in introducing unit trusts as financial investment products for consumers which stimulated both the growth of the fund management industry and funds channelled into the capital market (Singh and Yusof 2002). Second, the Malaysian government, through policy initiatives, also accelerated the pace of change. The privatisation of public companies in the late-1980s and early-1990s contributed to a deepening of the market and attracted the interest of a greater number of potential investors to the equity market. Finally, government policy also shaped the nature of change. The Finance Minister, for instance, allowed banks to provide up to 100 per cent loan support for share purchases in August 1985 in order to enhance the liquidity of the market despite persistent warnings from BNM against giving out loans for share speculation (Khor 1987). While the need to reinvigorate the then ailing stock market was the stated reason for this decision, some have questioned whether the move was ultimately targeted at providing financial assistance to well-connected business individuals who had suffered when the stock market had earlier declined in value (Lim 1985), thus suggesting the role of the 'polity' or institutional context of policy making. The banking sector was also permitted to participate directly in capital market instruments at a time when it helpfully coincided with the government's push to privatise public corporations (Lin 1994, p.118). Regardless of the political motivation that underpinned these policy moves, they contributed to increasing liquidity in the capital market thus facilitating its expansion.

As the capital market expanded and deepened, Malaysia's financial sector increasingly acquired attributes associated with that of a liberal market model. However, as in Korea, the role of the state was instrumental in this process through its influence on the diversification of the financial sector and the growth of the market. The state's involvement

[7] In 1981, Amanah Saham Nasional Bhd launched Skim Amanah Saham Nasional (ASN) to promote savings in the *bumiputera* community and encourage *bumiputera* ownership in the corporate sector. In 1990, the Bumiputera Trust Fund (ASB) replaced the ASN. These institutional investors are under the control of the Ministry of Finance. See Gomez and Jomo (1999, p.36) for details.

in the financial sector was however not always used to promote economic growth but sometimes also political ones. This is the subject of the following section.

Policy lending and government intervention

Governments intervening to actively direct credit in order to promote their desired development outcomes is a feature that is frequently noted in the literature on the Asian developmental model. However in the case of Malaysia, with the exception of export credit and some relatively minor financial institutions, there was little evidence that the Malaysia government had used financial policy as an instrument to promote industry (Chin and Jomo 2000). Thillainathan (2003) noted that there was no *overt* policy of 'directed lending' to big firms. There were, however, since the mid-1970s guidelines on lending to 'priority sectors' which have included small-scale enterprises, agricultural food production, individual housing loans and the manufacturing sector (Yusof et al. 1994, p.284).[8] The guidelines were kept broad-based and individual financial institutions were given considerable discretion in assessing and monitoring credit. The guidelines also did not distort interest rates since the fixed rate reflected the actual cost of funds to the banking institutions and when the BLR was introduced in 1987, interest rates on priority lending were pegged to it, subject to a maximum margin. Although there was a requirement for banks to extend credit to the *bumiputera* community, bank lending to this sector had exceeded minimum 'requirements' by the late-1980s and the guidelines were therefore no longer binding (Hamilton-Hart 2002, p.122) – the government's policy orientation towards the bumiputera community is discussed shortly.

Although these guidelines did not target lending to 'big firms' and might not have constituted 'industrial policy' proper, the government was nevertheless partial to a planned approach to economic development, as opposed to leaving matters to market forces alone. Its commitment to a high growth policy based on a high ratio of investments to GDP led eventually to the promotion and financial support of certain 'mega' projects in the 1980s when Mahathir Mohamed was Prime Minister. Since it was implicit that the government would not let those

[8] As recently as 2005, priority sectors were mentioned in BNM's annual reports which at that time encompassed lending to SMEs, *bumiputera* SMEs and for the purchase of low cost houses. Since the 2006 edition, BNM's annual reports no longer mention priority sectors although the central bank continues to champion access to credit for SMEs.

projects fail, commercial lenders made their decisions based on not just project cash flows but also on collaterals and implied government support. More importantly, explicit policies of 'directed lending' were not important when the government, through its statutory agencies, held significant equity in domestic financial institutions as well as controlled 'development finance institutions' that were explicitly mandated to provide medium- to long-term financing to investment projects that require long periods of gestation.[9]

The Malaysian government's most significant policy intervention in the market has been its intercession on behalf of the *bumiputera* community that embraces the ethnically Malay majority and a variety of other indigenous ethnic groups,[10] which in turn is a manifestation of the broader racial politics of the country that has become a main referent point for most studies of Malaysia's politics and political economy. Following racial riots in May 1969, wherein economic disparity between racial groups was a main point of contention, the government introduced the New Economic Policy (NEP) that became a cornerstone of national development between 1970 and 1986. The NEP had two principal goals: to reduce poverty and to reduce the identification of race with specific types of employment. In practice, it is understood as an affirmative action instrument to redress the economic imbalance between the majority *bumiputera* – mostly Malay – and the wealthier Chinese minority of the population. In 1971, the *bumiputera*, comprising 64 per cent of the population, owned a mere 2 per cent of national wealth, defined as ownership of company share capital at par value.[11] The NEP set long-term targets for *bumiputera* ownership of share capital in limited companies (30 per cent by 1990) and employment in manufacturing and management. Although many strictures of the NEP were relaxed after 1986, and the policy was subsequently replaced by the National Development Policy (NDP) in 1991, aspects favouring the *bumiputera* community continue to be in force. The new NDP for instance envisaged the creation of small and medium-scale *bumiputera*

---

[9] In a survey conducted in 2004, three Malaysian banks responded that more than 30 per cent of its loans went to the public sector on instruction by the government. See Parreñas (2006) for details.

[10] *Bumiputera* comes from Sanskrit and can be literally translated as 'son of earth'.

[11] While Chinese ownership of corporate equity was greater than Malay ownership, its 27 per cent paled in comparison to foreign ownership which stood at about 63 per cent. See Yun (1987).

businesses through state-funded venture capitalism, the granting of franchises and other assistance programmes.[12] The political importance of economic policies that favoured the *bumiputera* community (and the discourse thereof), and that conversely discriminated against other ethnic groups, persists until the present day. This is an outcome of the 'polity' of Malaysia's political economy as we will see in our discussion on the evolution of the financial sector in the post-crisis period.

While the stated socio-political goals of the NEP/NDP are 'developmental' in nature, in that they were intended to eradicate poverty and improve the wealth holdings of a large subset of the population, over time, aspects of the implementation of the policy goals took the form of 'patronage politics'. This became particularly acute under the Prime Minister-ship of Mahathir (1981–2003) as he sought to promote the advancement of specific *bumiputera* individuals in the corporate sector as a means of achieving the spirit of the NEP/NDP goals (Gomez and Jomo 1999). While corruption and nepotism undermined economic growth and efficiency, the ascendance of *bumiputera* 'entrepreneurs' to the height of Malaysian industry and corporate life had political traction, at least for a brief period of time, as 'proof' of the ability of *bumiputera* individuals to succeed in a modern capitalist economy. However, over the course of time, patronage politics changed the 'polity' and politics of the country; perverted the developmental element of the NEP/NDP and kept the state embroiled in the market with outcomes that most would assess to be less than positive.[13]

Returning to the financial sector, the government's active direct intervention in finance began with the establishment of Bank Bumiputera in 1965 to provide commercial loans to Malay entrepreneurs. The government later become a major shareholder of Malayan Banking in 1969 after a run on the bank in 1966. By 1976, when the then United Malayan Banking Corporation (UMBC) came under government control, the government dominated the banking system, owning the three largest commercial banks in the country. The government, through either management or ownership, had control of 77 per cent of the combined paid-up capital of 21 Malaysian banks by 1986 (Yun 1987). Within just two decades after the NEP, eight of the top ten local commercial banks

---

[12] For a brief account of the implementation of the NEP and how the effects of the policy contributed to the dynamics of the financial crisis in Malaysia, see Doraisami (2005). For a more recent succinct critique of the NEP, see Gomez (2005).

[13] See, for instance, the volume by Gomez and Jomo (1999).

were brought under the control of state-owned companies and politically connected *bumiputera* individuals (Gomez and Jomo 1999, p.62).

Although the macroeconomic development goals and the socio-economic objectives of the NEP are conceptually distinct, the policies implemented to attain both were frequently intertwined in Malaysia. Commercial banks under the control of state-owned companies and politically connected *bumiputera* individuals were used to facilitate the implementation of the NEP as well as the industrialisation programme that the government launched in 1981 (Chin and Jomo 2003). This was achieved by lending to favoured Malay and a selected few non-Malay business elites on highly concessionary terms (Economic Analytical Unit 2002, p.135; Shari 2003), coupled with the award of major public projects and lucrative licences as well as other business opportunities including the privatisation of public corporations (Gomez 1994). Such practices would and did lead to inefficient economic outcomes but government intervention was motivated by not just considerations of economic growth but also political ones: the emergence of major *bumiputera*-controlled conglomerates in the early-1980s was an important indicator of progress and development, as understood in a peculiar Malaysian manner within the context of NEP politics. The institution and adoption of policies and strategies that not just promoted but also ensured *bumiputera* participation in the economy were quite clear in the capital market. Firms issuing shares to the public were required to offer and maintain 30 per cent of their equity to the *bumiputera* community after 1976.[14] Due to government intervention, the prices of shares issued to Malay interests were usually set below market levels to ensure positive returns to and accelerate the acquisition of corporate assets by *bumiputera* individuals and organisations on behalf of the *bumiputera* community. The Foreign Investment Committee (FIC) also became an important government body to monitor and influence non-*bumiputera* and foreign-owned corporations to restructure their equity to comply with NEP's ownership regulations.[15]

---

[14] This requirement was only relaxed in the period after the financial crisis as discussed later in the chapter.

[15] The FIC was set up in 1972, in part, to rule on proposed new investments or corporate transactions to ensure that Malay interests owned at least 30 per cent of a new corporate entity. Property purchases are also scrutinised by the FIC. It is neither a statutory body nor a government authority. It is run by civil servants but its recommendations do not have the force of law. The FIC does not have explicit guidelines directing its action, only broad principles, and as such, rulings can be inconsistent. See Jayasankaran (2003a).

Despite these significantly discriminatory and arguably restrictive policies, the government was also always careful to ensure that the broader private sector continued to play a vibrant and important role in the economy. This has historically been a major, if not primary, contributor to economic growth in Malaysia. Since the government's distributive policies were largely made politically possible by a growing economic pie, the government had to be careful not to, as it were, kill the goose that laid the golden eggs for it to achieve its political goals. Thus, for several decades prior to the crisis, the Malaysian government managed what was effectively a 'dual economy' in which more liberalised market niches were established to attract foreign direct investors while local markets were protected in order to promote 'national economic goals' (Jesudason 1989, pp.173–6; Rasiah 1995).[16] This 'productive synergy', it was argued, helped Malaysia secure economic growth against a relatively more muted racially-based competition over wealth and resources in contrast to the 1969 racial riots that first prompted affirmative action policies (Salleh and Meyanathan 1993), the costs of re-distributional policies introduced under the NEP notwithstanding. In the financial sector, despite government interference in state-owned institutions, privately owned banks, other than those belonging to politically connected *bumiputera*, did not become very entangled in business conglomerates partly due to effective regulation that attempted to preserve some arms-length relation between the banks and corporate interests and to check their market power.[17]

In short, state policies and intervention had shaped the landscape of the Malaysian financial sector. While the banking sector was once dominated by foreign-owned banks, by 1997, their share of the

---

[16] Menon (2001) argued that the openness of the Malaysian economy to trade and foreign investment was a key force behind its rapid economic growth. Export-oriented foreign firms were exempted from the employment quotas and ownership restrictions of the NEP. There was a decisive policy shift towards greater outward orientation in the late 1980s according to Athukorala (2001), although export-oriented industrialisation was promoted from the early 1970s.

[17] Banks were limited to holding 10 per cent of the equity in any one firm and bank officials were barred from sitting in any company board of directors. Furthermore, the banking sector's emphasis on extending loans on the basis of collateral, rather than project viability, had favoured loans to the real property sector and for share purchases and consumption rather than production, particularly when the property and stock markets have been bullish, see Yun (1987). Until 1997, no more than about a third of commercial bank lending went to manufacturing, agriculture or other productive activities, see Chin and Jomo (2003).

banking systems' total assets had dwindled to only about 15 per cent, largely the result of a policy decision to heavily regulate foreign-owned banks.[18] Conversely, state-owned companies and politically connected *bumiputera* individuals increasingly controlled a number of large local commercial banks, which the government used as instruments to achieve policy, social and political goals (Gomez and Jomo 1999). Notwithstanding these interventions, a dynamic financial sector thrived to meet the needs of the economy, particularly since the government took a decisive step towards greater market liberalisation in the late-1980s. This is in no small part due to the regulatory and developmental efforts of the central bank (Hamilton-Hart 2002). Thus in 1997, prior to the crisis, Malaysia had a relatively vibrant financial sector that included one of the top three biggest capital markets in East Asia (Demirgüç-Kunt and Levine 1996). Although the state interfered and influenced the financial sector, market dynamics were also strong. This mirrored the real sector where despite frequent intervention and regulation to serve political goals, a thriving export-oriented market 'enclave' existed that drove economic growth. In the financial sector, active state interference over the market is channelled through more direct influence over a selected number of financial institutions while broader market dynamics were promoted and regulated by the central bank. There was therefore a 'dual economy' or 'hybrid' system where elements of both LME and SiME ideal types co-existed. The nature of state–market dynamics in the financial sector was the result of a combination of policy decisions to develop the market dynamics of the sector, the institutional context ('polity') of Malaysia's multi-racial society and the private interests of patronage politics.

The Asian financial crisis

While short-term foreign debt was a critical factor in the financial crisis experienced by Korea and Thailand, in Malaysia, commercial bank lending for property development and stock market investments were

[18] The opening of new branches of foreign-owned institutions has been virtually proscribed while the installation of off-premises Automated Teller Machines (ATMs) by foreign banks was strictly controlled. Although, foreign banks could acquire an equity interest in a local banking institution, the acquisition had to be approved and aggregate foreign shareholding in the target bank could not exceed 30 per cent.

understood to be the main reasons for Malaysia's economic problems during the 1997–8 financial crisis (Jomo 2006).[19] In the decade before the crisis, greater competition in the lending market, partially induced by BNM's attempts at market consolidation (elaborated later in this chapter), had led to the expansion of financial credit by an annual average of nearly 30 per cent. A significant proportion of this went to less 'reliable' customers as large corporations turned to the increasingly developed equity market and no longer relied as much on banks for capital. At the end of 1997, over 40 per cent of commercial bank lending was extended for property development and stock market investments (Ong 1999, Table 5.4). These developments – the diversification of the banking business and the equity market acting as an alternative source of funding – were facilitated by the liberalisation efforts discussed in the earlier sections.

Although Malaysia had the most open economy in the region after Hong Kong and Singapore, its foreign borrowings and share of short-term loans in total borrowings were far less than in the more closed economies of Indonesia, Korea and Thailand. According to Athukorola (2001, p.21), Malaysia's foreign debt in the period 1989–97 remained at 25–30 per cent of GDP and its ratio of debt payments and interest payments to export earnings varied in those years from 6 to 8 per cent. These indicators, Athukorola contended, were 'remarkably low by developing country standards' and were the result of fiscal discipline and prudent macroeconomic management on the part of government. Furthermore, strict controls were imposed on Malaysian private borrowing from abroad (Jomo 2006, p.495; Radelet and Sachs 1998), attesting in part to the strength and capability of the Malaysian central bank to regulate the market. In addition, domestic interest rates were lower than those in the international markets thus minimising market incentive to borrow from abroad.

In the years prior to the crisis, official indicators suggest that the soundness of the Malaysian financial system had been improving significantly: the ratio of NPLs to total loans in banks and finance companies fell from 20 per cent in 1990 to about 3.8 per cent for banks and 4.7 per cent for finance companies in 1996 (Lindgren et al. 1999). The banking sector was well capitalised with the risk-weighted capital ratio at 12 per cent, significantly above the minimum requirement of 8 per

---

[19] For a critique of more endemic and longer term problems faced by the Malaysian economy at the time of the crisis, see Rasiah (1998).

cent.[20] At the time, Malaysia had also already complied with 22 of the 25 BIS Core Principles (Zamani 2006, p.269). However, the persistent pace of credit expansion in the 1990s to the private sector, leading to high loan exposure in non-tradable sectors, rendered the financial system vulnerable when the economy slowed and asset values declined. As the regional crisis deepened, concerns about the true conditions of the financial system increased, a matter not helped by measures announced by the authorities to relax the manner in which NPLs were classified (Chin 2004, see Table 8.1).[21]

Government response to the crisis

In contrast to the case of Thailand, where more market-based approaches were initially adopted, the Malaysian response to managing the financial crisis of 1997–8 was state-led from the beginning. Since external debt was manageable, the government decided against turning to the IMF for fear that many of its existing policies would be affected by IMF conditionality. Nevertheless, for about the first year of the crisis, the Malaysian government, on its own accord, followed an orthodox IMF-style approach in responding to the crisis in an attempt to regain the confidence of investors (Khor 2005). It focussed its efforts on addressing the current account deficit, containing inflationary pressures from the depreciation of the Ringgit, stabilising the exchange rate, preventing large outflows of short-term capital, and reducing public expenditures.[22] Nevertheless, the Ringgit continued to depreciate and market capitalisation in the KLSE continued to decline. More importantly, these policies together with heightened sensitivity to corporate risks and a 'capital crunch' as bank capital was depleted led to a decline in the growth of loans and subsequently a general contraction of the economy (Domac, Ferri and Kang 2005; Gan and Soon 2001).

In the face of this deflationary effect on the economy, the Malaysian government decided to changed tack. The statutory reserve ratio was

---

[20] This refers to the Basel capital framework that weighs both on- and off-balance sheet items according to their perceived level of risk.

[21] During the period of the crisis, BNM flip-flopped on the classification of NPLs. On 18 October 1997, loan classification rules were tightened from a six month to a three month delinquency, which was the recognised standard being adopted across the region. On 23 September 1998, BNM reverted to the former six month standard to allow banks 'breathing space'.

[22] For more detailed accounts of measures taken by the Malaysian government in the wake of the financial crisis, see Yap (2001); Jomo (2006).

reduced to make more funds available for bank lending; and the central bank's three-month intervention rate was lowered to reduce the cost of funds and the debt service commitment of firms as well as promote investment activities. However, the most controversial measure adopted by the Malaysian government in its new strategy towards managing the crisis was the introduction of capital controls on 1 September 1998. This eliminated offshore speculative activities and curbed external portfolio capital outflows. Much has been written about these measures and it is beyond the scope of this chapter to discuss them, however it suffices to note here that their introduction insulated the economy from the continued adverse external environment and allowed policy makers to regain some monetary autonomy.[23]

With capital controls in place, the government deployed its administrative capacity more extensively. It established two new state agencies, Danaharta and Danamodal, that together with the Corporate Debt Restructuring Committee (CDRC) formed an institutional framework that was employed to rehabilitate the commercial banking system through the use of public funds to acquire NPLs and recapitalise commercial banks while at the same time facilitate the restructuring of corporate debt. Whilst Danaharta was established as a public asset management company in order to purchase non-performing loans, Danamodal was a limited liability company wholly-owned by BNM that was tasked with the objective of injecting new capital in ailing banks.

Among the three countries in this study, the method adopted by Malaysia's asset management company, Danaharta, for dealing with NPLs was the most assertive and yet generous.[24] The carrot in this arrangement was that banks would not bear any losses that might arise from the eventual sale of distressed assets to Danaharta but would receive an 80 per cent share of the gains. In the other two economies, banks would share in both gains and losses. The stick however was that although the government did not make it compulsory for banks to transfer NPLs to Danaharta, banks had to write-down their NPLs to 80 per cent of the price offered by Danaharta if they chose not to participate in the scheme. No other national asset management companies had such

---

[23] See, among others, Jomo (2004); Doraisami (2005). For a recent view on the use of capital controls to address financial market volatility, see Anderson (2009).

[24] For details see, Smith (2008).

a harsh condition. This was a very aggressive and powerful incentive designed to encourage banks to participate in the public programme. As further encouragement, only banks that sold NPLs to Danaharta were permitted to access funds from Danamodal to recapitalise their institutions. However, as a shareholder in banking institutions that needed recapitalisation, Danamodal was eventually employed as a catalyst to facilitate the restructuring of banking institutions via merger exercises. This reflected the state's desire to exercise control over the banking institutions in order to achieve a long-standing policy goal.

BNM had been attempting to consolidate the fragmented banking industry since the late-1980s with the aim of improving its competitiveness and encouraging the emergence of more professional management through the dilution of individual ownership. BNM's view was that small Malaysian banks would not be able to survive once the financial market was liberalised following the country's commitment under the General Agreement on Trade in Services (GATS) in the WTO (Jayasankaran 1997). The BNM also thought that two huge banks in the market would make monetary policy easier to manage as the smaller banks would find it more difficult to ignore the larger banks' lead in setting central bank-prescribed interest rates (Jayasankaran 2001b). However calls for banks to merge voluntarily since the late-1980s had been largely ignored as lucrative oligopolistic bank profits, largely assured by banking regulation, have meant that the desire to retain independent banking licences remained strong. The most recent scheme prior to the crisis adopted by BNM to encourage institutional consolidation in the financial sector, the Two-tier Regulatory System,[25] did not produce the desired result and was pronounced a 'dismal' failure by the central bank Governor, Ali Abdul Hassan Sulaiman (Bank Negara Malaysia 1999b).

The financial crisis of 1997 provided BNM with another opportunity to achieve its desire of consolidating the banking sector, this time through the use of more assertive means as it was able to 'encourage' the process through Danamodal in the latter's role as a strategic shareholder in recapitalised banking institutions (Chin 2005). BNM outlined a radical restructuring plan in July 1999 to consolidate the country's then 21 commercial banks, 25 finance companies and 12 merchant banks down to six groups each built around an 'anchor' bank (Bank Negara Malaysia 1999a). Although BNM considered the plan to be a 'guided merger', it was highly directive: the central bank identified the likely anchor

[25] See Ito and Hashimoto (2007b) for details.

institutions – three of which were state-owned – and how they would be built. As many as four of the six new banks would continue to have significant government equity, thus maintaining, if not increasing, the government's ownership-levels in the financial sector. All banking institutions were required to sign preliminary merger agreements by the end of September 1999 and tax incentives were offered to facilitate the merger process. While few would have contested the need to consolidate the financial sector, the speed and scale of the merger and the manner of their official orchestration alarmed many both within and outside the banking industry (Jayasankaran 1999; Wall Street Journal 1999). Furthermore, significant differences in ownership structure, size, reputation and earnings of the acquirers and their merging partners caused the announcement to be poorly received by a majority of the banks' shareholders (Ahmad and Sieh-Lee 2000). For instance, in one case, it was proposed that a small 'Malay' bank would take over eleven other institutions including one that was eight times its size.[26] In addition, there remained uncertainty over the impact of the mergers on the asset quality of the newly formed groups, particularly on the anchor companies.

Although it was argued that the government was using the merger plan to demonstrate its commitment to economic reform and to prove that the 'visible and strong hand of government' was just as good, if not better, at this task as the 'invisible hand of markets' (Lopez 1999), the way with which the government chose to implement the consolidation exercise led many to view the process as being politically oriented rather than targeted at resuscitating the ailing financial industry following the crisis, let alone improving the efficiency of the sector. For instance, the most contentious political issue was the effect the consolidation exercise would have had on banks owned by ethnic Chinese interests. Under the NEP, the Malay interests in the banking sector had grown dramatically, primarily at the expense of foreign and to a lesser extent (Malaysian-)Chinese banking institutions. The proposed consolidation would have drastically reduced the number of Chinese-controlled banks from eight to two (Lopez 1999).[27] It was also suggested that two of the Chinese-owned banks were being 'victimised' for their close connections with former-Deputy Prime Minister, Anwar Ibrahim,

---

[26] The proposed anchor bank in question was Multi-Purpose Bank controlled by a businessmen said to be close to then Finance Minister, Daim Zainuddin.

[27] Although this represented roughly the same proportion of Chinese-owned bank equity as before the proposed merger, see Jayasankaran (1999).

who had, in the course of the crisis, fallen out with then Prime Minister Mahathir (Jayasankaran 1999).

The fact that the consolidation plan was driven by politics became explicit in October 1999 when Prime Minister Mahathir signalled that the plan might be modified (Banoo 1999). It was reported that the Prime Minister and the National Economic Action Council (NEAC) had disagreed with the central bank on whether the number of anchor banks should be determined in advance (Mansor 1999),[28] and the plan was subsequently modified to allow for a larger number of 'anchor' institutions, though initially unspecified. The banks were then given until 31 January 2000 to submit their merger proposals and the Prime Minister said that the government would not 'ram (the process) down (the banks') throat' (Banoo 1999). Furthermore, all domestic banking institutions merging into groups were permitted to choose their own 'anchors' but the Prime Minister warned that the government would step in if the banks could not agree among themselves. On 14 February 2000, the government granted approval for the formation of ten banking groups to be led by ten anchor banks and the process of consolidation was completed in March 2002 when the last deal was sealed between RHB Bank Berhad and Bank Utama Malaysia Berhad. With their formation, the number of domestic banking institutions was substantially reduced to 29 (ten commercial banks, ten finance companies and nine merchant banks).

Although consolidation resulted in larger and better capitalised domestic banking institutions that were more efficient and productive (Njie 2007), it has had little or no impact on the market concentration of the top three banking institutions with their shares of total assets, loans and deposits remaining roughly the same in 2003 when compared with 1998 (Lum and Koh 2006, p.294) – see also the 'bank concentration indicator' in Table 4.3. Furthermore, consolidation did not have any significant effect on the composition of the ownership structure in the banking industry, an outcome that was largely by design in order to assuage the varied political interests in the process.

Controversies

There is general agreement that the roles played by Danaharta and Danamodal in managing NPLs gave banks the ability to restore their

---

[28] The NEAC was chaired by the Prime Minister and comprises cabinet ministers and public and private sector representatives. It was set up in January 1998 as a consultative body to the Cabinet to come up with innovative strategies for economic recovery.

lending capacity and to focus on providing credit to viable corporate ventures. The response of the two state agencies was generally acknowledged to have been rapid and well-coordinated, which subsequently set the financial system on a much more solid foundation (World Bank 2004). However, the state agencies' roles have also been controversial.

First, there was a lack of transparency in the operations of these agencies. Although Danamodal claimed to have only recapitalised viable banking institutions based on assessments by financial advisors of international repute, the basis of deciding which banks were given priority to receive capital injection by Danamodal were not made public. A legal case that was brought against Danaharta suggested that it might not always have employed rational, or fair, economic calculations in resolving the bad debts (Jayasankaran 2003b).

Second, there were suggestions that the Minister of Finance, who oversaw the running of the agency, was using it for political purposes when he rejected a proposal to buy shares back, at a substantial premium, from the agency in February 2001.[29] Selected individuals and corporations, including Mirzan Mahathir, eldest son of then Prime Minister Mahathir, and the top protégés of Daim Zainuddin, then Minister of Finance, were perceived to have been 'bailed out' as part of the exercise (Haggard 2000, pp.162–71; Jayasankaran 2001c; Case 2005). Many of these individuals were recipients of state largesse in the late-1980s and early-1990s when the Mahathir government was actively promoting the rise of *bumiputera* 'enterpreneurs' (Gomez and Jomo 1999, Chapters 4 and 5). Similarly, in the bank consolidation exercise, at least one observer argued that the process was 'shaped by political interests that overshadow economic considerations' (Chin 2004, p.224).

However, the state's involvement was also seen as a means to remedy the failures of the past with the bail-outs being read as a move to replace the previous strategy of achieving *bumiputera* equity goals based on privatisation and 'owner-entrepreneurs' with one that relied more on institutional ownership and professional management (Jayasankaran

---

[29] The case involved RHB Capital's proposal to buy back RHB Bank's irredeemable non-cumulative preference shares from Danamodal. This was read as an attempt by the Finance Minister to oust Rashid Hussain from control of RHB Bank.

2002a).[30] In other words, the bailouts could be read as an attempt at rectifying the mistakes of the past. State agencies that held listed assets increased their holdings and reformed management structures, with the Malaysian state eventually becoming the largest holder of listed firms in the region after the governments of China and Singapore (Economic Analytical Unit 2002, p.136; Case 2005). Although such vast state ownership is often looked upon critically as a wellspring of corruption and inefficiencies, in the Malaysian case, the renationalisation of assets was viewed as an improvement, if only relative to the business practices of the prior owner-managers of the Malay business elites. However, as the government did not have an explicit strategy, much of their effort in this regard was ad-hoc and inconsistent (Haggard 2000).

The consolidation exercise also further demonstrated the continuance of a top-down approach to economic development and policy making that has been a feature of Malaysia, especially since Mahathir was elected Prime Minister. Although the post-crisis merger and acquisition activities in Malaysia might have been a 'natural' market response to the financial crisis, it 'would have not happened at such a speed [less than two years] without strong government influence' (Ahmad 2007). BNM intervened and accelerated the pace of consolidation in the wake of the crisis in order to shape market outcomes and ensure the survival of national players, rather than leave the fate of domestic banks to market forces.

Thus, whether for economic or political ends, in the period immediately following the crisis, state intervention in the Malaysian financial sector was acute and revealed the intricate links between the government and the corporate sector, and thus the 'polity' or institutional context of policy making in Malaysia. Political patronage, which ostensibly began as a means of meeting socio-political goals, not only contributed to weaknesses in the economy but also coloured the way the crisis was resolved and managed. Thus, in the Malaysian case, state-interference in the market is heavily shaped by a socio-political bargain first made in 1970.

---

30 In May 2004, the successor to Mahathir, Abdullah Ahmad Badawi, announced a plan to consolidate more than 40 partially state-owned firms, or Government-Linked-Companies (GLCs), into a holding company that would be overseen by Khazanah, the government's investment arm established in 1993. The government intended to introduce performance indicators; employ depoliticised and professional managers and enforce higher standards of corporate governance.

Post-Crisis evolution of the financial system

How has the mix between significant state involvement and strong market dynamics in the financial sector evolved since the crisis of 1997–8? Has there been a shift in this balance and in which direction has it moved? I address these questions by analysing the change in the Malaysian financial sector firstly through the use of quantitative indictors. Then, I will provide a qualitative discussion of some of the major initiatives and developments that have taken place in the financial sector since the crisis. In discussing these developments, I will examine, by focussing on the dimensions of policy, 'polity' and politics, the extent to and the manner in which the state's past influence in the financial sector continue to persist and whether patronage politics continue to affect the implementation of policy.

Quantitative indicators of change

A decade on from the financial crisis of 1997–8, many of the features identified above endure. As we can see from Figure 4.1 and Table 4.2, the relative sizes of the banking sector and the stock market have remained relatively constant although the bond market has expanded considerably in relative terms. Foreign players continue to be a prominent feature, owning about a fifth of total banking system assets (see Table 4.3). With five main government agencies holding more than 40 per cent of the outstanding shares of six banking groups, the state also continued to have a substantive stake in the banking sector and, given the consolidation that had since taken place in the financial sector, has arguably strengthened its relative ownership levels (Lum and Koh 2007, Table 8).[31]

However, on closer inspection, there have also been significant material changes in the financial sector in the years since 1997–8. While the 'conventional' commercial banking sector is still important, its dominance has now been circumscribed by the emergence of Islamic finance and the growth of the bond market. The latter has increased by about

[31] The five government agencies were Permodalan Nasional Berhad (PNB), the Employees Provident Fund Board (EPF), Khazanah Nasional Berhad, Pertubuhan Keselamatan Sosial (PKS) and Kumpulan Wang Amanah Pencen (KWAP). PNB is the government's national capital corporation and Khazanah the Ministry of Finance's investment arm. EPF, PKS and KWAP are government agencies tasked with providing social security and pension funds. In three of the banking groups, these agencies held more than 50 per cent of outstanding shares.

Table 4.2 Malaysia: structure of financial systems (per cent of GDP)

	1996	1997	2002	2005	2006	2007
Deposit Money Bank Assets	129.64	146.05	128.09	113.77	111.60	106.84
Private Credit Extended by Deposit Money Banks and Other Financial Institutions	123.87	139.49	119.53	105.95	104.69	100.69
Stock Market Capitalisation	263.46	201.70	128.91	136.64	134.78	155.99
Bonds Outstanding	67.45	65.25	88.37	86.02	87.28	90.41

Source: Compiled from data extracted from The World Bank: Thorsten Beck et al.'s World Bank Database on Financial Development and Structure available from http://go.worldbank.org/X23UD9QUX0.

Table 4.3 Malaysia: banking sector assets (in MYR million)

	1996	1997	1998	2001	2005	2007	2008
Commercial Banks	360,127.6	481,114.1	455,542.7	530,374.2	886,094.8	1,145,813	1,275,401
– Domestic	*279,986.5*	*377,299.6*	*354,897.4*	*398,769.1*	*686,419*	*881,685.4*	*1,005,486*
– Foreign	*80,141.1*	*103,814.5*	*100,645.3*	*131,605.1*	*199,675.8*	*264,127.3*	*269,914.2*
Finance Companies	119,768.8	152,386.8	123,729.6	121,750.3	26,874.9	n.a.	n.a.
Merchant (Investment) Banks	34,072.8	44,300	39,249.5	41,077	46,631	75,614.4	58,708.2
Bank Concentration Indicator[1]	0.4090	0.4420	0.4011	0.4417	0.4143	0.4732	0.4851

[1] Refers to the ratio of the three largest banks' assets to total banking sector assets, extracted from Thorsten Beck et al.'s World Bank Database on Financial Development and Structure available from http://go.worldbank.org/X23UD9QUX0.

Source: Author's own calculations from data extracted from BNM's Monthly Statistical Bulletin (various issues).

30 per cent in size in the last ten years, from 67.45 per cent of GDP in 1996 to about 90 per cent of GDP at the end of 2007 (see Table 4.2 and Figure 4.2). Low interest rates and corporate debt restructuring in the period post-crisis contributed to the increase use of public and private debt securities. The greater market depth and liquidity of the bond

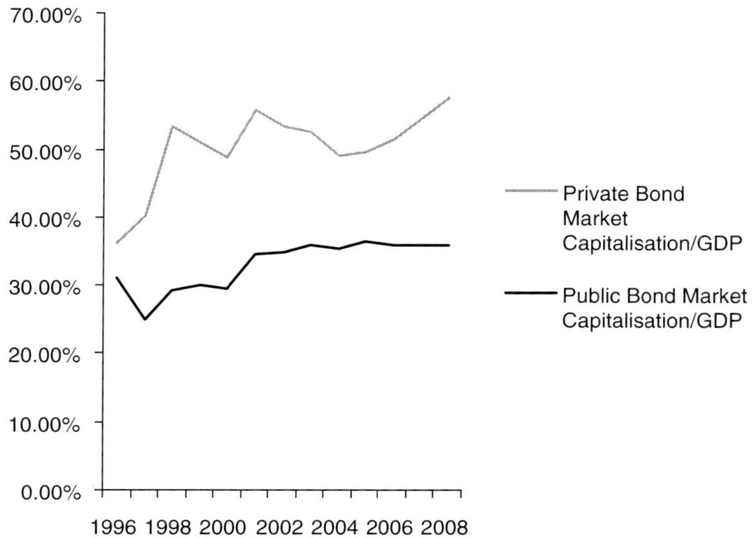

Figure 4.2 Malaysia: bond market capitalisation (per cent of GDP)

Source: Constructed from data extracted that was from The World Bank: Thorsten Beck et al.'s World Bank Database on Financial Development and Structure available from http://go.worldbank.org/X23UD9QUX0.

market suggests that it can better act as a 'spare tyre' to the banking sector unlike the pre-crisis period when it consisted almost entirely of government securities that were bought and held as opposed to being actively traded. The biggest change in the Malaysian financial system however has been the spectacular growth of Islamic finance. The sector practically doubled in the last decade, albeit from a low base. The size of Islamic banking currently represents under 15 per cent of total banking assets while over a third of outstanding bonds are now Islamic issues (see Table 4.4). The sector has also seen significant foreign participation in its development.

These changes – the greater diversity of sources of funding, the increasing sophistication of the various sub-sectors and the greater presence of foreign players – were all prescribed as market-enhancing developments in the wake of the crisis and a casual observer might quickly conclude that they have contributed to tilting the balance between the state and market in favour of the latter. However, two indicators of financial structure – Structure-Size and Structure-Activity – suggest that the opposite

Table 4.4 Malaysia: key indicators of islamic finance

	1999	2000	2001	2002	2003	2004	2005	2006	2007
Total No of Institutions	**52**	**49**	**38**	**37**	**33**	**29**	**29**	**23**	**25**
Islamic Banks	2	2	2	2	2	2	6	10	11
Banks Participating in Islamic Banking Scheme									
Commercial Banks	22	21	14	14	13	13	11	7	7
Investment Banks/ Merchant Banks[1]	5	5	5	5	4	4	4	4	6
Finance Companies[2]	16	14	10	9	7	3	1	n.a.	n.a.
Discount Houses	7	7	7	7	7	7	7	2	n.a.
International Islamic Banks	n.a.	n.a.	n.a.	n.a.	n.a.	n.a.	n.a.	n.a.	1
Assets, Financing and Deposits as a percentage of Total Banking System									
Total Assets	5.5	6.9	8.22	8.93	9.72	10.45	10.99	12.18	12.80
Total Financing	n.a.	5.3	6.53	8.13	10.27	11.30	15.06	12.37	13.96
Total Deposits	n.a.	7.4	9.51	10.13	10.41	11.16	11.24	12.19	14.02
Outstanding Islamic Bonds as a Percentage of GDP									
Government	0.00	1.12	1.13	1.30	1.67	2.13	2.32	3.76	4.67
BNM	0.00	0.07	0.28	0.49	1.31	1.05	1.34	1.74	3.19
Others	2.94	9.58	14.08	16.73	18.10	17.05	19.29	19.98	23.17
TOTAL	2.94	10.77	15.50	18.53	21.08	20.23	22.95	25.49	31.05

Notes: [1]With effect from 31 December 2006, all merchant banks merged with discount houses and stockbroking companies and were designated as investment banks.
[2]From 2006, finance companies merged with commercial banks under the concept of Banking and Finance Companies (BAFIN).

Source: Malaysia International Islamic Financial Centre, BNM Annual Report (2000), and BNM's Bond Info Hub (http://bondinfo.bnm.gov.my).

Table 4.5 Malaysia: indicators of financial structure

	1996	1997	2002	2005	2006	2007
Structure-Size	2.1269	1.4460	1.0784	1.2897	1.2875	1.5492
Structure-Activity	1.3894	1.0971	0.2428	0.3439	0.4095	n.a

Note: *Higher values indicate a more market-based financial system.*

Source: Compiled from data extracted from The World Bank: Thorsten Beck et al.'s World Bank Database on Financial Development and Structure available from http://go.worldbank.org/X23UD9QUX0.

conclusion, that is that the Malaysian financial system has become *less* market-based, might be closer to the mark (see Table 4.5).[32] In order to gain a better insight into the nature of changes in the financial sector since the crisis, let us turn to a more qualitative analysis.

The masterplans and financial sector development

In 2001, the Malaysian government issued two ten-year master plans for the financial system – one for the capital market and one for all other parts of the financial sector. While these plans were devised with the long-term goal of improving the financial system's effectiveness, competitiveness, resilience and dynamism in order to facilitate further liberalisation as well as improve the ability of domestic institutions to withstand greater competition; the immediate motivation were economic challenges that emerged on the back of the financial crisis of 1997–8: foreign investors and the Malaysian public had not reacted kindly to the statist interventions during the management of the crisis, in particular the capital controls and the perceived corporate bailouts. As a consequence, foreign direct investment began to weaken in late-2000 and the equity market failed to regain its earlier vigour. This prompted the government to turn to more market-based strategies. It let most of the capital controls package lapse leaving only the currency peg and the offshore trading ban in place and introduced more regularised procedures in both the public and corporate sectors. It was in this context that the master plans were devised and introduced.

While the goal of these plans was the promotion of greater market dynamics, they also demonstrated the persistence of the Malaysian state's conviction of its leading role in shaping and fostering economic activity through interventionist and directive means. The ten-year (2001–11) Financial Sector Master Plan (FSMP) covered all sectors of Malaysia's financial system and built on the earlier process of consolidation in preparing domestic financial institutions for the later introduction of new foreign competition. Although the FSMP acted as a guideline to the sequencing of policy goals, it was not clear on specific policies and

[32] Structure-Size is the ratio of Stock Market Capitalization to GDP divided by Bank Credit to GDP, while Structure-Activity is the ratio of Stock Market Value Traded to GDP divided by Bank Credit to GDP. The difference between these two indicators is that Structure-Size focuses on the total shares outstanding in the economy's stock exchanges, while Structure-Activity focuses on the liquidity of the exchanges. See Beck and Levine (2002).

timing. For instance, while the FSMP stated that restrictions on incumbent foreign banks would be 'gradually' lifted 'depending on the overall ability of the financial system to absorb these changes', it did not specify how the system's ability to absorb changes would be determined nor did the document elaborate strict deadlines for such measures to be effected (Bank Negara Malaysia 2001, p.36).[33] This ambiguity in the document is reflective of BNM's publicly stated approach to 'manage with flexibility to achieve the desired objectives'. However, given BNM's documented penchant to exhort domestic institutions into complying with its policy-desires within BNM-set deadlines, the absence of greater clarity in the FSMP is notable. BNM's Governor, Zeti Akhtar Aziz, instead pointed out that while greater market orientation and liberalisation could lead to more efficient allocation of resources, other objectives such as 'promoting growth, financial stability and social stability' were also important (Zeti 2003). Liberalisation, Zeti contended, should be 'sequenced and managed ... according to the stages of development of the domestic financial system' and guided by the objectives to develop a more diversified (real) economy. This absence of more specific commitments could therefore be read as an option to derogate from liberalisation measures should the need arise.

The central bank continued to push for greater consolidation and the BAFIA 1989 was amended in 2003 to enable this to take place within banking groups through the introduction of a new legal entity, called a 'Banking and Finance Company' or 'Bafin', that was permitted to conduct both finance and commercial banking businesses under one roof. While this policy move was intended to facilitate further rationalisation that would result in more competitive, one-stop financial centres for customers and improve the management of what had traditionally been riskier institutions (finance companies) through diversification and consolidation, the demarcation between commercial banks and finance companies had already narrowed considerably as a consequence of BNM's earlier efforts at market deregulation. Most services that could be obtained at a commercial bank could also be obtained from a finance company with the only major difference being the exclusive right of a finance company to offer car hire-purchase loans and its inability to provide interest-free current accounts (Kaur 2003). Thus, to some extent, this exercise merely consolidated changes that had already taken place

[33] The document does suggest rather loose timeframes, for example 'two to four years'.

in the market. Nevertheless, further institutional consolidation in the market remained on BNM's radar and at the beginning of the second phase of the FSMP, the central bank suggested that the existing ten banking groups might be further reduced to four large banks, much along the lines of universal banks, with another two to three transforming into more specialised roles, such as Islamic financing and development financial institutions. The first cab off the rank in this direction was the merger of two domestic banking groups, Bumiputera-Commerce Holdings Berhad and Southern Bank Berhad, in the first quarter of 2006, thus bringing the total number of banking groups down to nine.

As a stepping stone to BNM's long-term vision of universal banks, a new legal class of financial intermediaries – investment banks – was created in 2005. BNM's intention was that local intermediaries would upgrade their capabilities by consolidating and rationalising the merchant banking, discount houses and stock-broking industries into investment banking businesses. Foreign equity participation in investment banks were liberalised, from 30 to 49 per cent, as part of the overall effort to strengthen the latter's linkages globally and, more importantly, to accelerate the transfer of specialised skills and expertise to the Malaysian investment banking industry. When it became clearer of its specific goals, BNM once again resorted to imposing deadlines and all financial groups were given up to the third quarter of 2006 to undertake the necessary rationalisation in order to form full-fledged investment banks. By now, following BNM's earlier success at consolidation, industry players were more compliant. The flagging capital market and the impending liberalisation of Malaysia's financial sector under its obligations to the WTO provided further incentives for market players to see value in the mergers. More importantly, as investments banks were a whole new class of financial intermediary, there were few entrenched parties who felt threatened. On the contrary, the policy changes created new opportunities for well-connected individuals to funnel economic benefits into private interests. One of the most controversial cases that emerged involved Khairy Jamaluddin, the son-in-law of then Prime Minister Abdullah Ahmad Badawi. Khairy was made a director of ECM-Libra, a boutique investment bank, in July 2004, not long after Abdullah became Prime Minister. In December 2005, the three founding members of ECM Libra each sold 1 per cent of their shareholdings in the company to Khairy at what was perceived to be a very good price in Khairy's favour. A month later, it was announced that ECM Libra would take over Avenue Capital, a much larger government-linked company owned by the Ministry of Finance. Questions were raised as to the propriety of the exercise especially since the merger required the approval of the Minister of Finance, who then happened to also be Abdullah. Although a parliamentary Public Audit Committee investigation later found that the merger had complied with all statutory regulations, not all questions and issues were addressed and many critics were left unsatisfied (Beh 2006).

Capital market masterplan

While the FSMP focused principally on those institutions that come under the regulatory purview of BNM, which effectively means everything but the capital market, and proved to be more of a refinement of the already on-going process of consolidation in the financial sector, the Capital Market Masterplan (CMP) not only brought in new regulatory measures and a new orientation in the approach of supervising the capital market, but it also introduced the dynamics of consolidation, borrowed from the FSMP and the banking sector, into the capital market. However, unlike the FSMP, the CMP was relatively more explicit about its plans for the liberalisation of the capital market, albeit couched within the use of language such as 'targeted' or 'strategic' liberalisation. The implementation schedule for the CMP identified certain 'strategic and nascent' sectors – such as the investment management industry, venture capital industry, the Islamic capital market and the derivatives market – where early liberalisation should be taken as there was an 'immediate priority' to introduce greater competition and skills in those sectors. Other than the investment management industry, these sectors have few, if any, large established domestic players and Islamic finance had been identified by the Malaysian government as a market niche within the global financial system that it wished to develop. State intervention, as expressed within the CMP, can therefore be read as developmental in nature. Much like the FSMP, the CMP spoke of 'pragmatic sequencing' in relation to the deregulation and liberalisation of various segments of the capital market. It argued that 'appropriate preparatory measures must precede the facilitation of competition within the domestic market in order to enhance the resilience of market participants beforehand and to avoid severe economic displacement from a sharp increase in competition', thus, echoing the FSMP in arguing that liberalisation in favour of foreign actors would be meaningless if domestic players were unable to compete effectively. The state, though committed to greater market dynamics, still wished to shield the domestic market from global forces on developmental grounds, at least rhetorically, through its role as regulator and market creator.

Like the FSMP, the development of the CMP was motivated in part by the lingering effects of the financial crisis that had led to a decline in international competitiveness and a slow recovery in the Malaysian capital market (Securities Commission of Malaysia 2001, chapter 2). A 'crisis' in confidence had emerged following the imposition of capital controls that had contributed to a decline in foreign participation (Jayasankaran 2001a). While the malaise in the market was certainly a cause for concern, there was also an understanding that a growing economy and heightened global competition for business and investment would require a more advance and sophisticated capital market since it plays an important role in promoting investment flows as well as contributing towards a more diversified fund-raising environment that would safeguard the economy against external shocks (Securities Commission of Malaysia 2001; Jayasankaran 2001d). As such, there were real economic challenges that demanded responses beyond simple protectionist measures.

One key path forward, mirroring the banking and finance sectors, was market consolidation, with the 1997–8 crisis cited as proof of the need to have stronger, and by extension larger, market intermediaries (Securities Commission of Malaysia 2001, p.188). At the same time, the increasing conglomeration of financial services, partially the result of earlier liberalisation, was blurring the traditional boundaries between banks, fund management companies, insurance companies and securities brokers. Technological applications such as online broking, for example, had also revolutionised the intermediation function, providing end-users with faster, cheaper and more direct access to the market thus undermining the role of traditionally fragmented industry players.

The second key feature of the CMP was the reliance on foreign expertise to expedite the development of the market, especially in sub-sectors in which Malaysia had little or no experience. New liberalisation measures were announced in the 2005 Budget which included opening stock brokering activities to foreign players (initially allowing international brokerage licences to be granted to five major foreign brokerage firms), and permitting the entry of five global fund managers (World Trade Organization 2005, Para.19).[34] Full foreign ownership was also granted

[34] Fund management companies may be 100 per cent foreign owned if they provide services only to foreigners. If they provide services to both foreign and local investors, then foreign ownership will be limited to 70 per cent.

for a range of incipient sub-sectors with few entrenched domestic players: venture capital firms, venture-capital management corporations, futures brokerage firms, futures fund managers and futures trading advisers. Given the historical protection of the domestic financial market, this policy change demonstrated a measure of commitment on the government's part to the development of the market by leveraging on foreign expertise.

Expanding and diversifying the sources of funding in the capital market was the third prong of the CMP. In Malaysia, the use of the corporate bond market as a source of funding was still relatively low vis-à-vis the banking sector. In 1999, the outstanding value of bond issues amounted to under 67 per cent of GDP, half that of outstanding bank loans (157 per cent) (Securities Commission of Malaysia 2001, p.31). The regulators recognised that the high degree of reliance on bank-lending had contributed to funding mismatches during the crisis, resulting in a significant strain on the banking sector when many companies found themselves unable to service their debt (Securities Commission of Malaysia 2001, p.63). It was therefore important to deepen the bond market in the longer term, especially given the country's anticipated long-term investment needs. Following the recommendation of the CMP, new financial instruments such as asset-backed securities and residential mortgage-backed securities were introduced to help broaden the market. Electronic and technological enhancements were introduced to improve the accessibility and efficiency of the bond-trading systems and encourage secondary bond market activity. The approval process for bond issuance was shortened to 14 days with the introduction of the *Guidelines on the Offering of Private Debt Securities,* which came into effect in July 2000. Issuers were also given greater flexibility in timing issues when the shelf-registration scheme was introduced as it allowed eligible corporations to make multiple issues of debt securities within a two-year period instead of having to seek approval each time. The foreign exchange administration rules were further liberalised in 2004 to allow supranationals and multinational corporations to issue Ringgit-denominated bonds in the domestic market in an effort to further widen the issuer base and diversify credit risks in the bond market. Within 12 months of the new measures, the market saw two issues by multilateral development banks: MYR400 million Putra Bonds (fixed rate bonds) by the Asian Development Bank in November 2004; and MYR500 million Wawasan Bonds (Islamic debt securities) by the International Finance Corporation in December 2004. The second of these new issues were in the Islamic bond market that Malaysia had been aggressively promoting (more of which later).

The most controversial decision in the liberalisation of the capital market focussed on the requirements for *bumiputera* equity participation. As noted earlier, since the introduction of the NEP, companies that wished to list on the stock exchange had to ensure that at least 30 per cent of their equity was held by *bumiputera* investors. From 2002 onwards these requirements were progressively relaxed. In May of that year, the Securities Commission (SC) announced that multinational companies that had already established their presence in Malaysia need not comply with the requirement for 30 per cent *bumiputera* equity participation when seeking listing on KLSE via a reverse take-over of, or a back-door listing into, distressed listed companies (Securities Commission of Malaysia 2002). The equity requirement however still applied to new listings. Then in May 2003, companies that derived 50 per cent of their income from outside Malaysia no longer had to meet the 30 per cent *bumiputera* shareholding requirement. The amendment to this long-standing listing requirement is significant from a discursive point of view in the context of Malaysia's racial politics and demonstrates the government's commitment to liberalising the sector in order to revive economic activity.

Despite these selective dispensations of the rule, the economy still struggled to regain the shine of the years prior to the crisis. In 2006, when the UNCTAD World Investment Report revealed that Malaysia's FDI flow had not only contracted by over 14 per cent for the year but that the country's attractiveness as a FDI-destination had also fallen behind Indonesia for the first time, a member of the NEAC stated that the country had 'lost its competitive edge' (Omar 2006). In the lacklustre market environment of late-2008, when several companies found it difficult to attract *bumiputera* investors in the equity market, then Prime Minister, Najib Razak, announced in November that companies wishing to list would be *deemed* to have met the *bumiputera* equity condition even if there were no takers in the market provided that the issuing company had made a 'genuine' attempt to comply with the requirement. At this stage, the economy was struggling along with the global downturn. It would later be reported that FDI for January to May 2009 amounted to a mere MYR4.2 billion, as compared with MYR46.1 billion for the whole of 2008 (Bernama 2009b). It was in this context that even 'bolder' moves were made with respect to the *bumiputera* equity requirements. In April 2009, the 30 per cent *bumiputera* equity ruling was scrapped entirely for 27 services sub-sectors, though not for the financial sector, nor for the retail or utilities sectors where there were significant Malay employment. The listing requirement for most other sectors was subsequently lowered, at the end of June 2009, to what is effectively 12.5 per cent.[35] From a practical perspective, given the many exemptions and workarounds that had been introduced in the previous years to make Malaysia an attractive investment destination, the equity requirement had already become redundant by mid-2009. As one financial journalist noted, 'what remains of the 30 per cent rule is only its spirit' (Yeap 2009). These changes are however symbolically significant for Malaysian politics. The willingness of the government to even contemplate and then introduce liberalisation measures in an area that has long been considered sacred from the perspective of Malaysian politics demonstrated the importance of the market's contribution to economic growth but more significantly, how long-held state preferences can be altered by changing market conditions even though the revised policies may result in political costs.

Nevertheless, the government was not averse to intervening in non-market oriented ways, despite veering increasingly towards market dynamics. For instance, in January 2003, the government set up a new investment fund, Value Capital, owned by three state agencies and declared that it was prepared to support the capital market, and 'make it more efficient', by buying stocks of 'good companies' that were perceived to be undervalued (Jayasankaran 2003c). The initiative stemmed from frustration over a stock exchange that did not appear to mirror what was perceived to be the country's underlying economic fundamentals. In June 2009, during the same speech in which the Prime Minister announced the liberalisation of the *bumiputera* equity requirement for listed companies, he also launched a private equity fund, Ekuinas, that would focus on nurturing *bumiputera* businessmen in sectors considered to be of high growth such as education, tourism, oil and gas and ICT. The fund was given an initial capital of MYR500 million from the federal budget but would eventually grow to MYR10 billion. This was read as a move to 'contain a potential *bumiputera* backlash' in reaction to the liberalisation of various policy measures that concerned the *bumiputera* community (Yeoh 2009), but it was unclear whether this method of nurturing a class of *bumiputera* businessmen

---

[35] More strict equity restrictions continue to operate over companies in 'strategic' industries such as energy, transport, water and communications.

would be different from the discredited approach used in the 1990s. What is notable is that the creation of this fund and state interference in the market were influenced by the politics and 'polity' of Malaysia where policy makers constantly balance economic goals with the political demands of the *bumiputera* community.

Islamic finance

The most significant development on the landscape of the Malaysian financial system in the last decade is probably the spectacular growth of Islamic finance.[36] It is also the most recent attempt, one that is arguably very successful, by the Malaysian government to not just steer but also actively develop a vibrant market that had hitherto been relatively small and inactive. The growth of Islamic finance further contributed to the diversification of the financial sector of Malaysia as well as greater competitive dynamics in the market. It further revealed how the growth of both the market and market dynamics can be the result of state intervention and influence.

Although Islamic banking first appeared in Malaysia in 1983 when the first Islamic bank, Bank Islam, was established, there was not much activity in the sector until the period after the financial crisis. Since then, Islamic assets, financing and deposits have more than doubled between 1999 and 2007 (see Table 4.4). Islamic principles of finance have now emerged as an integral part of the overall Malaysian financial system, operating in parallel with the conventional system, and covering banking, insurance, the money market and capital market. The capacity of Islamic banking institutions to arrange and offer products with attractive features and competitive pricing that are comparable to conventional products has been enhanced so much that today Islamic financial products and services have wide appeal to both Muslim and non-Muslim customers.[37]

Given that more than half of Malaysia's population professes the Islamic faith, it is not surprising that Islamic finance is popular in the

---

[36] The key feature of the Islamic financial system is the prohibition of the payment and receipt of *riba*, the equivalent of 'interest' in the conventional financial system. For a primer on Islamic finance, see Warde (2000). See also Lena Rethel's (2011) account of Islamic finance's 'emulation' of the existing global financial order that accompanied its recent global growth.

[37] According to a report in The Edge (2002), the chairman of a major local bank claimed that half of his customers for Islamic banking facilities were non-Muslims.

country. However, the emergence of Islamic banking in Malaysia is also an extension of the politics in the country. The state actively supported and promoted the emergence of a parallel Islamic financial system as it was an instrument with which the ruling coalition, Barisan Nasional, and in particular its main component party, the United Malays National Organisation (UMNO), could build and claim its Islamic credentials in order to legitimise its claim to government among the majority Malay-Muslim population. This was particularly important with the challenge increasingly posed by the opposition Islamic party, PAS, in the 1990s (Md Khalid 2004). In this context, Islamic finance was also a means to reconcile the appeal of religion with the materialist aspects of economic development (The Economist 1993). Its emergence in Malaysia also occurred against the backdrop of rising pan-Islamism internationally and similar introductions of Islamic finance in a number of other countries (Warde 2000).

While there are underlying domestic political reasons for a market in Islamic finance, the state's more intensive support for and promotion of Islamic finance after 1997 can be traced to policy makers' reaction to the financial crisis. In the post-crisis period, then Prime Minister Mahathir outlined ways in which lending practices sanctioned by Islam, in which the levying of interest charges are replaced with a profit sharing system that links lenders and clients as partners, may help to discourage speculative activities and asset bubbles that figured so prominently in the financial crisis (Case 2005).[38] Through profit-sharing arrangements, he argued, lenders have a greater stake in the long-term viability of investment projects. As such, Islamic finance can be seen as a functional reaction to the weaknesses of conventional banking. In addition, in the post-crisis period, the development of Islamic finance was a means by which Malaysia could re-energise its financial system and carve out a niche for itself in the global economy, a strategy that was flagged in the FSMP.

In order to develop and promote the Islamic banking sector, initially, all commercial banks that were already operating in Malaysia were permitted to set up Islamic banking windows where Islamic banking operations resided either within the conventional banking entity or a full-fledged Islamic banking subsidiary. Foreign equity participation of up to 49 per cent was allowed in Islamic banking subsidiaries and new *takaful* (Islamic insurance) companies in Malaysia, in contrast to the

---

[38] For a more recent articulation of similar arguments, see Chapra (2008).

ceiling of 30 per cent in conventional banking.[39] When the growth of the Islamic banking sector exceeded initial expectations under the first phase of the FSMP, BNM decided to bring forward by about three years the third phase of the liberalisation of the Islamic banking sector in which foreign capital and expertise were further leveraged to enhance its development (Bank Negara Malaysia 2004). Three new Islamic banking licences were issued in 2004 to fully foreign-owned financial groups from the Middle East. In April 2009, it was further announced that two new Islamic banking licences would be issued to foreign investors to establish new Islamic banks with paid-up capital of at least USD1 billion (Bank Negara Malaysia 2009b). The foreign equity limit for existing domestic Islamic banking institutions was also increased from 49 per cent to 70 per cent to further encourage international interest and build on the progress that had already been made, the government, in presenting the 2008 budget, announced that Islamic fund-management companies, in contrast with institutions managing non-Islamic assets, can be wholly owned by foreigners. A series of Islamic fund management licences were issued to both domestic and foreign institutions in 2008 and by May 2009, the SC had allowed eight foreign Islamic fund-management companies to start operations in Malaysia (Liau 2008). Again, given the restrictions that have historically been imposed on foreign players, the fact that foreign actors could not only acquire a greater share of domestic institutions but also establish their own institutions via these new licences was a significant indicator of policy makers' commitment to developing the sector as part of the country's overall development goals.

The growth of Islamic finance also extended to the bond market where the government invested effort in developing markets for both Ringgit-denominated instruments and also Islamic-compliant foreign currency-denominated debt, the latter by allowing foreign issuers to tap the Malaysian capital markets. The Malaysian government was the first to issue a sovereign *sukuk*, or Islamic security, in the global market in 2002. Through tireless government promotion, Malaysia has successfully created a niche market in this area. The country is the world's largest market for *sukuk*. It is estimated that 85 per cent of the total global Islamic bonds have been issued in Malaysia (Ibrahim and Wong 2006). According to a 2008 report by Moody's Global Corporate Finance arm,

[39] Locally incorporated foreign banks were permitted to own up to 100 per cent of their Islamic bank subsidiaries.

Malaysian Ringgit-denominated issues accounted for almost 61 per cent of global outstanding *sukuk* as of year-end 2008 (cited in Gearen 2009). Domestically, the issuance of Islamic bonds eclipsed conventional bonds in 2001 (Ibrahim and Wong 2006).

With these developments, Malaysia is now considered an important 'hub of innovation' for Islamic financial services (Thomas 2007). Kuala Lumpur is home to the Islamic Financial Services Board that was established in 2002 to promulgate international prudential standards for Islamic finance contributing to the development of an international Islamic financial architecture (El – Hawary, Grais and Iqbal 2007). A Boston-based research firm specialising exclusively in the financial services industry recently stated that 'Malaysia now possesses the most highly developed regulatory structure for Islamic finance in the world' (Cerulli Associates 2008). That the World Bank and the International Finance Corporation both chose to issue Islamic financial instruments in the Malaysian market, as noted earlier, was a significant endorsement.

The development of Islamic finance in Malaysia thus attests to the outcome that can be achieved by policy makers who saw this as 'good' policy for economic development. While it leveraged on market actors and dynamics, it is clearly the result of state-led developmental policy. The sector would not have developed with such rapidity if not for the incentives, regulatory changes and support provided by the financial authorities, all of which stood in contrast to the more tentative foreign liberalisation measures in the conventional banking sector. It also demonstrated that where no entrenched interest groups exist, greater economic liberalisation could proceed at a faster pace. Of course, the fact that Islamic finance was a new market in which policy makers felt Malaysia had a particular comparative advantage and that coincided with the political discourse on Islam domestically was also helpful. The growth of Islamic finance also contributed to diversifying the financial sector of Malaysia as well as promoting greater competition and market dynamics. The substantial and rapid change seen in Islamic finance stand in contrast to foreign liberalisation measures in the conventional banking sector to which the chapter will now turn.

Foreign banks

Since independence, the Malaysian government had intentionally sidelined foreign banks in order to promote the development of domestically-owned institutions. Various restrictions were imposed on the activities of foreign-owned banks. They were prohibited from opening new branches or building ATM networks. There was also the requirement that 40 per cent of any bank lending to foreign-owned corporations had to be provided by Malaysian banks, thus curbing the market opportunities of foreign-owned ones.[40] Although no foreign conventional bank has been granted a banking license since 1973, some, in particular, Japanese banks, have acquired minority holdings in local financial entities as a means of gaining entry as foreigners were allowed to own up to 30 per cent of a Malaysian financial institution.

From the 1990s onwards, the protectionist measures on the domestic financial market was reversed, albeit selectively and marginally. During the Uruguay Round of multilateral trade negotiations of the GATS in 1994, Malaysia committed to raising limits on foreign equity ownership in stock broking companies and measures related to the entry of highly skilled labour, but no commitment was made in the commercial banking sector that formed the bulk of the country's financial sector. In December 1995, Malaysia also entered into the ASEAN Framework Agreement on Services, one aspect of which was to develop commitments on financial services liberalisation. Most of Malaysia's commitments were again marginal and in sectors other than banking. The continued restriction in the banking sector was motivated by the view that the Malaysian banking system was already very open with foreign-owned banks accounting for about a fifth to a third of commercial banking business and almost 40 per cent of the financial system's capital (Jayasankaran 1995). This position has not changed substantially in more recent times and the following quotation from the Governor of the central bank summarises Malaysia's current position with regard to foreign liberalisation (Zeti 2006):

> While liberalisation in the traditional sector will continue, its already highly liberalised status and its higher level of capacity relative to the economy does not introduce urgency to the liberalisation compared to the new growth areas. These traditional sectors may lead to overcrowding. The focus of a more rapid liberalisation is where significant market development are [sic] likely to take place. Emphasis would be towards attracting foreign players who are recognised as specialist in specific segment [sic].

Thus liberalisation for foreign actors would and has been taking place only in nascent sectors where it would more likely contribute to

[40] This restriction has been gradually relaxed over time and completely removed in 2003.

development and help Malaysia's financial sector to be both regionally and globally more competitive. Much of the focus of liberalisation has therefore been in sectors other than conventional banking. For instance, as we saw earlier, in the capital market, foreign ownership limits on investment banks were raised from 30 to 49 per cent of shareholding as a means of providing opportunities for emerging investment banks to explore tie-ups and joint ventures with foreign parties to leverage on the latter's expertise and distribution network. Similarly, in the Islamic finance sector, extensive foreign liberalisation was undertaken in order to develop this nascent sector and help Malaysia achieve its aspiration to become a regional Islamic financial centre. In short, where it coincided with policy makers' developmental goals, foreign participants were viewed as useful allies. However, where entrenched local interests exist, restrictions on foreign players continued to apply as in the conventional commercial banking sector where foreign participation has been heavily restricted since the 1970s.

Nevertheless, the government did commit to gradually liberalising the conventional banking sector in the FSMP, albeit again also selectively. From January 2006, incumbent foreign banks were allowed to open up to four new branches a year, thus abolishing the previous long-standing freeze on the number of branches a foreign bank could set up in Malaysia (Bank Negara Malaysia 2005b). This was however subject to certain conditions imposed by the central bank. For example, foreign-owned banks were required to open up to three branches in 'semi- and non-urban areas' as a means of levelling the playing field with domestic banks, as the latter had long been required to meet geographical branching requirements, and as a way of extending financial services to underserviced areas. BNM argued that this was meant to 'integrate' foreign-owned banks with the domestic economy in order that they can 'better serve' the needs of the country (Bank Negara Malaysia 2005a). In addition, several key foreign banks were permitted to form a shared ATM network in 2005 that connected to the existing domestic electronic payment system network (MEPS), thus improving their infrastructure and market reach into the retail banking segment. While these measures point to greater market liberalisation, they are nevertheless somewhat modest in nature. BNM felt that domestic banks still had to be afforded some protection as foreign banks had proved to be formidable competitors in the Malaysian market despite the restrictions that have long been in place (Zeti 2002). Notwithstanding the government's protection of the domestic banks, foreign-owned banks' market share has not only been maintained at a substantial level but has arguably also increased in recent years (Chee and Tan 2006).

Although the Malaysian government was keen to manage and control how the market was liberalised, it was also pressured into making policy moves by changes in the economic environment as we saw in our earlier discussion of the capital market where liberalisation was undertaken in the face of poor market performance. Similarly, even though changes had been presaged in the FSMP, the document was vague in terms of timeline and detail and it was not until the difficult economic environment of late-2008 and 2009 that details of dramatic policy changes were announced, which included the granting of five new commercial banking licences to qualified foreign players (Bank Negara Malaysia 2009a) and raising the cap on foreign ownership of insurers and Islamic and investment banks (Bernama 2009a). Even then, the cap on foreign ownership of conventional commercial banks was maintained at 30 per cent (The Star 2009).

These measures again highlight the selective and targeted manner in which policy makers have approached market liberalisation in Malaysia. Where domestic actors have a large presence but are not yet able to compete with foreign actors, liberalisation has been more tentative. Where domestic actors have comparative advantage, as in Islamic finance, or have a less significant stake, as in the nascent sub-sectors in the capital market, liberalisation measures have been more aggressive in order to leverage on foreign expertise to attain development goals. The Governor of the central bank stated in an interview with the *Far Eastern Economic Review* that since Malaysia did not aspire to be an international financial centre, liberalisation and deregulation at a faster pace was therefore not as important (Jayasankaran 2002b). Malaysia, she said, wanted a system where at least 50 per cent of market share was held by domestic institutions. Ultimately, from BNM's perspective, 'key considerations for the strategic opening up of the financial sector would be to steer the financial sector towards increased competition whilst ensuring domestic financial institutions are not marginalised by the liberalisation process' (Zeti 2006).

Regulatory and supervisory changes

Before concluding this chapter, I will briefly review key changes in the regulation and supervision of the financial sector since the crisis given the importance of its contribution towards market stability.

Apart from Singapore, Malaysia was known to have one of the better regulated financial sectors in the region, with the central bank having long had a reputation for the pursuit of a high level of regulatory and supervisory standards (Hamilton-Hart 2002). The Basel I framework was introduced in the Malaysian financial system in 1989, well before the 1997–8 financial crisis (Zamani 2006, p.269). The Malaysian central bank had the capability and capacity to restrict banks' and corporations' access to foreign borrowings, thus partially explaining why borrowings from foreign banks were not a destabilising factor in the crisis (Chin and Jomo 2003). While scandals and failures were not unknown in the financial sector, they were not as detrimental to the economy as in other developing countries and Malaysia's record in this regard was said to have been 'exceptional' (Hamilton-Hart 2002, p.127).[41]

Nevertheless, the financial crisis demanded that regulatory and supervisory arrangements be reviewed, and BNM has since revised and issued a number of regulatory guidelines covering a range of issues from credit limits to the provision of bad debts. Two of the more important regulatory guidelines that have significant impact on the banking industry cover the appointment of directors and the issue of financial statements (Lum and Koh 2006). Underlying these changes is the progressive introduction and adoption of more market-based approaches to risk management. There is an increasing shift towards more institution-based risk management approaches, in line with current international practice, where financial institutions monitor and report their exposure to risks. In this spirit, quantitative limits on bank activities have increasingly been removed in favour of risk assessment procedures that are institution-based. For instance, prior to the financial crisis, BNM imposed caps on lending to the broad property sectors and on share financing that were based on the respective institution's outstanding total loans. Post-crisis, banking institution's risk exposure to these sectors is now based on the respective institution's own risk assessment and management. This move from a predominantly 'rule-based' towards a 'principle-based' approach to regulation is intended to both conform to international best practices as well as to promote competition and innovation in the Malaysian financial sector (Zeti 2004). The 'principle-based' approach facilitates the latter goal since it is supposedly more adaptable to changing market circumstances and business practices and stands in contrast with the previous rule-based approach where there was more

[41] BNM is by no means independent from political influence. During the crisis, political pressure led its Governor and Deputy Governor to resign as they had disagreed with Prime Minister Mahathir on policy direction, see Hamilton-Hart (2002, p.168).

control by the regulators. Supervisory activities are similarly now premised on a risk-based framework that provides for a structured and forward-looking approach in assessing banking institutions' risk profiles and the effectiveness of risk management systems. In line with these developments, Malaysia has also adopted the Revised Capital Adequacy Framework (Basel II) that became effective from January 2008 for the Standardised Approach.

For market-based regulation to be effective, transparency and public disclosure of financial institutions' activities are important features. In this regard, a recent survey scored Malaysian banks relatively highly compared with their counterparts in Korea and Thailand (Parreñas 2006). All Malaysian banks in the survey reported formal disclosure policies and relatively high levels of disclosure in the area of market risk and credit risks, while Korean and Thai banks exhibited lower levels of disclosure. On the other hand, Malaysian banks scored lower than Thai banks in terms of the frequency of their public disclosures. Nevertheless, a study of Malaysia's regulatory regime post-crisis concluded that 'the Malaysian capitalisation, loan classification, and provisioning regime is more stringent than in many Asian countries', if still lagging those in the United States (Walter 2008, p.108). Thus, in general, the strength of banking regulation in Malaysia appears to have been maintained, if not strengthened.

Similar developments were observed in the capital markets. With the introduction of the CMP, the SC's regulatory role was strengthened and the Commission began to emphasise executive professionalism over entrepreneurial acquisitiveness in listed firms. 'Firewalls' were imposed between managerial roles and corporate ownership and the SC gave new attention to strengthening the voice of minority shareholders (Economic Analytical Unit 2002, p.145). A Minority Shareholders Watchdog Group was set up in mid-2000 with shareholders drawn from the five biggest state-owned fund managers in the country. Although the membership of the Watchdog Group might lead one to question the independence of the body, its establishment nevertheless reflected a growing recognition of the importance of corporate governance to the functioning of the local stock market.

As with the banking sector, the regulatory system of the capital market displays significant conformity with current international best practices. During the first phase of the CMP, the Malaysian stock exchange began to enforce listing requirements which, in the view of some analysts, came to be regarded as among the best in East Asia (Case 2005). Similarly, new accounting standards, introduced by the Malaysian

Accounting Standards Board, were evaluated as exceeding US standards. In mid-2000, new rules made it compulsory for all listed companies to submit quarterly results, complete with balance sheets and profit-and-loss statements, a requirement that even Singapore and Hong Kong had not yet implemented at the time. The SC also moved from merit-based regulation to disclosure-based regulation in order to reduce its involvement in assessing the merits of investment opportunities while shifting the onus onto investors, and thus the market. This required companies to adopt higher standards of information disclosure and governance and enhanced the role of issuers, their advisers and investors in the allocation of capital and decision-making. While the introduction of these new measures helped improve the operation of the market, there were suggestions that they might have also deterred domestic firms, particularly medium sized ones, from listing on the stock exchange as the regulations were perceived as being too invasive and too onerous for smaller firms to implement.[42] A similar observation was made about Thailand when a number of companies voluntarily de-listed from the SET after disclosure requirements were tightened (Walter 2008, p.86). Of greater concern is the fact that this move towards a market-based system of regulation, requiring a relatively open and rules-based framework, stands in contrasts to the discriminatory principles of the NEP/NDP. As such, regulatory enforcement has, unsurprisingly, sometimes been inconsistent (Gomez 2004, pp.60–6; Gomez and Jomo 1999).

Conclusion

In reviewing changes in the Malaysian financial sector through the lens of quantitative indicators earlier in the chapter, I observed that there had been a movement towards greater market orientation on account of the growth in the diversity of sources of funding, the increasing depth of the various sub-sectors and the greater presence of foreign players. To this extent, the Malaysian financial sector has become more liberalised and adopted more features associated with the LME ideal type. However, as observed in the subsequent more qualitative institutional analysis, these changes have emerged as a result of state-led efforts to restructure and develop the financial sector, largely in reaction to difficult economic conditions, both during and after the financial crisis of 1997–8.

---

[42] Interview with a senior executive of the SC in November 2007.

In analysing the policies that led to the growth of the capital market and the increasing participation of foreign actors, I noted that the state's preference, in particular that of the regulators of the financial sector, for a more developed financial sector was a key factor. The expansion of the capital market was guided and shaped by the government's vision as manifested in the CMP and 'resolute' policy changes contributed to rapid growth (Zhang 2007). The authorities made provisions to consolidate institutions, issued public securities to foster the growth of the bond market as well as revised a range of legislation to facilitate the implementation of the master plans. It was policy makers' desire to leverage on market forces to further develop the financial sector that in part led to selective amendments being made to long-standing legislative positions on both foreign ownership in financial institutions and the *bumiputera* equity requirement on publicly listed firms. The expansion of the Islamic finance sub-sector in the last decade provides the clearest example of the government's interventionist role in successfully nurturing and developing the market through the use of a range of policy changes, public funds and fiscal incentives.

The nature of state interference was however also coloured by the 'polity', or institutional context of policy making in Malaysia. The amendments made by Prime Minister Mahathir to the consolidation process of the banking sector first proposed by the central bank reflected the constraints imposed on policy making by the racial and patronage politics of the country. Similarly, the government had to establish a private equity fund, Ekuinas, with money from the federal budget to invest solely in *bumiputera* business ventures in order to 'compensate' the *bumiputera* community for liberalising the *bumiputera* equity requirement on listed firms. The constraints posed by the institutional context of Malaysia's racial politics also reflect the persistent salience of the discourse of racial politics in policy making, even if it has no correspondence in economic 'facts'. For instance, even though the legal *bumiputera* equity requirement had been progressively undermined by exemptions and workarounds such that all that remained of the rule was its 'spirit', its formal removal nevertheless provoked opposition from within the *bumiputera* community that had to be placated through the establishment of the Ekuinas fund. The consolidation exercise that took place from 1998 to 2002 was also affected by the discourse of racial politics although here it was the Chinese community that felt marginalised. The consolidation exercise also demonstrated how the private interests of owners of financial institutions and their connections to political parties affected the nature of the Malaysian state's management and implementation of policy. The continuing protection of the domestic banking sector is also a reflection of the private interests of domestic banking institutions and not just the result of the central bank's concern over issues of development and market stability. In short, 'polity' and politics explain the nature of political interference into the formulation and implementation of economic policies as well as the qualified independence enjoyed by BNM and the SC (Hamilton-Hart 2002, Chapter 5).

The Malaysian state therefore still significantly influences and intervenes in the financial sector and thus cannot be said to operate like the state conceived within the LME ideal type. Nevertheless, the Malaysian government has always been careful to chart 'a fairly even course between statist interventions and market forces, producing 'middling' amounts of corruption and reasonable levels of governance', resulting in a 'twin orientation' or 'dual economy' where vibrant, largely market-led economic growth facilitates political patronage and economic redistribution (Case 2005). In other words, the Malaysian state is historically both 'pro market' and 'pro state-intervention', which in part explains the inconsistencies in policies or forms of state intervention. The developments in the last decade confirm the continuing interplay of both state and market forces in the evolution and development of the Malaysian financial sector.[43] Consequently, convergence towards a LME model, at least in the form that critics had expected, has not taken place and state interference remains significant.

[43] See also Rethel (2010a).

5
Thailand

Despite being the first casualty of the Asian financial crisis, and the focus of so much analysis and criticism, a couple of key weaknesses identified in the Thai financial system remain unaddressed. The Thai financial sector remains predominantly bank-based. Although the capital market has expanded and foreign participation in the banking sector has increased in the intervening years, so too has the share of the state's stake in both the banking sector and capital market. So, while the Thai state had previously played a more restrained role in the Thai financial sector, relative to most other East Asian economies, its participation in and influence over the financial sector has expanded since the financial crisis. Therefore, instead of moving towards a liberal market model, the Thai financial sector appears to be moving in the opposite direction.

This chapter explores how the Thai state has asserted itself in the financial sector with a stronger and more prominent role than ever before, almost in contradiction to the criticisms and observations raised in the aftermath of the 1997 financial crisis. As with the previous chapters, I will begin with a brief discussion of the historical roles of the state and market in the Thai financial sector in order to provide background and context to our subsequent discussion. This will then be followed with a review of changes in the financial sector of Thailand through the use of quantitative indicators. Then, as in the previous two chapters, the discussion will proceed with a more qualitative assessment, focussing on the three P's (policy, 'polity' and politics) of key changes in the financial sector since the crisis of 1997–8. The discussion in the later part of this chapter will be structured along the key issues of the financial sector master plans, the participation of foreign banks and changes in regulation and supervision since the financial crisis of 1997–8.

History

The history of commercial banking business in Thailand dates back to 1888 when British-owned Hong Kong and Shanghai Bank opened a branch in Bangkok to facilitate international trade. A private Thai bank – the Siam Commercial Bank – operating under the management of the Minister of Finance was only first established in 1904 to serve the non-European population and break the British domination of the market (Doner and Unger 1993). The competition between local and foreign banks were resolved in favour of the former in 1932, when restrictions were imposed in an attempt to reduce Chinese and Western economic influence on the financial sector and the economy more generally. All but two banks closed following these initiatives, however by 1950, Chinese-owned banks once again dominated the industry controlling ten out of eleven commercial banks. These institutions were heavily involved in commodity exports, which was central to the country's economy, and were eventually consolidated in the 1950s forming the core of five large business groups whose economic power laid not only in their control of credit and rice but also in a variety of other activities such as insurance, shipping and light manufacturing.

These financial institutions became important sources of funding for the competing factions that then dominated Thai politics (Doner and Unger 1993). The linkages between the state and the financial institutions were such that top government officials would sit on the boards of directors of banks and related firms and protect them against Thai nationalist threats, while the banks in turn helped to finance state enterprises. This nexus afforded the commercial banks relative freedom from the state, which persisted even after the coup in 1957 that installed the authoritarian regime of Sarit Thanarat. Despite a revised *Commercial Banking Act* in 1962 that expanded the powers of the central bank, the Bank of Thailand (BOT) was unable to exercise its powers on the more influential Thai banks other than through moral suasion. This was reflective of the broader private sector's ability to resist statist intervention at the time, reinforced by general public opposition to the dominance of the state (Doner and Unger 1993). For the commercial banks specifically, their relative freedom was the harvest reaped from having invested heavily in political relationships, first with military dictators and then later with political parties. Thus, while the Thai banking sector was not state-centred, large local banks closely associated with leading diversified conglomerates, owned mainly by

Sino-Thai businessmen, were well-connected with the political system (Crone 1988). This state–business nexus was largely mutually beneficial even though the military leaders resented the latter's power despite being greatly enriched by their alliances with the banks during the era of military rule (Overholt 1999).

The relative independence of local commercial banks grew throughout the 1960s. Government or government-related shareholdings in three commercial banks declined during this period while the sector became increasingly concentrated in four to five major banking families (Doner and Unger 1993). As was the case in Malaysia from the 1970s onwards, the growth of domestic banks in Thailand was in part facilitated by government policy on foreign banks. In 1964, Thailand banned the entry of new foreign banks and limited existing ones to one branch each (Dobson and Jacquet 1998, p.324). Foreign bank branches were also eventually required to maintain exposure to Thailand of no less than 70 per cent of total deposits and borrowings raised in the country; and the ceiling on foreign ownership of local banks was capped at 25 per cent. Off-site ATMs were defined as bank branches thus strictly limiting foreign banks' ability to leverage on technology to overcome the restriction on single branching. The protection of domestic oligopolies in the banking sector through the use of various government policies was also mirrored elsewhere in the economy (Phongpaichit and Baker 1995).

The state therefore influenced but did not 'govern' the financial sector, as it is understood in the context of the developmental state model. However, this was not a liberal market even though the Thai financial sector had greater independence from the state than was the case in Korea, or even Malaysia, as a close state–business nexus existed. According to Hewison (2005), Sarit's regime foreshadowed a developmental 'social contract' in which authoritarianism was a pre-condition for the stability required to attain economic growth. Private initiative was promoted while state investment was limited to the development of infrastructure. The state felt no need to be 'predatory' as it had comfortable sources of fiscal revenue. Furthermore, the historical experience of other countries in the region had suggested to Thailand that unless the government maintained prudent and responsible macroeconomic policies, their independence from foreign powers would come under threat. As such, young technocrats were promoted in the central bank, as well as in the Ministry of Finance (MOF), and they were given relative independence to manage the economy on technocratic grounds (Doner and Unger 1993).

State intervention and initial liberalisation

It was not until 1973 that the authoritarian aspect of the government was challenged by growing but discontented middle-class citizens led by university students. The military government was ousted and replaced with a democratically elected government that lasted three years. During this period, a broader range of business interests gained access to political and economic resources. The process of democratisation also led to pressure for expansionary policies as more Thais began to see a need for a more active role of the state to stimulate and anticipate future economic demand as well as curb excessive concentrations of market power, particularly in the financial sector. Furthermore, a reduction in external flows, as a result of the withdrawal of the US military in 1975 and a diversion of Japanese capital to other countries, pushed the central bank toward a more expansionary and developmental set of economic strategies. Public expenditures and tariffs rose and price controls were introduced. It was at this stage that the government implemented the country's first large-scale mandated credit allocation programme which required that commercial banks extended a certain percentage of their total deposits as credits to farmers. This policy was introduced in response to increased political competition for rural votes as well as popular concern with urban–rural economic disparities.

The establishment of a new type of financial institution, finance companies, was encouraged by the state in the 1970s in order to meet the private sector's increasing financial needs while simultaneously intensifying competitive pressures on commercial banks (Doner and Unger 1993). Their number grew from 17 in 1971 to 113 in 1979. Regulation however did not keep pace with this development and the rapid and unregulated growth of finance companies resulted in increased manipulation, insider trading and improper loans that eventually contributed to the collapse of the Securities Exchange of Thailand (SET) in 1978 and the failure of a major finance company the following year. The finance companies were only brought under formal control with the passing of the *Commercial Banking Act* in 1979 which also included provisions requiring banks to limit the scope of their investments in non-banking businesses, channel more of their credit into priority development sectors and compel banking families to divest themselves of large direct holdings. The reforms also provided the BOT with additional instruments of monetary control through the regulation of capital to asset ratios and minimum cash requirements. These changes were intended to strengthen the financial sector while decreasing the relative dominance of the commercial banks. It was also an attempt by the state to assert its power over the financial sector.

Thus, over the course of the 1970s, the state's influence over the financial sector increased, partially in response to regulatory concerns but also political demands. Nevertheless, as compared with other East Asian countries, state intervention in the Thai economy was less 'activist'. The state attempted to influence the direction of economic activity through the use of broad policy instruments such as tariffs, tax regimes, export incentives, reform of customs procedures and regulations and the provision of good infrastructure in 'export processing zones'. The state also played a more active role in the agricultural sector for development purposes,[1] and a number of developmental agencies such as the National Economic and Social Development Board, the Board of Investment and the Budget Bureau were established with this goal in mind (Phongpaichit and Baker 1998b). Although the government devised and published a series of development plans from 1961, it did not engage in detailed sectoral policies nor did it have a coherent or coordinated industrial policy. The government, through the Board of Investment, attempted to promote capital-intensive, large-scale activities but there was a lack of coherence in its practices in the 1960s and 1970s when the focus was on import substitution (Christensen et al. 1993, pp.10–11). The government was more successful in the 1980s when it shifted its focus to export promotion. However, even then it did not appear to make use of extensive industrial credit policies but relied instead on more broad-based fiscal incentives such as exemptions from duties and taxes. By and large, the Thai state sought to facilitate market activity by maintaining stable macroeconomic conditions while the private sector, or more specifically the well-connected oligopolists, decided on the details. In other words, the former provided an enabling environment for the latter to flourish. Coordination in the market was partially fulfilled by commercial banks that not just developed close ties with, but also acquired equity in, their clients (Christensen et al. 1993, p.30; Lauridsen 2000).

The Thai state's behaviour was an extension of the 'tradition of a small, passive and cautious government' that was constrained by a limited budget as a consequence of a restricted ability to tax due to

[1] The issue of economic development in the northern regions of Thailand continues to be a salient political issue to the present day and is most vividly seen in the protests mounted by the 'Red Shirt' protestors in Bangkok in 2010.

foreign treaties, and a reluctance to borrow from abroad for fear that financial instability would lead to foreign intervention (Jansen 2001). The Thai governments were therefore hesitant about investing heavily in the economy and very cautious in their financial and monetary policies. The choice for a market-oriented development strategy rather than one based on greater state intervention is also explained by the relative absence of cohesive social groups within the Thai polity (Unger 1998). Until the 1990s, there was no political elite with a unified view on development strategy while social pressure for redistributive policies was in general low. Furthermore, from an institutional perspective, the short-lived nature of coalitional politics in Thailand when the democratic era began in the 1980s made it difficult for governments to implement long-term policies, and a weak and fragmented bureaucracy could not control the private sector. All of which resulted in limited government intervention leaving the private sector with considerable freedom.

This institutional arrangement where the Thai state stood relatively more in the background, when compared with Korea or even Malaysia, while the private sector led the direction of economic growth and activity was nevertheless read as a 'developmental social contract' that delivered significant, if unequal, benefits to all social sectors (Hewison 1996, 2001b). Since the government helped to cultivate protected oligopolies in banking and other key sectors, the Thai 'polity' has been interpreted as a variant of the East Asian developmental model (Phongpaichit and Baker 1995, 1998b; Christensen et al. 1993).[2] The state thus influenced the economy but in a much less active nature as compared to, for instance, Korea. Nevertheless, this state–market nexus was part of the economic landscape of the Thai economy that produced about 7.7 per cent average real GDP growth per annum between 1960 and 1995 and a decline in the proportion of the population under the poverty line from about 60 per cent to less than 15 per cent during the same period.

The relatively more passive role of the state meant that by the early-1990s, 'state-owned financial institutions play only a modest role in

[2] In 1993, the three largest local banks in Thailand accounted for 50 per cent of banking assets while the ten richest families in Thailand controlled roughly 50 per cent of the stock market in market capitalisation terms, see Claessens, Djankov and Klingebiel (1999). The 15 banks in existence before the crisis were still mainly characterised by concentrated family ownership, for details see Charumilind, Kali and Wiwattanakantang (2006).

the banking system. To the small degree that state officials have pursued an interventionist industrialisation strategy, they have tended to rely on fiscal rather than financial policy tools' (Doner and Unger 1993, p.93). There were few credit allocation requirements and the state imposed only loose controls on international capital account movements.[3] However, despite these more liberal policies, the state continued to extend its protection to the domestic banking sector from a range of sources of competition: financial markets abroad, foreign banks in Thailand and other types of domestic financial institutions and markets (Okuda and Mieno 1996). Financial regulators maintained lending and deposit rate ceilings and limited entry by new firms into the financial sector. There was little substitute to bank deposits for the household sector and similarly for the corporate sector, bank loans were the primary source of funds. The capital market was underdeveloped and could not function as an effective alternative destination for investment or source of funds other than for large companies. The nature of the Thai 'polity' characterised by a small number of private sector actors who have strong relationships with key actors in the government, and the preferences of these actors, largely explain the state's more accommodative policies towards the oligopolies. Conversely, the state's access to adequate levels of revenue meant that it had little incentive to act in more predatory ways.

Further financial liberalisation in the 1990s

A series of massive finance company and bank failures in mid-1980s served as prelude to a decade of change in the financial sector. During this crisis, the MOF found itself rescuing 32 finance companies and three banks – accounting for a quarter of total financial institutions' assets – and the BOT revoked the licences of 15 other finance companies that had collapsed. In addition, changes in the international environment – trade in financial services being introduced in the Uruguay Round of trade negotiations; pressure from developed countries and the

---

[3] According to Muscat (1995, p.121), the 'only large-scale sectoral credit allocation policy in Thailand concerns agriculture'. At its peak in the mid-1980s, agricultural credit represented no more than 7.5 per cent of total commercial bank lending, see Muscat (1995), Table 4.2. Although the BOT operated a rediscount facility to directly channel credit to specified classes of borrowers, this has been used more to fund working capital and current transactions rather than fixed investments. The volume of credits extended by the BOT provided only marginal amounts of direct financing for industry and is unlikely to have had any significant effect on investment decisions, see Muscat (1995, p.123).

IMF; and the turn towards market-orientation in Indochina – also motivated the Thai monetary authorities to liberalise the financial sector (Vajragupta and Vichyanond 1999). More importantly though, it was the government's ambitious desire for Bangkok to become a regional financial centre that formed the basis for the first long-term financial reform plan (1990–2) and accelerated the pace of financial liberalisation (Nidhiprabha 2003, p.40).

The process of liberalisation was spearheaded by a group of technocrats, educated in the US in free-market policies who were promoted into the cabinet during the regime of General Prem Tinsulanonda from 1980 to 1988 (Phongpaichit and Baker 1998a). General Prem's ascent to power also narrowed the number of claimants on state resources which facilitated the technocrats' greater control of macroeconomic policy (Doner and Unger 1993). The consensus over the need for financial liberalisation however went beyond central bankers and technocrats in the relevant ministries as it also included commercial bankers and independent think-tank economists who shared policy makers' aspiration to turn Thailand into a regional financial centre, albeit for more private motives where the commercial banks were concerned (Nidhiprabha 2003, p.40). From the policy makers' point of view, financial sector reform between 1988 and 1996 was intended to strengthen competition in the domestic financial system as well as prepare domestic financial institutions for the eventual global liberalisation of trade and services (Vichyanond 2007). Policy measures focussed on four major areas – (1) interest rate liberalisation; (2) foreign exchange liberalisation; (3) relaxation in the management of financial institutions' portfolios; and (4) expansion in the scope of operations of financial institutions – and were implemented in rapid succession between 1989 and 1992 (Bank of Thailand 1992).

Other liberalisation measures that were introduced in this period included the relaxation and eventually elimination of the requirement to hold government bonds as a prerequisite for the establishment of new branches (Vichyanond 1995). In June 1991, the definition of 'reserves', which the banks were required to hold for prudential reasons, was broadened in order that banks might manage their assets more flexibly and efficiently. The obligation of commercial banks to extend credits to rural borrowers was also relaxed to cover more related occupations and wider geographical areas, which incidentally also supported the government's strategy to broaden rural development (Muscat 1995, p.121).

A number of new frameworks and institutions were also formulated during this period of financial liberalisation and reform, including those that were focussed on the development of the capital market. The *Securities and Exchange Act* that was passed in May 1992 gave qualified limited companies access to direct financing through the issuance of common stocks and debt instruments. It marked a major step towards the establishment of a unified legal and institutional framework for the development of the capital market. The Act also established the Securities and Exchange Commission (SEC) as an independent agency responsible for supervising capital market activities related to equities, bonds and derivatives. In 1993 the government spearheaded the formation of a credit rating agency to help promote the issuance of bonds and other private debt instruments; and in 1994 private market actors organised a bond dealers' club to function as a secondary debt market, thus adding more liquidity to debt instruments. However, the Thai government's conservative fiscal stance meant that it did not issue any domestic bonds between 1987 and 1997 which inhibited the development of a risk-free benchmark, against which private issuers could price their bonds, subsequently impeding the development of the corporate bond market. So, prior to the crisis in 1997, the function of financial intermediation in Thailand still fell almost entirely on the banking sector despite the stated desire of policy makers to diversify the financial system. Funds were mobilised mainly through bank deposits, while direct financing through the domestic capital market, both public and corporate, was relatively small-scale and undeveloped. This was partly a reflection of the level of economic development in the country and, when compared with the contemporaneous expansion of the capital market in Malaysia, partly also the result of minimal effort to develop the Thai capital market.

While this range of measures led to some liberalisation and diversification of the financial sector, it was the promotion of greater competitive dynamics in this period that had the greatest impact on the Thai financial system. From March 1992 onwards, the BOT allowed all financial institutions to undertake a range of new related businesses (Bank of Thailand 1992). Commercial banks were permitted to expand their activities into areas such as debt underwriting and dealing, acting as securities registrars and custodians, selling public sector debt instruments, mutual fund management, financial consulting and feasibility studies. Finance and securities companies were similarly given entry into a range of new lines of operations despite the fact that they had performed badly in the 1980s, as the authorities felt that the move would help deepen the financial system in market segments which traditional banks were unwilling to adequately service. Finance and securities companies were thus allowed into leasing, management of provident/private/mutual funds, custodial services, and foreign exchange businesses as well as open branches outside the Bangkok region for the first time in March 1994, and in August 1994 even overseas. With these liberalising measures, finance companies began to look more like banks and were able to attract more business. However, unlike commercial banks, finance companies were not allowed to accept deposits but had to raise funds by issuing promissory notes or borrowing funds from banks themselves, which they then lend to customers. This restriction acted as an incentive for finance companies to undertake high-risk activities in order to generate higher returns to cover their relatively higher costs. Loan growth among the finance companies was a major conduit in the borrowing of short-term credit from foreign banks that subsequently fuelled a real-estate bubble.[4] This was a 'major structural weakness' of the Thai financial system that contributed to the 1997 crisis (Nakornthab 2007).

To summarise, there was progressive liberalisation of the Thai financial sector from the late-1980s to mid-1990s that was accelerated in the early-1990s as a result of state-induced policies in reaction to a number of domestic and external factors. This contributed to the growth and expansion of the financial market in terms of size, the number of players and the range of activities (Okuda and Mieno 1996). In the early-1990s, these policy changes were ultimately designed around policy makers' desire to transform Thailand into a regional financial centre. The jewel in the crown of this state-led process of liberalisation was the establishment of on-shore 'off-shore' international banking facilities. It is to this topic that we now turn.

International banking facilities

The establishment of an off-shore market, the Bangkok International Banking Facilities (BIBF) in March 1993 was the first step of a process aimed at turning Bangkok into a major regional financial centre (Bank of Thailand 1998, p.58). The concept was extended to provincial

---

[4] According to Fratzscher (2002), finance company loan growth grew at an average of 30 per cent per annum from 1988–1995, and according to Kawai and Takayasu (1999), by 1996 accounted for 21 per cent of credit extended.

areas in 1994 and called Provincial International Banking Facilities (PIBF).[5] IBF status allowed domestic commercial banks and foreign bank branches to accept deposits and lend in foreign currencies to both residents and non-residents, and to conduct foreign exchange transactions. Various tax privileges were granted to promote the development of the IBFs (Bank of Thailand 1993, p.54). Thailand also liberalised the foreign exchange market for current account transactions in 1992 with a concurrent liberalisation of capital account transactions as part of its strategy to promote the development of the IBF.[6] Although Thailand began to liberalise its financial sector later than many of the newly industrialised economies in East Asia, it went arguably much further than some of its neighbours by introducing full capital convertibility and establishing an on-shore international banking sector (Zhang 2003, p.1).

In March 1993, all 15 domestic banks and 32 foreign banks were licensed under the IBF scheme. The BOT unofficially encouraged foreign IBF licensees to maximise their lending by suggesting that some license holders, depending at least in part on the growth of their assets, would eventually be allowed to open local branches (Overholt 1999, p.71; Ito 2001), an inducement that was attractive due to the then prevailing restricted access to the domestic banking sector for foreign banks. Foreign banks consequently seized the IBF opportunity as a way to expand their presence in the Thai market. Thai finance companies that wanted to upgrade to the status of a full-fledged bank faced similar incentives. The entry of foreign banks through this channel further increased competition in the market which prompted many institutions to undertake more risky activities to make up for the reduction in their profit margins, further compounding the incentive for finance companies to undertake high-risk activities as elaborated earlier. In other words, BOT policies and encouragement not only contributed to the development of the IBF sector but also to the emergence of destabilising competitive behaviour in the financial sector.

---

[5] Both BIBF and PIBF institutions had to source funding from outside Thailand. While BIBF institutions could extend credit only in foreign currencies, PIBF could do so in both foreign currencies and Thai Baht.

[6] This followed Thailand's acceptance of Article 8 of the IMF Agreement in May 1990 that required that the country observe three conditions: (1) allow unrestricted payments and transfers with respect to international current transactions; (2) refrain from preferential treatment regarding international payments, including the use of a multiple exchange rate system; and (3) accept local currencies of other member countries through current transactions.

The BOT initially hoped that IBF lending would concentrate on 'out-out' activities – funds raised abroad and lent abroad, specifically to countries in Indochina – so that Bangkok could become a financial centre servicing regional economies. Instead, most of the flows were 'out-in' which fuelled the domestic economic bubble and led to a rapid increase in short-term foreign debt, both key factors that contributed to undermining the financial sector during the financial crisis of 1997–8. 'Out-in' lending formed about 80 per cent of total IBF lending between 1993 and 2005 with Thai banks being the major players (except in 1995) due to their stronger customer base, whereas foreign IBF bank units with no branches in Thailand dominated the 'out-out' business (Satsanguan and Lewis 2009). The growth in 'out-in' lending was attributed to the higher interest rates that then prevailed in Thailand relative to those in other markets, in particular Japan.[7] The problem of growing foreign debt was compounded by the provisioning requirements for risky assets under the Basel Capital Accord that had encouraged the supply of short-term over long-term debt at the global level as short-term lending to financial institutions in developing countries required only 20 per cent provisioning whereas long-term lending required 100 per cent provisioning. These factors created an incentive structure that contributed to Thai banks borrowing from foreign banks in US dollars, largely on short-term bases, and then lending domestically in Thai Baht. The lending frenzy that flowed from the IBF fed into speculative activity in both the stock and real estate markets. It also contributed to a rise in intra-affiliate lending or lending to clients with poor financial discipline and/or corporate governance (Sussangkarn and Vichyanond 2007). The level of external debt doubled in the period between 1992 and 1996 (Suehiro 1998). In the process, the private sector replaced the government as majority foreign debt borrower and by the end of 1996 total short-term foreign debt in Thailand was larger than the amount of official foreign reserves. This meant that Thailand was at risk of not being able to service its debt if short-term loans were not rolled over by foreign creditors, which eventually proved to be the case during the Asian financial crisis.

While easy access to foreign debt exposed Thailand's financial system to mismatches in the currency and term of funding, the resort to foreign borrowings by financial institutions were strongly driven by

---

[7] Although the Baht was fixed to a basket of currencies, with the US dollar having by far the largest weight in the basket, the BOT also tried to pursue an independent interest rate policy.

competitive behaviour in the domestic market.[8] This, together with poor supervision of domestic lending activity, underpinned the erosion of financial system stability. Supervisory forbearance was a systemic issue that undermined financial system stability (Siamwalla 2007). For instance, although the Bangkok Bank of Commerce (BBC) had been having problems for well over a decade before it collapsed in 1995, the BOT had not only shown extraordinary forbearance but had also injected funds, through the Financial Institutions Development Fund (FIDF),[9] to shore it up (Blustein 2001, pp.57–8; Sender and Lee 1998). The failure of the BBC also pointed to another source of weakness in the Thai financial sector: close state–business nexus and cronyism.[10] A study by Charumilind et al. (2006) found that in the period before the crisis, firms with connections to banks and politicians had greater access to long-term debt than those without such ties. Connected firms needed to furnish less collateral, obtained more long-term loans and appeared to use fewer short-term loans than those without connections.[11] The ability of financial institutions to carry on in such a manner is also a reflection of either forbearance or weak ability on the part of the BOT to supervise and regulate the financial sector. Laothamatas (1996) suggested that by the mid-1980s the supervisory capacity of the BOT was no longer immune from the 'incompetence and corruption that had long pervaded other agencies'. More broadly, it reflected the nature of

---

[8] Although Zhang (2003) argued that the gains of financial liberalisation did not materialise because deregulation efforts were focused on abolishing direct financial controls such as removing ceilings on interest rates rather than on actually increasing competition in the financial sector, a study by Okuda and Mieno (1996) demonstrated that interest rate differentials between banks and finance companies lending; bank deposits and financial companies' promissory notes; and domestic bank lending rates and LIBOR (London inter-bank offered rate) had all declined, especially after the IBFs were introduced in 1993. This suggests that competition had increased between the various segments of the financial market during this period of financial liberalisation. There were also indicators, as measured by the Herfindahl Index, that competition among the commercial banks alone had also increased.

[9] The FIDF was established in November 1985, in the wake of a series of crisis in the financial sector, to grant financial assistance to insolvent financial institutions. It is a separate juristic entity from the BOT though the Governor of the BOT serves as Chairman of its Board of Directors.

[10] Although the BOT took over the BBC in early-1996, no action was taken against corrupt owners and managers. Handley (1997) suggests that this may have been related to alleged credit extended by the BBC to BOT managers, and to the Chart Thai Party's successful 1995 election campaign.

[11] Similar observations were also made by Handley (1997); Sender (1997).

the Thai 'polity' in which state and market actors had developed such complex linkages that influence policy making and the processes of economic management.

These domestic practices and the dynamics of the IBF are two sides of the coin that is the financial crisis of 1997–8. The inefficient deployment of capital had increased imports of non-productive capital goods and consumption but failed to contribute proportionately to production and exports (Overholt 1999). Thai exports had also simultaneously lost their competitiveness to lower cost countries like China and India. This was not helped by the increasing strength of the US dollar to which the Baht was tied. The BOT attempted to support the troubled financial institutions through an infusion of liquidity through the FIDF but did not devalue the currency (Montreevat and Rajan 2001). As economic fundamentals began to weaken, a market perception was created that the Baht had to be devalued, so speculators began attacking the currency in waves. The BOT tried in vain to defend the currency and by the end of June 1997, almost all of the country's reserves had been used to this end. Thailand became effectively insolvent and the Baht had to be floated on 2 July 1997 while the country sought assistance from the IMF. The real-estate bubble; panic arising from the realisation by both domestic and foreign banks that debtors were not, or no longer, creditworthy; and mismatches in the currency and maturity of foreign debt can be identified as the immediate causes of the crisis.[12] However, ultimately, many blamed the way the financial sector was liberalised and (poorly) supervised as the fundamental reasons for Thailand's misfortune.[13] This in turn was in part a reflection of the 'polity' and politics of Thailand.

Managing the financial crisis

As was the case with Korea and to a certain extent Malaysia, the Thai government's broad objectives at the initial stage of the crisis were to manage bad assets, inject liquidity and close or restructure insolvent financial institutions.[14] However, unlike Korea and Malaysia where the respective governments led the effort in dealing with the crisis,

---

[12] For a brief and succinct account of the causes of the crisis, see Anwar and Gupta (2006, pp.23–6); Ito (2007).

[13] See, for instance, Vajragupta and Vichyanond (1999).

[14] For a detailed discussion of the Thai experience of the financial crisis, see, among others, Sharma (2003), Chapter 2.

Thailand's initial response to the crisis was more market-based or -led. There was a lack of public political support, at least initially, for the state to play the role of lender of last resort and this was consistent with the Thai state's historically less interventionist stance in the financial sector, when compared with that of Korea or for that matter Malaysia (Asami 2000). The Thai state has also traditionally faced a 'hard budget constraint' that discouraged mass public bailouts of weak firms (Doner and Ramsay 2003, p.130). Thus, Thai banks were initially encouraged to establish their own asset management companies (AMCs) to deal with NPLs. However, although bad assets were taken off the banks' books, the banks were reluctant to write down their bad debts as that would involve recapitalisation. This, together with the emergence of 'strategic NPLs', where debtors would evade repayment in the hope that their debts would eventually be written off,[15] contributed to a 'debt overhang' situation in the Thai financial system. A credit crunch subsequently emerged where banks were not extending new loans or would charge significantly higher margins to do so as they faced a shortage of capital on top of the difficulty of assessing the credit-worthiness of potential borrowers (Disyatat and Nakornthab 2003). The market's coordinating mechanism was thus unable to function properly or efficiently given the complexity of the situation thrown up by the crisis.

The restructuring of troubled finance companies was also complicated for much of the first half of 1997 by the close ties that some of these institutions, and business corporations, had with politicians in the ruling coalitions (Cook 2008). Progress in addressing NPLs was slow and creditors faced difficulties in converting debt into equity (IMF 2009b). The FIDF found itself injecting capital into a number of finance companies as politicised regulatory forbearance triumphed. Even when very weak finance companies were eventually closed down by the Financial Sector Restructuring Authority (FRA) that was set up to review their rehabilitation plans, the disposal of assets belonging to those institutions was also politicised as the FRA was unable to sell assets at prices that were perceived to be undervalued (The Economist 1998). In the end, the government had to rope in two new state-owned institutions, Radhanasin Bank and the Asset Management Corporation, as buyers/bidders of last resort for the lowest quality assets in order to avoid a fire sale (Sila-On 1998; Polkuamdee 1999).

---

[15] This was partly encouraged by the fact that under Thai law, creditors effectively had no way to seize assets that had been placed as collateral for loans to debtors who subsequently defaulted, see Overholt (1999).

A more active state role

From this point on, the state became increasingly involved in the resolution of the crisis and eventually also the reform of the financial sector. The state-owned Radhanasin Bank not only took over some of the assets of finance companies that the FRA had failed to sell off, but it was also subsequently used as a vehicle to take over the assets of some of the banks that the FIDF had earlier acquired in the process of resolving the crisis.[16] Another state-owned bank, Bank Thai, established late in 1998 with the FIDF as its largest shareholder (almost 49 per cent), was also designed as a vehicle to take over the remaining assets of failed financial institutions, in this case those of the Union Bank of Bangkok and a dozen finance companies that had failed in the course of 1998. In August 1998, the government installed new management in the state-owned Krung Thai Bank and instructed that it assumed the assets of First Bangkok Commercial and Bangkok Bank of Commerce, becoming in the course of these transactions the largest bank in the country. In the same month, the government also made public funds available to recapitalise other domestic banks, on condition of capital write-downs and management changes. Without new capital, financial institutions could not meet newly introduced asset classification and provisioning standards and thus could not extend new loans. However, few banks responded suggesting that there was a reluctance to dilute ownership in return for public money (Vichyanond 2007), symptomatic of the traditionally fierce independence of Thai commercial banks. Many preferred to raise capital privately in the market. So, in order to keep credit flowing, specialised state-owned financial institutions that had been virtually dormant for some years were resuscitated by the government to channel funds into the economy with a particular focus on 'priority sectors' (Phongpaichit and Baker 2001).

Hewison (2000) argued that the rescue operation and the subsequent generally 'gentle' approach to the banking sector and its massive debts reflected the continuing close links between the financial sector and the state, an observation which the IMF similarly made in a recent report (IMF 2009b). This was reinforced with the rise of Thaksin to power as nationalistic concerns with providing domestic capital the

---

[16] In the course of the crisis, the FIDF had taken over a number of domestic banks that failed including Bangkok Metropolitan Bank, Siam City Bank, First Bangkok Commercial Bank, Bangkok Bank of Commerce, Union Bank of Bangkok, Laem Thong Bank and Nakornthon Bank.

space and opportunity to survive and regenerate were important to Thaksin's political support base (Hewison 2005). Dixon (2004), on the other hand, pointed out that the government did allow large parts of the financial sector, other than the banks, to collapse. However, as he noted, there were really few alternatives given the inability of the sector to raise capital. Support was however clearly given to commercial banks where public funds were used for recapitalisation. Consequently, the state ended up with a larger stake in the banking sector and was saddled with a larger but weaker Krung Thai Bank; two new banks, one under the MOF (Radanasin Bank) and one, in practice, under the FIDF (Bank Thai); and three nationalised banks, Nakornthon Bank, Bangkok Metropolitan Bank and Siam City Bank, again under the FIDF.

Against this background of expanding state-ownership levels in the financial sector, a more 'activist' approach began to emerge in June 2001 following the electoral win of the Thaksin government and the promise that he had earlier made to the Bangkok business elite.[17] The government created a nationally owned Thai Asset Management Company (TAMC) to buy out bad loans from the banks including taking over the entire NPL portfolio of state-owned banks, totalling THB1.1 trillion. Private financial institutions and AMCs were also given the opportunity to transfer NPLs that had multiple creditors and were in excess of THB5 million to the agency but non-Thai banks and their branches were excluded from the process. Despite the invitation to private financial institutions to participate in the scheme, many were again reluctant to compromise on their independence by accepting state aid. Therefore, well over 80 per cent of assets acquired by the TAMC were sourced from state banks (Siamwalla 2007). A disjuncture subsequently emerged between state-owned and privately-owned banks in the resolution of NPLs where progress was much slower with the latter despite amended bankruptcy and foreclosure laws in order to encourage debt renegotiations. Corporate debt restructuring remained a lengthy and difficult process and it took about eight years (until 2005) before the ratio of NPLs in the financial system declined to below 10 per cent (Sussangkarn and Vichyanond 2007), although Siamwalla (2007) did not think that

[17] With the Thaksin administration, Thai politics saw the centralisation of power in the office of the Prime Minister as a result of provisions in a newly minted constitution designed to promote 'stability' in government. The rise of Thaksin to power also brought with it greater direct participation by business individuals in politics. For a recent succinct account, see Chaiwat and Phongpaichit (2008). See also Prasirtsuk (2007).

this should have been surprising given that assets classified as non-performing were about 40 per cent of bank assets at one point.

In the short period after the crisis first emerged, not only did the Thai state's ownership levels in the financial sector rise, eventually controlling close to one-third of total banking assets, but so too did that of foreign actors. Due to the pressing need to recapitalise domestic banks, parliament passed amendments to the *Commercial Banking Act* in October 1997 that permitted incumbent foreign banks or foreign banks with an IBF licence to hold up to 100 per cent of the assets of distressed local banks for a period of ten years.[18] The foreign ownership ceiling on non-distressed local banks was also raised from 25 to 49 per cent, also for a period of ten years. Foreign investors were quick to increase their stakes in the largest and best performing Thai banks. The banking sector attracted almost USD5 billion in aggregate FDI in 1998 and 1999 which represented well over half of total FDI during this period (Montreevat and Rajan 2001; Dixon 2004). The sale of nationalised banks to major foreign ones deepened the position of foreign banks in Thailand and allowed successful buyers to evade the one-branch limitation. This policy departure on foreign ownership in financial institutions, as well as the departure on extensive state involvement in the sector, emphasised the depth of the crisis and how it required the state to act against its traditional banking policy.

While this extensive liberalisation of the financial sector to foreign actors and the steps taken by the government are reactions to the averse circumstances in which the country found itself during the crisis, they were also coloured by the politics and polity of Thailand at the time. First, state management of the crisis was subjected to the unstable nature of multi-party government in Thailand as reform proposals were blocked, delayed or watered down by members of the government coalition or the Senate (Hicken 2008), thus leaving the market to initially fend for itself. The government's initial effort to reduce NPLs, encourage corporate restructuring and induce banks to restructure and resume lending moved much more slowly because of disagreements within the government about how to proceed (Pattnapong 1999).

Second, even though Chuan Leekpai's government supported the extensive liberalisation required by the IMF in the former's determination to eradicate 'crony capitalism' through market reform (Hewison

[18] Initially, the understanding was that after the ten year period, shareholding must be reduced to 49 per cent although it was unclear then how this was to be achieved.

2005), the steps taken by Thailand represented more of a reaction to immediate problems rather than a comprehensive path to greater financial liberalisation, as was the case in Korea where measures adopted during the crisis, even though part of an IMF programme, were an extension of earlier policy goals. Thus when the crisis struck, the approach of Chuan Leekpai's government had been to do what was necessary to cope rather than pursue a broad vision of reform (Overholt 1999). This absence of a more coherent strategy explains, for instance, the initially poor outcome in the management of NPLs and the subsequent need to change approaches. It was not until 2001, when Thaksin Shinawatra became Prime Minister and imposed a level of party discipline and party cohesion previously unheard of in Thailand's democratic history that a clearer vision of policy reform was articulated (Hicken 2006).

Finally, political issues took precedent over economic ones in the midst of the crisis. Following years of changing military and democratic governments, as well as rampant corruption, there was a broad public consensus that the foundation for economic reconstruction had to be change in the political arena. Economic issues were therefore relegated to a lower priority as the government focussed on writing a new constitution at the end of 1997.[19] The rise of Thaksin's *Thai Rak Thai* party to power was itself a reactionary response to public disenchantment with the way previous governments had managed the crisis, and the economy more generally (Hewison 2005). With Thaksin in government, the state not only played a more significant role in managing and resolving the crisis but also acquired much larger stakes in Thai financial institutions, thus marking the beginning of a process of transformation in the Thai financial sector.

Post-Crisis evolution of the financial system

I will now turn to the core question of this chapter and book: how has the Thai financial sector changed or been transformed in the decade since the crisis? As with the other case study chapters, I will address this issue by first looking at quantitative indicators of the financial sector before proceeding with an institutional analysis of the changes of the past decade.

---

[19] This process had begun before the crisis when the Thai parliament approved a bill in 1996 to convene a Constitutional Drafting Assembly. A draft was only produced in August 1997, after the crisis struck.

Quantitative indicators of change

As noted at the beginning of this chapter, despite the severity of Thailand's financial crisis of 1997–8, a quick glance at the Thai financial sector in 2009 might leave the casual observer with the impression that not much had really changed in the decade since that event. There were about the same number of Thai and foreign commercial banks in 2009 as there were ten years earlier (a total of 34 in 2007 versus 29 in 1996) (IMF 2009b). Commercial banks still remain the primary source of credit in the economy extending, as it did in the period before the crisis, about 70 per cent of total credit (Kubo 2006). Private Thai-owned banks continue to manage about the same level (about 40 per cent) of total financial assets in 2007, just as they did in 1996 (IMF 2009b). The six largest banks in the country have remained effectively the same, though two have since changed their names. The level of conglomeration in the banking industry has also remained about the same (see Table 5.1). Finally, state own deposit-taking financial institutions similarly retained their share of 12 per cent of the country's total financial assets between 1996 and 2007 (IMF 2009b).

The banking sector therefore continues to have a large presence in the financial sector and remains a primary source of credit for the economy (see Table 5.2). Its position in the market is reinforced with the almost complete disappearance of, and consequently competition from, finance companies. The finance companies, as noted earlier, were identified as one of the destabilising elements in the Thai financial system during the crisis as they had taken greater business risks and acted as a major conduit for short term foreign loans into the domestic market. From 91 institutions managing about 18 per cent of the financial system's total assets in 1996, there remained only four in 2009 with less

Table 5.1 Thailand: indicators of financial structure

	1996	1997	2002	2005	2006	2007
Bank Concentration Indicator[1]	0.4677	0.4691	0.4924	0.4454	0.4490	0.4715
Structure-Size[2]	0.4872	0.2677	0.3364	0.7627	0.7465	0.8332
Structure-Activity[2]	0.1777	0.1041	0.3864	0.5590	0.5598	0.5322

[1] *Refers to the ratio of the three largest banks' assets to total banking sector assets.*
[2] *Higher values indicate a more market-based financial system.*

Source: Compiled from data extracted from The World Bank: Thorsten Beck et al.'s World Bank Database on Financial Development and Structure available from http://go.worldbank.org/X23UD9QUX0.

Table 5.2 Thailand: structure of financial systems (per cent of GDP)

	1996	1997	2002	2005	2006	2007
Deposit Money Bank Assets	142.92	159.21	113.95	104.30	99.23	93.62
Private Credit Extended by Deposit Money Banks and Other Financial Institutions	137.44	154.08	97.13	90.55	87.11	82.71
Stock Market Capitalisation	66.96	41.24	32.68	69.06	65.03	68.91
Bonds Outstanding	9.20	9.56	32.73	41.53	46.07	50.72

Source: Compiled from data extracted from The World Bank: Thorsten Beck et al.'s World Bank Database on Financial Development and Structure available from http://go.worldbank.org/X23UD9QUX0.

than 1 per cent of total assets, thus leaving commercial banks and state-owned financial institutions as the primary sources of banking credit.

Ownership of commercial banks, on the other hand, has become more dispersed. Whereas the commercial banking sector was characterised by tightly held family-ownership before, there is now not only greater levels of state-ownership but also a very significant level of foreign-ownership. Of today's 14 Thai commercial banks, only 9 banks remain privately-owned by Thais, compared to 14 out of 15 before the crisis (Nakornthab 2007). The Sino-Thai banking families' presence in the banking sector has been significantly reduced (Hewison 2001a; Wailerdsak 2008). The government, through the FIDF, now has majority-stakes in two banks – Krung Thai and Siam City – and also hold significant shares in three other large local banks as well as a number of smaller banks. Banks in which the government has an equity stake accounted for 41 per cent of total commercial banking sector assets at end-2006 (IMF 2009b). Although local banks' share of the financial sector has remained roughly the same at over 70 per cent, the state now plays a larger role in these domestic institutions when compared with the period before the crisis.

Foreign-ownership and participation have also similarly expanded in the Thai banking sector. Although, the number of foreign-owned banks appears to have changed relatively little since the crisis, the nature of those institutions is now quite different. The restructuring of permissible types of institutions by the BOT under the Financial Sector Master Plan (discussed later) has done away with the IBFs and all foreign-owned institutions are now streamlined into either 'subsidiaries' or 'branches'. More significantly, as we saw in the previous section, the need to recapitalise several former domestic commercial banks has resulted in 'hybrid' banks that have large domestic networks but are foreign-owned, a phenomenon that was previously impossible due to government restrictions. UOB (Thai), Standard Chartered (Thai) and CIMB Thai fall into this category. But even among the remaining nominally Thai private banks, foreign ownership has also increased significantly (Nakornthab 2007, Table 1; Wailerdsak 2008, Table 1.2).

Although the banking sector still remains a very significant source of credit, there has been considerable growth in the size of the capital market in the last decade. Net funds raised in the capital market by both the public and private sectors have risen from 8.5 per cent of GDP in 1997 to over 146 per cent of GDP in 2008 (see Table 5.3). Despite the fact that the total assets of the Thai banking sector has grown in absolute terms, the competition increasingly posed by the capital market implies that there has been a decline in the *relative* importance of the banking sector (Nakornthab 2007) – see also Table 5.2. The ratio of assets held by deposit money banks to GDP while still considerable has nevertheless fallen from 143 per cent in 1996 to approximately 94 per cent in 2007 (see Table 5.2). Conversely, the size of assets managed by the stock and bond markets combined now exceed those of the deposit money banks, unlike the situation in 1996 when assets in the capital market were dwarfed by those managed by deposit money banks by a factor of two. The financial sector has therefore gained both breadth and depth since the crisis and this is reflected in the indicators of financial structure (see Table 5.1).

This relative growth of both bond and equity markets points to a changing disintermediation on both the asset and liability sides of banks. Not only has there been a gradual shift towards greater capital market financing, but the rise of asset management companies in recent years also suggest that savers may no longer be relying as much on bank deposits as they once did (Disyatat and Nakornthab 2003). The capital market has become an increasingly important source of fund raising since the crisis although as with the banking sector the role of the state is also significant. About two-thirds of the stock of assets in the capital market in 2008 was public securities and with the exception of 2003, new issues of public securities have consistently exceeded those of private securities (see Table 5.3 and Figure 5.1).

Table 5.3 Thailand: capital market (in THB million)

	1997	1998	2001	2003	2005	2007	2008
SET Market Capitalisation	1,098,869	1,243,556	1,607,310	4,789,857	5,105,113	6,636,069	3,568,223
As % of Total Outstanding Securities in Capital Market	64.57	54.75	44.48	60.63	54.39	50.78	35.25
New Issues in the Capital Market							
New Issues of Public Securities	239,286.19	501,677.69	772,069.58	752,354.77	5,129,683.89	5,129,683.89	10,039,601.28
New Issues of Private Securities	163,430.97	431,832.14	340,391.17	830,636.74	3,069,841.83	3,069,841.83	3,286,470.64
– *Of Which Stocks*	*63,297.34*	*329,980.59*	*102,745.81*	*184,664.44*	*107,758.63*	*107,758.63*	*44,972.08*
Net Funds Raised by both Public and Private Sectors	402,717.16	933,509.83	1,112,460.75	1,582,991.51	8,199,525.72	8,199,525.72	13,326,071.92
As % of GDP	8.51%	20.18%	21.67%	26.75%	115.60%	96.54%	146.40%

Source: Author's own calculations from data obtained from the Bank of Thailand's website (last updated July 2009).

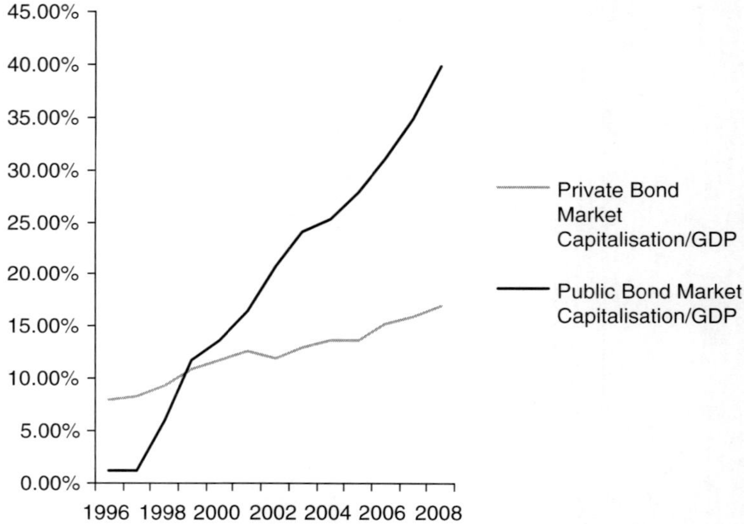

Figure 5.1 Thailand: bond market capitalisation (per cent of GDP)

Source: Constructed from data that was extracted from The World Bank: Thorsten Beck et al.'s World Bank Database on Financial Development and Structure available from http://go.worldbank.org/X23UD9QUX0.

What do these developments mean in terms of our discussion of convergence and change in economic models? The significant expansion of the capital markets and the increased participation of foreign actors in the banking sector indicate that, with increasing diversification, the Thai financial sector is moving towards the liberal market end of the spectrum. However, a study conducted by Kubo (2006) suggested that there might have been no changes to the competitive environment in the banking sector, despite the changes in ownership structure, and at worst a decline in competition might have even emerged as a result of the process of consolidation and the pursuit of economies of scale by the larger players. This echoed an earlier study by Laeven (2005) which indicated that the degree of competitiveness in the Thai banking sector is the lowest among a number of East Asian economies. Within the group of Thai commercial banks, the industry has become slightly more concentrated, with the Herfindahl index increasing from 0.118 to 0.123 and the combined asset shares of the six largest banks rising from 74.7 to 80.5 per cent (Nakornthab 2007) – see also Table 5.1.[20] Large foreign players have also become larger relative to their foreign peers. The top five foreign banks now control 75 per cent of foreign banks' total assets, up from 42 per cent a decade ago (Nakornthab 2007). In other words, the dispersion and diversification of types of ownership in the banking sector, although a welcome development from a liberal market model perspective, has not actually contributed to improved competitive dynamics, at least not yet. This is probably not helped by the increased state-ownership levels in the banking sector. Similarly, the expansion of the capital market has been accompanied by significant levels of state participation (see Table 5.3). Therefore, despite having taken on aspects of an LME, the Thai financial sector's change towards that ideal type is problematic based on this analysis of quantitative indicators.

The remainder of the chapter will investigate changes in the Thai financial sector in greater depth by adopting an institutional analysis approach. I will begin with a discussion of the master plans that were promulgated to provide direction to the development of the financial sector. I will then discuss in more qualitative terms the increasing prominence of foreign participation before concluding with an analysis of changes in regulation and supervision. Throughout the discussion in the remainder of this chapter, I will focus on the three P's (policy, 'polity' and politics) of these key issue areas in order to discern the nature and extent of changes in the financial sector, in particular where it concerns the role of the state in the market. In the process, I will uncover the factors that conditioned the manner in which the financial sector has evolved in the last decade and the role that the state has played in this process.

The financial sector master plans

At the turn of the century, two different master plans were formulated for the financial sector: one targeted at banking institutions and the other the capital market. The broad goals of the former were to

---

[20] The Herfindahl Index is a measure of the size of firms in relation to the industry and is used as an indicator of the level of competition among them. It is defined as the sum of the squares of the market shares of the 50 largest firms within the industry, where the market shares are expressed as fractions. The Index can range from 0 to 1.0, where an Index of 1.0 implies a single monopolistic firm. Increases in the value of the Herfindahl Index generally indicate a decrease in competition and an increase of market power.

improve public access to financial services as well as to consolidate financial institutions as a means of addressing weaknesses identified in the financial sector. With the master plan for the capital market, the authorities wanted to expand the range of sources for corporate funding and the options for private investment by diversifying the financial sector. Together, both plans were ultimately designed to modernise and improve the market dynamics of Thailand's financial sector. In this section, I will discuss the plans designed for the banking sector, leaving those for the capital market to the following section.

The Financial Sector Master Plan (FSMP) was the result of the deliberations of a committee comprising government, financial sector, consumer and public representatives, among others, organised in February 2002 to evaluate the need for the reform of, and develop a vision and framework for, the Thai financial sector. One of the bases for the committee's deliberations was a nationwide survey conducted in 2002 that had suggested that 23 per cent of SMEs and 58 per cent of people with low income lacked access to credit (Bank of Thailand 2006, p.10). The desire to expand access to financial services for low-income households and SMEs was reflected in the three 'visions' embodied in the FSMP when it was unveiled in 2003: (1) to broaden general access to financial services, especially for rural and low-income households; (2) to increase the efficiency of the financial sector; and (3) to protect consumers by promoting information disclosure of financial institutions and introducing a deposit insurance scheme.

While there certainly was legitimate demand for credit and financial services that had not previously been met, it was also politically astute for the Thaksin administration to pump credit into rural areas and the SME sector in order to gain popular support, especially since its ascent to power had depended significantly on the rural vote.[21] State-owned and specialised public financial institutions (SFI) such as the Government Savings Bank, the Government Housing Bank, and the SME Development Bank became instrumental in carrying out the government's policy of spreading credit to the grassroots and SME sector. In fact, two new SFIs, SME Bank and Islamic Bank, were established in 2002 for this purpose. Between 2000 and 2005, lending of these SFI to households and businesses expanded by 15.2 per cent on average compared to an average growth of only 4.2 per cent for lending by commercial

[21] Chris Baker (2005) called Thaksin's brand of politics 'pluto-populism' referring to a grand scale of populist policies that were initiated by 'tycoon politicians', thus creating a rich-poor alliance.

banks and finance companies to the same group (Sussangkarn and Vichyanond 2007). The lending of Government Savings Bank and SME Development Bank to households and SMEs grew particularly rapidly at an average of 32.2 per cent and 72.4 per cent per annum, respectively, between 2000 and 2005. In the housing market, the SFIs have garnered almost half of the market share since commercial banks could not, or would not, provide mortgage loans (IMF 2009b, p.42). State agencies nevertheless attempted to encourage commercial banks in the private sector to extend loans to retail customers and the SME sector. The BOT, for instance, lowered the risk-weighted reserve requirements for these types of transactions (The Nation 2004b). In late-2009, it dangled a further carrot when the central bank's governor stated that new licenses would be granted to companies who could provide 'microfinance' to the low-income population and SME sectors (Chan 2009; Bank of Thailand 2009).

While the need to meet consumer demands was important, so too was addressing weaknesses identified during the crisis. The key measures suggested in the FSMP to improve efficiency and stability in the banking sector were the rationalisation of the licensing structure and the introduction of a 'one presence' policy for financial institutions. This strategy was meant to both reduce the number of small players and eliminate regulatory arbitrage since a major structural weakness of the Thai financial system before the 1997 crisis was the many finance and credit foncier companies that had undertaken extremely risky activities. This weakness was to be corrected by removing the regulatory boundary between commercial banks' and finance companies' activities and providing a transition path to strengthen financial institutions via mergers and upgrading or orderly exit (Watanagase and Financial Institutions Policy Group 2006).

In contrast to the previous licensing structure that recognised a variety of types of financial institutions, the new regime under the FSMP recognised only four types of financial institutions: commercial and retail banks for domestically owned institutions; and foreign bank branches and subsidiaries for foreign-owned institutions. Commercial banks may provide most types of financial services to all groups of customers, but were not permitted to engage in insurance underwriting and brokering, or trading and underwriting of equity securities. They were required to maintain a higher minimum of tier-1 capital than retail banks (THB5 billion v. THB250 million). Retail banks, on the other hand, were expected to exclusively serve retail customers and SMEs and they cannot conduct business related to foreign exchange and derivative products. By acknowledging only two types of domestic banking licenses, the BOT was implicitly encouraging financial institutions to consolidate their range of services. This was reinforced with the 'one presence' policy that was designed to eliminate duplications of services offered by different types of financial institutions within a single conglomerate so that financial institutions fully benefitted from economies of scale. The idea was to reduce the number of licenses held by any one conglomerate and to increase the scope of commercial banks, thereby reducing regulatory arbitrage in the system.

A similar form of consolidation was imposed on foreign banking institutions. Under the FSMP, full branches of foreign banks were still permitted, while IBFs were replaced by subsidiaries of foreign banks. Both full branches and subsidiaries of foreign banks may engage in the same scope of business as commercial banks, but they differed in capital requirements and branch allowances. The establishment of foreign subsidiaries was a new phenomenon in Thailand and represented the BOT's response to pressures for further financial liberalisation. Subsidiaries were required to maintain a minimum of THB4 billion in capital and they were given a choice between keeping a maximum of four branches in the country (one of which was allowed inside Bangkok and metropolitan areas, and the remaining three outside) in addition to one head office; and merging or acquiring another institution in order to upgrade its status. Full branches of foreign banks, on the other hand, required a minimum of THB3 billion but were not permitted to open any branches. These new licences were intended to restructure the role that foreign banks had formerly played in the Thai economy via the IBF. Licenses for IBFs were discontinued and IBFs attached to commercial bank were asked to merge with their parent companies while stand-alone IBFs had to upgrade to foreign full branch or subsidiary or to return their licence.

After the FSMP went into effect in January 2004, several financial institutions 'upgraded' from finance company or credit foncier status to commercial banks (for example Tata Iron and Steel Co Ltd, Kiatnakin, Asia Credit) or retail banks (e.g. GE Money, AIG Finance, Thai Keha, Land and House). Two IBFs were allowed to convert to full branches (Société Génerale and Bank of Tokyo-Mitsubishi UFJ). The BOT had initially hoped that major foreign players such as Citibank and HSBC might choose to become subsidiaries, however, in the end, only one foreign-owned branch requested to upgrade into a subsidiary (International Commercial Bank of China, now known as Mega International Commercial Bank). Interviews conducted by Jittamai, Nakornthab and

Poshyananda (cited in Nakornthab 2007, p.23) revealed that most banks needed a network of 20 to 40 branches to be cost effective, implying that the five branch limit on foreign subsidiaries was uneconomical and thus, represented a commercial barrier.[22] The first phase (2004–7) of the FSMP nevertheless achieved one of its major goals, that is the rationalisation of the structure and roles of financial institutions. The number of financial institution in the system contracted significantly (Bank of Thailand 2005), and by March 2006, IBFs ceased to exist in Thailand.

While the consolidation of financial institutions was a means to gain a better handle on institutional actors in the market, the FSMP also featured several points of liberalisation over regulation governing the operations of banks in Thailand. An earlier policy that required banks planning to open branches in dense, well-serviced areas to open a corresponding branch in a rural area was eliminated with the FSMP. It also removed the requirements that provincial bank branches lend at least 60 per cent of the total amount of deposit within their operating region, and that foreign bank branches lend and maintain exposure in Thailand of not less than 70 per cent of their total deposit and borrowings raised in the country. The second phase of the FSMP, from 2010 to 2014, aimed to further reduce the operating costs of financial institutions; increase competition among financial institutions and non-bank entities through the expansion of the scope of business permitted; and improve market architecture with the development of limited deposit insurance and greater variety in risk-management instruments (Nijathaworn 2009; Bank of Thailand 2009). Public access to financial services will again be a focus of the new phase of the plan with importance given to expanding retail banking businesses and promoting new microfinance business models and players.

Although the FSMP has been considered the 'most far reaching Thai banking reform document for a generation' (Linklaters 2004), it is also, compared to those of Korea's and Malaysia's, rather modest. The Thai FSMP harboured no ambitious goal of becoming a regional or global financial centre nor did it really strive to improve the competitiveness of the Thai financial sector at the global level, whereas the governments of Korea and Malaysia aspired to transform their financial sectors into regional, if not international, centres. It also stands in stark contrast to

---

[22] During interviews conducted in September and October 2007, several finance industry professionals also suggested that foreign banks preferred to focus on cultivating business in the Bangkok region where the wealth of the country was concentrated.

the ambitions announced with the establishment of the onshore international banking facilities a decade earlier. The country's experience with the IBFs in the 1990s that, as noted earlier, had contributed to the weakening of the financial sector prior to the crisis; and the fact that the financial sector was particularly hard hit during the crisis understandably explain the relatively more inward-looking orientation of the Thai FSMP. Pridiyathorn Devakula, who was hand-picked by Thaksin and made Governor of the BOT in May 2001, felt that the master plan should have a narrower scope that better reflected the country's limitations and economic reality (Bank of Thailand 2006, p.3). This absence of a more ambitious developmental steering of the financial sector also harks back to the more laid-back approach adopted by the Thai government prior to the 1990s, before the desire to achieve regional financial centre status via the introduction of the IBFs surfaced.

The plan nevertheless still reflected a strong attempt by the state to shape the banking sector while simultaneously addressing its weaknesses, first in terms of rationalising the range of institutions in the market; and second, in its attempt at addressing the needs of large segments of the population who felt that they were underserved by the financial sector. However, the increased role of the state in the banking sector suggests that market dynamics might have been compromised. Compared to commercial banks, SFIs were more lax in lending discipline due to policy-directed lending and more primitive credit risk management capabilities. Sussangkarn and Vichyanond (2007) voiced concerns about the rapid growth of credit to the grassroots and SME sectors, fearing that they would either go to unproductive uses or lead to oversupply of similar goods.[23] They also noted that levels of debt in the rural areas had risen and that the precedent set by the government to forgive the debt of these sectors may lead to an eventual loss of market discipline. This is particularly worrying given that SFIs' share of total financial assets has risen from 7 per cent in 1996 to 14 per cent in 2007 (IMF 2009b). The increasing importance of SFI credit could also distort the market and create barriers for commercial banks to compete effectively (Nakornthab 2007). These developments merely compounded the concern that competitive dynamics in the Thai

[23] A case in point: Government Housing Bank had the worst asset quality with an NPL to loan ratio doubling in the third quarter of 2008 from the previous year to 16.40 per cent. The bank was employed by the Thaksin government to extend loans to build houses for the poor. For details, see Satsanguan and Lewis (2009).

banking sector have deteriorated since the crisis, as indicated by the studies cited earlier. In short, the implementation of state policies on improving public access to financial services may have undermined both market and competitive dynamics, a point to which I shall return later.

The capital market

The government's attempt at steering and developing the financial sector is more apparent in the capital market, a sector that had remained relatively underdeveloped before the crisis. The earlier discussion using quantitative indicators suggests that the Thai capital market has expanded significantly in the last decade. Net funds raised in the capital market by both the public and private sectors have risen from 8.5 per cent of GDP in 1997 to over 146 per cent of GDP in 2008 (see Table 5.3). The size of assets managed by the stock and bond markets combined now exceed those of the deposit money banks (see Table 5.2). The capital market has thus posed increasing competition to the banking sector and the relative importance of the latter has consequently been in decline. How did this development emerge? Does it contribute to improving market dynamics in the Thai financial sector and push it closer to the liberal market model?

Prior to the crisis, there were relatively few developmental initiatives in the capital market. The SET was then perceived as an unlimited source of funds and an opportunity for unbridled capitalism. Manipulation was not unusual, and regulation was slack. Regulatory interventions were rare, unwelcome and were denounced as the 'bureaucratic elite trying to prevent the new generation from enriching itself' (Handley 1997, pp.104–5). Since commission rates were fixed by the SET, there was little incentive to develop other business activities. Instead, brokerage firms relied heavily on retail sales at fixed commission fees for revenue and were not active traders in the capital markets. They also limited their underwriting services to the equity market. The brokerage industry in Thailand was also relatively small and poorly capitalised which did not help market development. The market also suffered from limited issuance activity and shallow secondary markets. One of the reasons for the latter was the small size of the institutional investor community in Thailand. Private savings were concentrated in the banking sector with stock market investments accounting for a mere 1.74 per cent of Thailand's total savings prior to the crisis (Thai News Service 2001a). Mutual funds in Thailand largely invested in government debt while private pension investment was low.

The financial crisis of 1997–8 presented policy makers with both a reason and an opportunity to promote the growth and expansion of the capital market in order to mitigate the economy's over-reliance on the banking sector. Furthermore, as in Malaysia, the focus on the capital market was also a reaction to a sluggish economy characterised by poor returns on deposit investments due to low interest rates and the shortage of credit as banks became more cautious in their lending (Polkuamdee 2002). Two development plans were presented in 2002 and 2006 by the Securities and Exchange Commission's (SEC) to guide its effort to revive and develop Thailand's capital markets. Given the relatively underdeveloped nature of the Thai capital market at the time of the crisis, the first phase of the capital market master plan (2002–5) focussed largely on relatively basic issues, that is enhancing the attractiveness of the market to local investors and increasing market liquidity.

Public interest in the equity market emerged rather slowly (Polkuamdee 2003). Although market capitalisation and the number of firms listed increased in the first couple of years of the master plan, the number of new investment accounts opened had been much lower than expected (Bangkok Post 2003). Contemporaneous developments on the external front – the collapse of Enron, the US–Iraq war, global accounting scandals and the SARS epidemic – were identified as some of the factors that kept investors at bay. Domestic factors such as the general public's lack of familiarity with equity investment, the lower level of sophistication among Thai consumers and the perceived higher risks of investing in the stock market were also important. Given the poor public response, the government turned to more aggressive approaches, such as the establishment of a new Thai Opportunity Fund in 2002, with THB30 billion, in collaboration with the SET, a state-run bank (Krung Thai) and government pension administrators, to help revive the moribund stock market as well as support politically connected firms in the market (The Nation 2002). This followed an earlier initiative in 2001 called the Equity Thailand Fund that had begun with a much smaller capital of about THB11 million (Thai News Service 2001b).

The low level of activity in the equity market at the turn of the century stands in contrast with that in the bond market. Although the bond market was relatively less developed than the equity market prior to the crisis, with the market for corporate bonds being then virtually nonexistent, this had changed completely a decade later. In the first quarter of 1997, the issuance of debt from the corporate sector amounted to only THB3.7 billion but in the second quarter of 2008, this had risen to around THB400 billion Baht (Satsanguan and Lewis

2009). However, the share of corporate bonds of total bonds has been in decline since 2001 (Ruengvirayudh and Panyanukul 2006). The limited number of large, quality corporate issuers with financial standing strong enough to meet the rigorous public disclosure and external rating agency requirements meant that there was a higher total cost of funding through debt issuance relative to bank lending for most firms. This problem was compounded by the fact that banks, which derived a large part of their profits from lending, were reluctant to underwrite bond issues. As a result, only a limited number of issuers (mainly companies with strong credit profiles) turned to the bond market for funding purposes. Other reasons for the poor development of the bond market included the ineffectiveness of the role of market makers due to relatively illiquid market conditions and imperfect market information; fragmentation in the clearing and settlement systems; the lack of hedging instruments that would facilitate risk and liquidity management; and the absence of a full range of benchmark government bonds. These issues relate to matters of coordination and collaboration that required, in part, active involvement of the regulators and/or the state to resolve. Nevertheless, there has been relatively more growth in the size of the bond market as a percentage of GDP than in the SET a decade after the crisis (see Table 5.2), and this is largely attributable to government activity (see Figure 5.1). As with the other 'crisis countries', the initial rapid growth of local bond markets over the last decade has been a by-product of the financial crisis as the government had to finance the cost of post-crisis restructuring. Government securities however continued to drive growth in the domestic bond market beyond this initial catalytic effort, in particular since 2004, as a result of a policy decision to issue bonds regularly in order to help establish a risk-free benchmark against which private issuers can price their bonds as well as improve market liquidity (Satsanguan and Lewis 2009).

The state's role in the growth of the bond market was also observed in a range of developmental efforts and attempts at shaping the market. A high-level Domestic Bond Market Development Steering Committee, originally established in 1998, was reorganised in January 2005 to enhance its role in promoting the development of the domestic bond market. The chair of the committee, originally held by the Director General of the MOF, was replaced with the Finance Minister to reflect the importance of this endeavour to policy makers. The BOT was entrusted with the responsibility for developing an active secondary market and, in collaboration with other authorities and market participants, mapped out a multi-year strategy and a plan of action that focussed on improving efficiency and reducing transaction costs in the bond market; increasing market players' ability to lend and borrow securities; enhancing participants' ability to hedge risks; streamlining and enhancing the function of primary dealers in their role as market-makers; and broadening the investor base by increasing market access for both domestic and foreign players (Watanagase and Financial Institutions Policy Group 2006). New markets and systems were also created to improve liquidity, facilitate trade and market efficiency. For instance, the Bond Electronic Exchange (BEX) was established in November 2003 to shift trade off the exchange floor or over the counter where it had deterred small and some institutional investors from investing because of the lack of transparency for both pricing and quantity. An electronic trading platform for all types of bonds, called 'Firsts', was also put in place in 2006.

The authorities also created new types of markets to diversify the range of sources for raising capital and the range of financial products that could be bought and sold in the market. The Market for Alternative Investment (MAI) was set up to provide SMEs, which represented a predominant proportion of Thailand's businesses, with access to long-term funding. It started securities transactions in June 1999. In May 2004, with the promulgation of the *Derivatives Act* of 2003, the Thailand Futures Exchange began to trade as a centre for transactions of financial futures contracts or derivatives, thus providing an important hedging tool for market participants. The government also extended tax incentives to firms wishing to tap funds from domestic capital markets and special treatment was given to long-term institutional investors such as retirement mutual funds. In order to encourage greater participation and activity in the capital market, the SET established the Securities Investor Protection Fund in 2004 to provide greater protection to Thai investors.

The number of retail investors in the equity and bond markets has since risen vis-à-vis institutional investors (Kasikorn Research Center 2005). On the supply side, retail investors' access to securities has improved as a result of various policy changes and the introduction of more efficient trading systems, such as the BEX (Thai News Service 2006c). More securities have been offered for sale to the general public particularly by larger, more well-known companies. On the demand side, low interest rates have driven investors to find alternative investments to bank deposits. A large number of asset management companies and pension funds have since emerged to meet this demand (IMF 2009b).

The most recent master plan for the capital market, 'Thailand's Capital Market Development Master Plan 2006–2010', extended these developments with the principal goal being to further address liquidity issues in the bond market and stability issues in the equity market by enhancing institutional participation (Thai News Service 2006b). Large state enterprises were encouraged to issue securities in local stock markets, as were companies that received privileges from the Board of Investment. The SET also reduced transaction costs and terminated listing fees to promote listing in the local bond market. Amendments were also made to the 'free float' requirement, where a certain proportion of shares of a listed company had to be held by retail investors who were not strategic shareholders, in order to help boost liquidity as well as strengthen market dynamics in the equity market (Thai News Service 2006a). Perhaps one of the most aggressive measures in this more recent plan was the intended liberalisation of brokerage commission fees in 2010, then deferred to 2012, as preparation for the full liberalisation of the entire securities industry though whether this will come to pass remains to be seen as a similar effort in late-2000 resulted in excessive competition that led to financial losses for many brokers (Polkuamdee 2002).

To summarise, growth in the capital markets since the crisis has been largely led by government initiatives through the investment of public funds in the market and the issue of public securities. Market participation outside of selected institutional investors and large corporations is generally weak, attributable perhaps to the country's level of economic development and its traditional reliance on bank credit. The issuance of government bonds helped to catalyse the growth of the bond market and subsequent policy initiatives contributed to the broadening and deepening of the capital market. When private sector actors shied away from the equity market, the government funnelled public funds to the market in order to provide liquidity and support its growth. In the bond market, the issuance of government securities continue to exceed that of the private sector, by a factor of almost three to one in 2008 in terms of value of issue (see Table 5.3). Although growth of the capital markets point to a diversification of the financial sector, this has largely been state-led due to the absence of more broad based market participation outside of selected institutional investors and large corporations. State influence in the evolution of the capital market has therefore been very important.

Foreign banks

As noted earlier, in the midst of the financial crisis, Thailand lifted foreign shareholding limits on banks for a period of ten years from

November 1997. Following this policy change, a wave of foreign banks acquired majority stakes in several Thai banks between 1997 and 1999, the first of which was Singapore's state-owned Development Bank of Singapore (DBS), which raised its holdings in the struggling Thai Danu bank from 3.4 to 52 per cent. In mid-1998, ABN Amro, a foreign bank holding an IBF license, acquired a 75 per cent share in Bank of Asia 1998, thus boosting its branch network from 1 to 121. However, as DBS and ABN Amro faced short-term problems in their mergers with their Thai acquisitions, not least of which was the lack of agreement over how existing NPLs would be managed, other prospective foreign buyers were more reluctant in proceeding with their purchases. In the end, only two of the remaining five nationalised banks were sold to major foreign banks, both in 1999. The first was Nakornthon Bank in which Standard Chartered acquired a 75 per cent share in September 1999 and expanded its branch network from 1 to 68. Similarly, 75 per cent of Radanasin Bank was sold to the United Overseas Bank (UOB) of Singapore in November 1999 giving the latter a 65-branch network. Both banks struck a deal with the FIDF in which the latter would be responsible for 85 per cent of losses accrued over the following five years from NPLs and would receive 95 per cent of the profits from any NPLs that resulted in gains.

There would be no more major sale to foreign banks until 2007 when Bank Thai sold a major stake to TPG Newbridge in order to raise fresh capital, making the investment company the second largest shareholder after the FIDF. The FIDF's remaining holding in Bank Thai was eventually sold to a Malaysian banking group, CIMB, in 2008. Special dispensation from the Minister of Finance was required as the sale resulted in foreign holdings in Bank Thai to rise beyond the then prevailing 49 per cent foreign shareholding limit. The transaction was considered crucial for Bank Thai's financial health, as the bank had been hit by losses on foreign debt investments, including collateralised debt obligations backed by US sub-prime mortgage assets (Yuthamanop 2008). TPG Newbridge's share in Bank Thai was also eventually sold to CIMB Group leaving the latter the majority shareholder at 94 per cent (Banchongduang 2009).

While these foreign banks made in-roads into the Thai financial sector, a number found themselves moving in the opposite direction. Some foreign banks withdrew entirely from the market due to disappointing returns (e.g. ABN Amro) while others, like Sakura Bank, the Industrial Bank of Japan and Dresdner Bank, changed their business strategies and wound up their operations in Thailand.[24] DBS Thai Danu Bank eventually merged with the Thai Military Bank (TMB) in 2004 overturning the foreign buy out of Thai Danu.[25] ABN Amro followed in DBS' footstep and sold ABN Amro Bank of Asia to Singapore's UOB in 2005.[26] ABN Amro now holds a full foreign bank branch licence and is back to a sole branch. At the end of 2009, with the exception of Standard Chartered, UOB, CIMB Thai and Mega International Commercial (a small Taiwanese bank registered as a foreign subsidiary), all other foreign banks were confined to one branch only, although most Thai banks have substantial foreign shareholdings. While the branching restrictions on foreign banks have been criticised as a barrier to commercial activity, some foreign banks have successfully employed outsourced distribution channels with support from internet banking and telemarketing to penetrate the Thai retail market (IMF 2009b). Most foreign banks are however focused on the wholesale market.

Recognising that there will be increasing pressure from external sources for greater liberalisation of foreign ownership in Thai financial institutions, Thai policy makers felt that the financial sector's best interest would be served by a gradually managed process of liberalisation in order to provide Thai banks the opportunities to strengthen their capital base, improve core banking business and promote an organic growth.[27] So in August 2008, further liberalisation of foreign ownership was facilitated when the *Financial Institutions Business Act* (FIBA) came into effect. The bill raised the limit of foreign ownership in Thai financial institutions to 49 per cent, up from 25 per cent, but this new limit can be further breached with permission from the MOF and recommendation by the BOT, as was the case with CIMB's purchase of its stake in Bank Thai in 2008–9. Whether this change in legal provision would have the desired effect is debatable as it had already been possible in the past to structure deals in order to get around ownership limits (Pandey 2006; Sarawuth 2007), and in this sense, the new legislation

---

[24] According to Kawai, Ozeki, and Tokumaru (2002, p.87), Sakura Bank merged with Sumitomo Bank in October 1999 and and decided to focus on domestic, that is the Japanese, market and retrench their overseas operations.

[25] DBS was left with 16 per cent of the larger Thai Military Bank.

[26] Bank of Asia was merged into UOB. ABN Amro was reported to have realised 'five years of low returns' on its investment in Bank of Asia, see The Nation (2004a).

[27] See for instance Bangkok Post (2006).

merely formalised what had been de facto ownership in the market. For instance, TPG Newbridge's stake in Bank Thai was bought as part of a 'consortium' whose combined ownership exceeded the permissible 25 per cent but none of the individual members breached the legal ownership limit.

Despite these liberalising measures, other restrictions continue to exist for foreign banks in the Thai financial sector, as noted earlier in the section on the FSMP where foreign banks, unless they were 'hybrid' banks that had earlier helped recapitalise Thai institutions, were restricted in their number of branches. However, even the 'hybrid banks' have been thought to face stricter supervision than did domestic commercial banks (Dixon 2004). The Thai central bank argued that restrictions continue to be maintained because 'the financial crisis taught Thailand about the downside of unencumbered liberalisation' (Bank of Thailand 2006, p.22). The persisting nationalist sentiments about the 'fire sale' of Thai assets to foreigners probably also contributed to the implementation of such polices. Politicians were also not averse to limiting the participation of foreign actors as banks were no longer channelling as much money to political parties as it did in the past with the increasing foreign ownership levels in banks (Prasirtsuk 2007).[28] Nevertheless, despite domestic opposition, it has been necessary under adverse market conditions to turn to foreign players in order to extend the lease of life of domestic institutions not only during the 1997–8 crisis but also as recently as 2008 when Bank Thai was sold to Malaysia's CIMB Group. Otherwise, as in Korea and to an extent Malaysia, the Thai state's position with regard to foreign actors has generally been cautious and in favour of domestic actors.

Regulation

Being a signatory of the Basel accords, the Thai regulators have been progressively implementing more market-based risk management systems. The BOT introduced a market risk supervision policy in line with the Basel standard in December 2003 which ensured that movements in interest rates, in addition to foreign exchange and equity, were taken into account in commercial banks' trading books when assessing their net positions, thus pushing banks towards risk management practices that were more sensitive to market indicators (Watanagase

---

[28] The new landscape of Thai politics that emerged with the rise of Thaksin meant that political funding came increasingly from new Thai business-politicians.

and Financial Institutions Policy Group 2006). The introduction of a forward-looking risk-based supervisory framework further encouraged financial institutions to be proactive in assessing and managing their own risks, relying largely on their own analysis, auditing skills and risk management tools, while authorities were responsible for overseeing systematic risks and maintaining the stability of the whole financial sector and the economy. In general, Thai regulatory systems have been moving towards a greater focus on the process and principles of risk, rather than on the letter of the law, which is regarded as critical in the face of contemporary complexity in financial innovation.

At the same time, the regulators have also been rationalising their institutional structures and processes to better meet with current international best practices. Policy formulation and decision making processes at the BOT have been reformed since the crisis in the hope of achieving more effective decision making, transparency and accountability, while ensuring better coordination with other relevant agencies. The monetary policy-making process and financial sector supervision are now conducted under the Monetary Policy Committee and Financial Institutions Policy Board, both of which have well-defined mandates and accountability. The Governor and Deputy Governors of the BOT sit on both boards in order to ensure effective information sharing and promote synergy in decision making, while experts from the industry and academia are invited to join the boards to help promote transparency and keep check and balances in place, in addition to providing intellectual input.

Since the crisis, the BOT has also placed greater emphasis on including financial institutions in the process of setting risk-based principles in order to ensure greater understanding of the issues and to encourage close, regular dialogue between regulators and financials institutions (Watanagase and Financial Institutions Policy Group 2006). The BOT and the financial sector, for instance, were working closely in preparation for the adoption of Basel II that went into effect in 2009. Consultative processes have also been institutionalised for most key policies, such as those on provisioning, new derivative products and market risk guidelines. Closer communication and cooperation among supervisory agencies, such as the Department of Insurance and the Office of the Securities and Exchange Commission, have also been formalised since the financial crisis of 1997–8.

While these various policy changes were important in improving the supervisory system of the financial sector, legal regulatory reform was not enacted until a number of critical bills addressing legal and regulatory shortcomings of the Thai financial system were passed by the Thai parliament in December 2007. The most anticipated of these were the amended *Bank of Thailand Act* and the new *Financial Institutions Business Act* (FIBA).[29] While the introduction of both these pieces of legislation have long been coming, with the drafting of the amended *Bank of Thailand Act* beginning as far back as when the crisis first emerged, changes of government in the last decade and differences of opinion between the two primary agencies, the MOF and the BOT, have led to delays in both the introduction and the parliamentary approval of the legislation (Horn 2000). These two pieces of legislation were critical in strengthening the supervisory power of the central bank through the consolidation of the supervision of all types of financial institutions under its purview. With the emergence of large banking conglomerates in Thailand, partially the result of the BOT's effort to rationalise the banking sector under the FSMP, consolidated supervision has become critical in promoting the stability of the overall financial system. The FIBA also gave the BOT legal power to enforce Basel II and prompt corrective actions to address weaknesses in troubled banks. Prior to FIBA, the BOT had to use a combination of moral suasion and contractual conditions, such as imposing certain conditions when banks applied for permits and licenses, to perform its supervisory responsibilities. FIBA however explicitly anchors the prompt correction action framework in the law and the central bank was given full operational independence with its objectives explicitly spelled out.[30]

Despite these changes in regulatory and supervisory provisions that introduce contemporary best practices, the state's control and ownership of financial institutions in the market have affected the credibility of supervisory practices. First, the BOT, as bank regulator, finds itself in a difficult position vis-à-vis the state-owned banks held under the FIDF. Although the FIDF is an independent juristic entity, and the MOF has assumed the FIDF's liabilities, in practice, the FIDF is run within the organisational framework of the BOT and managed by a board chaired by the Governor and staffed by both the BOT and MOF (IMF 2009b).

---

[29] FIBA was introduced to replace the *Commercial Banking Act*, and the *Act on the Undertaking of Finance Business, Securities Business and Credit Foncier Business*.

[30] These are: to achieve monetary stability, payment system stability and financial stability. Selection and dismissal of the BOT Governor and the length of term of the Governor and Board Chairman have also been more clearly defined.

This puts the BOT in a situation where it is required to supervise the banks with whose ownership and management function it is intimately involved. This arrangement creates, at the minimum, the appearance of a conflict of interest for the BOT as both an owner and bank supervisor, if not an actual conflict. Second, government ownership of deposit-taking SFIs and equity stakes in several private commercial banks have created the appearance of an unlevel playing field and selective regulatory forbearance (IMF 2009b, p.8). The deposit-taking SFIs, which in practice, operate alongside commercial banks, are regulated under separate, SFI-specific laws that come under the purview of the MOF. Although the Ministry has delegated authority to the BOT to examine the SFIs on an annual basis, the overall supervision of these deposit-taking SFIs still remains with the MOF. This bifurcated approach to examination and supervision of SFIs creates a potential source of 'reputation risk' for both the BOT and the MOF as it is potentially the source of sub-optimal, inefficient, costly and inconsistent supervision and regulation, a fact that is compounded by the increasingly blurred business lines between different types of financial institutions (IMF 2009b). During the Thaksin Administration, the MOF floated the idea that a new monetary authority should be set up to oversee all financial institutions leaving the BOT solely responsible for monetary policy in light of the latter's failings during the crisis (Satsanguan and Lewis 2009). However, given the BOT's ability to revive much of its credibility and independence since the crisis and the difficulty of establishing a new agency with enough credibility to gain the confidence of the market, supervision was eventually left with the BOT (Sussangkarn and Vichyanond 2007).

In short, while regulatory and supervisory systems are increasingly adopting international best practices, there is still more work to be done. At present, the fragmented regulatory structure, government ownership in financial institutions and government policy to encourage, if not direct, certain types of credit undermine the effectiveness and consistency of regulation and supervision. There is therefore inconsistency in terms of the introduction of regulatory systems and the compliance with norms that are generally associated with an LME ideal type. This is also mirrored in the broader agenda of corporate governance. Although Thailand's formal standards of corporate governance now approach or meet best regional practices, in contrast to the period before the crisis in which the notion of corporate governance was little known or understood, there are still significant weaknesses in the area of enforcement and the quality of compliance by companies (Walter 2008, Chapter 4).

The Thai regulatory system is therefore still quite a long way from approaching the LME ideal type.

Conclusion

The Thai financial sector has acquired features that are usually associated with the ideal type of an LME in the decade since the financial crisis of 1997–8. It has become much more diverse with the expansion of different markets, products available and the range of participating actors. The growth in the size of the capital markets also points to a deepening of the financial sector. Regulatory institutions have also been restructured to better conform to current international best practices. While these developments contribute towards reinforcing the market orientation of the Thai financial sector, and this is reflected in the indicators of financial structure (see Table 5.8), it is difficult to conclude that the Thai financial sector is becoming more like an LME because the state has come to increasingly shape and play a significant role in its evolution and operation in the decade since the crisis.

The significance of the state's participation in the financial sector was already apparent in the quantitative indicators. Not only is the state the dominant issuer of securities in the capital markets (see Table 5.3 and Figure 5.1), but it also now has majority stakes in two banks as well as significant shares in a number of other banks such that banks in which the government has an equity stake accounted for 41 per cent of the total commercial banking sector assets at end-2006 (IMF 2009b). An institutional analysis, focussing on the three P's, further revealed the extent and nature of state involvement in the financial sector in Thailand. A range of policies introduced by the state to reform and develop both the banking sector and capital markets have influenced and shaped how the financial sector has evolved and developed, although the views of market actors were sometimes also sought through consultation and workshops (Thai News Service 2004). More importantly, the state's determination to broaden the provision of financial services to under-serviced social groups has led it to actively participate in the delivery of financial services through specialised public financial institutions (SFIs), a development that has attracted concerns over the distortion of market dynamics, market stability and the consistency of supervision.

While policy goals were an important element of state intervention in the financial sector, the 'polity' or institutional context also shaped the nature of the state's involvement. On one level, the greater role of the state in the market was 'pre-ordained' by the devastation inflicted by the crisis on domestic banks. Without state assistance, the resolution of NPLs in the financial sector would have taken much longer. However, more active state intervention was also induced by the changing structure and dynamics of Thai politics in the post-crisis period that were underwritten by the capture of the state by business interest groups represented in Thaksin's Thai Rak Thai political party. Thaksin's ascendance to the Prime Minister-ship was accompanied with a significant change in policy orientation towards both the business and rural sectors that implied greater state intervention in the financial sector, as we saw in this chapter. This change in the Thai 'polity' also reflects an evolution of clientelistic politics that was already operating in the financial sector prior to the crisis except that under Thaksin, the government was courting the public for votes and the business sector, rather than the commercial banks, for political funding.[31] State interference in the financial sector was now a means to generate not just political but also electoral support. This was one of a number of key policies that earned the Thaksin government the description of 'pluto-populist' from a long-time observer of Thai politics (Baker 2005).

In short, it is difficult to conclude that the Thai financial sector has become more like a liberal market model since the financial crisis although the growth in the capital market, the increased participation of foreign actors in the financial sector and the diversification that this represents may signal the beginning of a longer-term evolution towards the ideal type of an LME, especially if the state intends for its holdings and interference in the banking sector to be temporal. For now, the marked increase in state intervention in the financial sector since the crisis, contrary to its historical role, suggests that if anything the Thai financial sector has so far been moving in the opposite direction towards greater state influence in the market.

---

[31] For an account of Thai political economy prior to the crisis, see, among others, Phongpaichit and Baker (1995); Phongpaichit and Baker (1998b).

6
Financial Systems in East Asia

The role of the state in the evolution of the financial systems has been significant in Korea and Malaysia as noted in the preceding chapters. The Korean state both owned and controlled banking institutions until at least the 1980s when they were privatised. Even so, the Korean state still intervened in, or at least influenced, the lending decisions and appointments of bank managers and directors. Although the Malaysian financial system was characterised by a number of privately owned banks, the state's involvement in the banking sector through state agencies and politically connected individuals has also been significant. While state intervention has been more modest in Thailand, a thick state–business nexus meant that the state was implicated in shaping the nature of the market not least in sheltering privately owned domestic banking institutions from foreign competitors.

Banking systems in our three case studies, as in most East Asian economies until the mid-1990s were large and, with the exception of the case of Malaysia, were the primary sources of financial intermediation in their economies (Claessens and Glaessner 1997) – see Table 6.1 and Figure 6.1. Even though Malaysia had the distinction of having one of the three largest equity markets in the region (measured as a proportion of GDP), the banking system was still a significant source of new funds raised in 1997 (see Figure 4.1). This reliance on bank loans to fund business activities, which earned these economies the label of a 'high debt model' (Wade and Veneroso 1998), required greater cooperation or linkages between banks, firms and the state to coordinate activity in the market. However, these very same linkages were criticised for sheltering less productive activities and promoting cronyism and corruption, a weakness that was acknowledged by even those who were sympathetic to the East Asian high-debt, high-growth

Table 6.1 Structure of financial systems (per cent of GDP)

	Deposit Money Bank Assets			Stock Market Capitalisation			Bonds Market Capitalisation		
	1996	**2005**	**2007**	**1996**	**2005**	**2007**	**1996**	**2005**	**2007**
Korea	50.8	94.9	107.6	29.0	72.8	101.5	50.3	98.4	106.9
Malaysia	129.6	113.8	106.8	263.5	136.6	156.0	67.5	86.0	90.4
Thailand	142.9	104.3	93.6	67.0	69.1	69.0	9.2	41.5	50.7

Source: Compiled from data extracted from The World Bank: Thorsten Beck et al.'s World Bank Database on Financial Development and Structure available from http://go.worldbank.org/X23UD9QUX0.

model (Wade and Veneroso 1998; Jomo 2007). In the aftermath of the financial crisis, many argued that greater market-dynamics and a retrenchment of the activist and interventionist role of the state in the financial sector would help address these perceived weaknesses in the Asian forms of economic management, especially if the affected countries wished to continue participating in the global economy without leaving themselves vulnerable to future financial crises, or at least the worst effects thereof. It was argued that not only were there different forms of managing and organising financial sectors, and more generally economies, but that there were also better and worse, rather than just different, ways of doing so. In the contemporary global political economy, the liberal market economy (LME) model, in particular the neoliberal variant, was held up as the one to emulate not only because it was argued to be better at managing economic affairs but also because it was understood to be most suited to the contemporary global economy and thus one on which all economies were expected to eventually converge.

While the more recent global financial crisis of 2008–9 did subject this expectation to further examination and criticisms, there has so far been little to suggest that in practice much of the economic orthodoxy that has guided policy makers since the 1980s is being seriously challenged. As noted earlier in this study, while many acknowledged that there are serious issues with the way in which the international financial market operates, by and large, the focus on corrective measures thus far has been on improving regulatory oversight and finding ways to make the market work better rather than imposing greater controls on market activity and changing the underlying nature of the economic model. Current debates can therefore be seen as more a 'development than as a refutation of the Washington Consensus' (Williamson 2009),

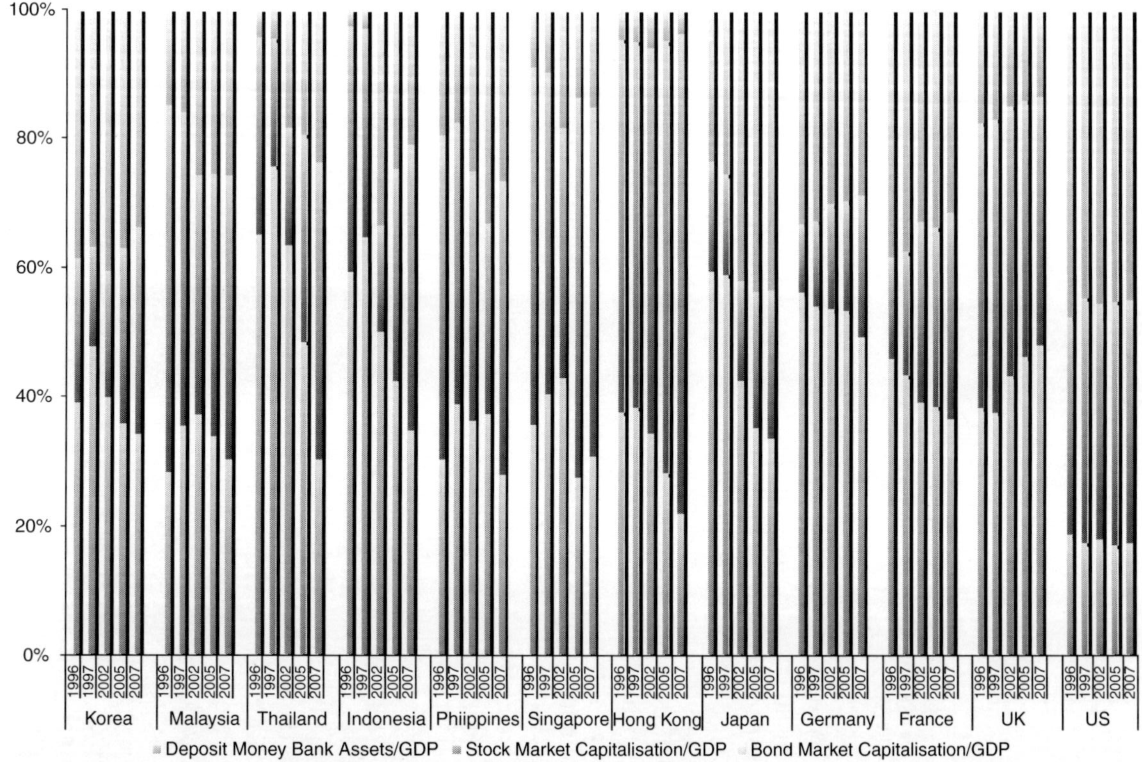

Figure 6.1 Structures of financial systems

Source: Constructed from data that was extracted from The World Bank: Thorsten Beck et al.'s World Bank Database on Financial Development and Structure available from http://go.worldbank.org/X23UD9QUX0.

and thus the liberal market model. As such, the expectations that were applied to the East Asian economies in the late-1990s are still relevant, albeit with minor adjustments, in particular in the realm of regulation and supervision.

In light of these debates, this study sought to ascertain, with respect to Korea, Malaysia and Thailand, the changes in the financial sectors since the financial crisis of 1997–8. What has become of the role of the state? Has there been convergence onto the LME model in the financial sector? Or do the financial sectors remain closer to the SiME ideal type? The preceding empirical chapters provided responses to these questions informed by both a quantitative analysis as well as an institutional analysis that focussed on the three P's (policy, 'polity' and politics) of key issue areas. My objective in this chapter is to summarise and synthesise the conclusions of the preceding chapters. I do so by first drawing on the detailed accounts of the earlier chapters to provide a comparative analysis of the evolution of the financial sectors of Korea, Malaysia and Thailand. In addition to analysing the nature of changes in the three financial sectors since the Asian crisis, I will also discuss some of the implications of these changes for market dynamics. This discussion will focus on four key areas of interest: changes in the banking sector, market diversification, foreign participation and regulation and supervision. Where relevant, I will also draw on secondary observations of the financial sectors of other countries to provide a wider basis for contrast and comparison. As I argued in the previous chapters the state still has considerable influence in the financial sectors of all three economies and, in fact, intervenes even more actively in the financial sector of Thailand than it has in the past. Following this summary discussion on changes in the financial sectors, I will provide a more systematic account of the ways in which the state still intervenes in the financial sectors of Korea, Malaysia and Thailand.

Changes in the financial sectors

This section will evaluate the nature of the changes in the financial sectors of Korea, Malaysia and Thailand drawing on both an analysis of quantitative indicators as well as an institutional analysis. The discussion is structured around four issue areas that have been the focus of debates during the crisis: the banking sector, the diversification of the financial sector, foreign participation and finally changes in regulation and supervision.

The banking sector

In the three economies that are the focus of this study, banks still play very significant roles in their financial systems (see Table 6.1). While the banking sector still has an important share of the market in Korea, there is now greater parity between deposit money banks, the stock market and the bond market when compared with 1996. In Malaysia however, assets in deposit money banks have become relatively larger than the capitalisation of both the stock and bond markets since the financial crisis of 1997–8. Although assets in the deposit money banks in Thailand have become relatively smaller than in 1996, they nevertheless still out-strip those in the stock and bond markets by quite a considerable margin.

The continuing significance of the banking sector in these financial sectors can also be gleaned by looking at another set of figures. At the end of 2007, bank credit still represented a primary source of funding in all three economies, especially for Thailand (see Table 6.2). In Korea, domestic bank credit stood at 106.9 per cent of GDP, on par with outstanding bonds but slightly exceeding stock market capitalisation at 101.5 per cent. Bank loans as a percentage of GDP in Malaysia have declined over the decade, amounting to approximately 99.5 per cent of GDP in 2007 compared with stock market capitalisation of 156 per cent of GDP and bond market capitalisation of 90.4 per cent of GDP. In Thailand, banks remain the primary source of credit in the economy with approximately 84.1 per cent of GDP worth of credit outstanding in 2007 compared with 69 per cent and 50.7 per cent of GDP for stocks and bonds outstanding respectively.

While it appears from these indicators that banks continue to play significant roles in these formerly crisis-afflicted economies, it should be

Table 6.2 Sources of finance (per cent of GDP)

	Bank Credit			Stock Market Capitalisation			Bonds Market Capitalisation		
	1996	**2005**	**2007**	**1996**	**2005**	**2007**	**1996**	**2005**	**2007**
Korea	50.1	91.2	106.9	29.0	72.8	101.5	50.3	98.4	106.9
Malaysia	129.5	107.3	99.5	263.5	136.6	156.0	67.5	86.0	90.4
Thailand	140.4	91.3	84.1	67.0	69.1	69.0	9.2	41.5	50.7

Source: Compiled from data extracted from The World Bank: Thorsten Beck et al.'s World Bank Database on Financial Development and Structure available from http://go.worldbank.org/X23UD9QUX0.

noted that the shares of total deposit money bank assets in these economies are not unusual in global terms (see Ghosh 2006, Figure 1.2) – see also Figure 6.1. Furthermore, much is hidden behind the statistics. For instance, despite the continuing dominance of the banking sector, the market dynamics of the sector have changed as a result of the significant restructuring that has taken place since the crisis. Merchant banking corporations and finance companies have all but disappeared in Korea, Malaysia and Thailand, leaving commercial banks as the only significant players in the banking sector in all three economies. Furthermore, as a result of the restructuring of the financial systems – state-led in both Korea and Malaysia and with significant state-involvement in Thailand (see individual chapters for details) – the number of banks has declined in Korea and Malaysia. The number of nationwide banks declined from 16 to 7 in Korea, and 22 to 9 in Malaysia. The number of commercial banks has actually risen in Thailand, increasing from 29 to 34, in part the result of the rationalisation of the bank licensing structure that induced finance companies to upgrade to a commercial bank status, and more importantly because the state took a much less aggressive approach to bank restructuring, attributable to its continuing close links with the financial sector (Hewison 2000; IMF 2009b).

With the reduction in the number of financial institutions, and the simultaneous conglomeration of banking institutions due to the liberalisation of activities that may be undertaken, there has been increasing concentration of assets in a small number of banks in all three economies (see Tables 6.3 and 6.4). In Korea, the share of financial institution assets that belong to financial conglomerates in general has grown substantially from 56.4 per cent in 1996 to 87.8 per cent in 2006 (Hahm 2007, Table 2), suggesting a reduction in competitive dynamics in the

Table 6.3 Measures of consolidation and diversification of banking sector activities

	Median Size of Assets (USD billions)		Median Size of Deposits (USD billions)		Median Market Share of Assets (%)	
	1998	**2004**	**1998**	**2004**	**1998**	**2004**
Korea	16.7	61.9	10.2	42.1	4.0	5.8
Malaysia	1.9	7.4	1.3	5.0	1.3	2.7
Thailand	4.4	13.4	4.1	11.8	3.9	6.9

Source: Ghosh 2006, Table 4.4.

Table 6.4 Bank concentration indicator[1]

	Indonesia	Korea	Malaysia	Philippines	Thailand
1996	0.3837	0.2557	0.4090	0.7629	0.4677
2007	0.5804	0.5268	0.4732	0.5636	0.4715

[1] Refers to the ratio of the three largest banks' assets to total banking sector assets.

Source: Extracted from The World Bank: Thorsten Beck et al.'s World Bank Database on Financial Development and Structure available from http://go.worldbank.org/X23UD9QUX0.

market. Even in Thailand, where the number of commercial banks have risen since the crisis, a couple of studies have noted a deterioration in the competitive environment following changes in ownership structures and regulations (Hosono 2005; Kubo 2006). This finding is supported by the results of a comparative study where it was concluded that Thailand was of most concern when it came to market competition, while Malaysia ranked middle in the sample of seven East Asian economies and Korea fared best among the three economies that are the focus of this discussion (Laeven 2005). Other studies however suggested that it was too early to evaluate the impact of these structural changes on competitive dynamics (Ghosh 2006; Corbett 2007).

Although the consolidation and conglomeration of banking institutions in Korea, Malaysia and Thailand have been partially driven by state-led policies, the rationalisation of the banking sector is not unique to these crisis-afflicted economies. It is a phenomenon that has occurred throughout the region, as well as more generally globally, driven by competitive pressures arising from deregulation and technological advances (IMF 2001; Ghosh 2006, p.7). In Table 6.5, we see that the bank concentration indicator has risen for a range of countries between 1996 and 2008. Aside from the potential impact on market competition, these developments also raise issues for supervision and regulation as consolidation also affects risks in the market. Cross-country empirical studies have found that not only do larger banks take on more risk than smaller ones but that higher concentration in banking systems are associated with higher levels of systemic risk (Ghosh 2006, pp.93–4). While, consolidation can augment the size, market power and profits of banks, thus creating incentives for banks to avoid imprudent risk-taking, they may also become more leveraged and take on greater risk, knowing that they can rely on policy makers to help when faced with adverse shocks. In other words, the increased conglomeration and consolidation of commercial banks in all three countries begs the question as to whether the 'too big to fail' argument that was believed to have

Table 6.5 Bank concentration indicator

	1996	1997	1998	2006	2007	2008
Korea	0.2557	0.2425	0.3832	0.5131	0.5268	0.5410
Malaysia	0.4090	0.4420	0.4011	0.4617	0.4732	0.4851
Thailand	0.4677	0.4691	0.5077	0.4490	0.4715	0.4967
Indonesia	0.3831	0.4334	0.4014	0.5254	0.5804	0.6370
Philippines	0.7629	0.7205	0.6732	0.4119	0.5636	0.7940
Singapore	0.7353	0.6177	0.8060	0.8573	0.9367	1.0000
Hong Kong	0.4800	0.4040	0.4313	0.6819	0.7572	0.8525
Japan	0.3347	0.3390	0.3255	0.3880	0.4553	0.5399
Germany	0.5094	0.5159	0.6310	0.6827	0.7133	0.7437
France	0.4228	0.4301	0.4829	0.6162	0.5834	0.5543
UK	0.7292	0.7309	0.7020	0.5029	0.5990	0.7225

Source: Compiled from data extracted from The World Bank: Thorsten Beck et al.'s World Bank Database on Financial Development and Structure available from http://go.worldbank.org/X23UD9QUX0.

significantly influenced government bail-outs, as well as promoted 'moral hazard' issues in the Asian financial sectors, might not now become even more pertinent.

In short, in all three markets, the policy decision to consolidate the financial sector, introduced with the aim of restoring confidence and stability into the financial system, has strengthened the market share, and possibly market power, of the commercial banks. As a result of this changing institutional structure, it is likely that market dynamics in the banking market has been impaired with potentially negative outcomes while the prospect of moral hazard continues to be an issue that needs to be reviewed and managed by financial sector regulators and supervisors.

State ownership in the banking sector

Market dynamics might also have been impaired by another development that has accompanied the consolidation of the banking sector during the crisis: the persistence of, and in the case of Thailand increase in, state ownership and influence in the banking sector. The rise of broader state ownership in Thai financial institutions meant that banks in which the government has an equity stake accounted for 41 per cent of total commercial banking sector assets at end-2006 (IMF 2009b). More importantly, the state's role in the Thai financial system has increased through greater use of state-owned and specialised financial institutions, including two new ones established in 2002 to channel credit to lower-income groups and the SME sector. This policy emerged, and took on a particularly populist dimension, during the Prime Minister-ship of Thaksin Shinawatra. Given the recurring turmoil in Thai politics since late-2007, it is difficult to ascertain whether this development in the state's role in the Thai financial system will continue. Since there is a genuine need for credit in the lower-income groups and the SME sector that is not being fulfilled by the commercial banks, the state's role is likely to persist in some form or other. It is however difficult to tell whether the state will divest its broader equity stakes in the commercial banks. While the Thai bureaucracy favours divestiture given its historically more arms-length relationship with the banking sector (Bank of Thailand 2009), it is difficult to judge how politicians will decide given the current instability in Thai politics.

In Malaysia, the state continues to have a substantive stake in the banking sector with five main government agencies holding more than 40 per cent of the outstanding shares of six banking groups. The state's relative ownership has arguably also strengthened with the consolidation in the financial sector (Lum and Koh 2007, Table 8). This has been an enduring characteristic of the Malaysian banking sector as a result of the dynamics arising from the 'polity' and politics of both patronage and the socio-economic goals embodied in the NEP/NDP. In Korea, government ownership of banks at the end of 2009 is limited to the Korea Development Bank, the Industrial Bank of Korea and Woori Bank, where only the last is a commercial bank that came into the government's fold as a result of the process of market restructuring following the crisis. The Korean government has long stated its intention to sell its stake in Woori Bank but has encountered difficulties in finding politically acceptable buyers (Na 2008). Although government ownership of banks has been largely divested since the introduction of greater liberalisation measures in the 1980s, the Korean state had nevertheless found indirect means of intervening in banking operations throughout the 1980s and 1990s. Signs of such influence appear to persist in the period since the Asian financial crisis, the effect in part of the historical and cultural dimensions of the Korean 'polity'. This includes the use of indirect means to control the management of financial institutions and moral suasion to direct credit (Parreñas 2006; Kim 2009a).

While state ownership of banking institutions was a concern raised in the debates about the financial crisis, a review by Mihaljek (2006) found no decisive evidence that private sector banks performed better than state-owned banks in the years following the crisis since standard prudential and efficiency indicators for banks improved across the board. Similarly, a study by Fan and Wiwattanakantang (2006) found that banks' performance and efficiency in Indonesia, Korea, Malaysia and Thailand were unrelated to their corporate governance characteristics. Since the study also concluded that corporate governance structures were significantly related to ownership and control structures, we can infer that the banks' performance and efficiency were also unrelated to ownership and control structures. In other words, public or private ownership had no statistically significant bearing on bank performance or efficiency. Notwithstanding these results about the actual economic performance of banking institutions, these studies do not address the criticism that the availability of credit was often decided on political considerations in state-owned banks or in institutions where the state had considerable influence.[1] It is possible that thus far, politically influenced extensions of credit have not had a negative impact on bank performance for any number of reasons, including the possibility that politically influenced loans are now also being assessed on their ability to contribute to the banks' 'bottom line'.

On the other hand, the level of foreign-ownership in commercial banks has increased in all three economies and this was expected to contribute to the improvement of banks' performance, market-orientation and lower the likelihood that political considerations would factor as significantly in the decision making processes of banking activities (see also the section on foreign participation). Moreover, although the banking sector still comprises a significant slice of the financial system, growth in the size of the capital market, that is equity and bond markets combined, has begun to challenge the dominance of the banking sector (see Table 6.1), and the diversification of sources of funding that this represents should lower the relative ability of the state to influence the distribution of finance in the economy. However, it is clear that state ownership in the market is still significant, particularly in Malaysia and Thailand, and that this does not conform to the LME ideal type.

Market diversification

If one of the main sources of weakness in the Asian financial systems was the absence or insufficient number of 'spare tyres', then this issue has certainly been addressed in the last decade. The financial sectors of all three economies that are the focus of this study have both broadened

[1] The case of Korea from the 1980s onwards demonstrated that the state did not have to have ownership in financial institutions in order to influence the direction of credit.

and deepened with significant growth observed in the bond market,[2] and to a much lesser extent in the equity market.

Growth in the bond markets of all three economies between 1996 and 2007 has been uniformly impressive. In Malaysia, the capitalisation of the bond market has increased by about a third, from 67.5 per cent of GDP in 1996 to about 90 per cent of GDP at the end of 2007. Bond market issuance in Korea rose from just over KRW400 trillion in 1998 to almost KRW1,000 trillion in 2007 (see Table 3.2), and bonds outstanding more than doubled within the decade (see Table 6.1). The growth of bonds outstanding in Thailand was even more impressive, rising from 9.2 per cent of GDP in 1996 to 50.7 per cent of GDP in 2007. Despite these changes, it has been noted that 'given their per capita incomes and the extent of their financial deepening overall, countries in East Asia lag behind in the importance of their bond markets, particularly of the corporate bond market, relative to the other financial segments' (Ghosh 2006, p.4), with perhaps the exception of Malaysia whose bond market trailed only those of Japan and the US in relative size (as a percentage of GDP) in the survey conducted by Ghosh (2006, Table 5.2) for the World Bank. However, a different dataset obtained from the World Bank, compiled by Beck et al., indicates that bond market capitalisation in Korea has been larger (in terms of percentage of GDP) than that of Malaysia since 2002 (see Table 6.1 and Figure 6.1). While this might suggest that the level of 'underdevelopment' of the bond market in Korea might not be as bad as Ghosh suspected, it is important to note that much of the growth in the Korean bond market is accounted for by government rather than corporate activity, a point that was stressed by Ghosh (see also discussion in Chapter 3).

Indeed, the role of government has been important in the development of the bond market in all three countries, especially in Thailand. Government securities account for a significant proportion of bonds outstanding in all three markets (see Table 6.6),[3] not least of which were those issued by the state in the course of managing and resolving the crisis. Government activity in the bond market has played a significant catalytic role in the growth observed. Each country has also actively attempted to add depth and breadth to its own domestic market through policy changes, the provision of fiscal incentives as well as issuing government bonds to help set benchmark yields in the market. In the case of Malaysia, the government's decision to develop the

[2] See also the discussion in Rethel (2010b).

[3] See also Ghosh (2006), Table 2.

Table 6.6 Composition of bond market capitalisation (per cent of GDP)

	Korea			Malaysia			Thailand		
	1996	**2005**	**2007**	**1996**	**2005**	**2007**	**1996**	**2005**	**2007**
Private Bonds	38.17	53.55	58.82	36.22	49.68	54.51	8.00	13.59	16.00
Public Bonds	12.08	44.81	48.11	31.23	36.34	35.89	1.21	27.94	34.72

Source: Compiled from data extracted from The World Bank: Thorsten Beck et al.'s World Bank Database on Financial Development and Structure available from http://go.worldbank.org/X23UD9QUX0.

Islamic finance sub-sector also contributed substantially to the expansion of the bond market. Finally, inter-state regional cooperation in East Asia has also facilitated the expansion of the bond markets as local and cross-border impediments have been addressed by the respective governments through the sharing of experiences and technical expertise (Ibrahim and Wong 2006).[4]

The size of assets managed by the stock and bond markets combined now exceed those of the commercial banks in all three markets (see Table 6.1). Although the global financial crisis of 2008–9 has led to a contraction in the capitalisation of equity markets in all three economies, the Korean stock market had displayed tremendous growth up to 2007, with capitalisation (as a percentage of GDP) increasing by more than threefold since 1996. While growth of the stock market (as a percentage of GDP) has been negligible in Thailand, Malaysia's stock market has represented a significant component of its financial sector, with market capitalisation as a percentage of GDP rivalling the size of those in the US and the UK (Ghosh 2006, Table 5.1) – see also Figure 6.1. The market dimension of all three financial sectors has been strengthened with this combined growth in the capital markets, since market diversification is argued to be a source of market stability, efficiency and competitiveness. However, the continued significant role of the state in this very diversification might prompt a more cautious evaluation

[4] Three regional forums have been at the forefront of financial development in the region, namely the Asia-Pacific Economic Cooperation (APEC), the Association of Southeast Asian Nations Plus 3 (ASEAN+3) and the Executives' Meeting of East Asia and Pacific (EMEAP) Central Banks. For more details, see Ghosh (2006), Chapter 2.

especially given the sizeable proportion of funds raised in the capital market attributed to state activity in all three countries (see Table 6.6).

As a result of the competition from the capital market, there has been a declining *relative* importance of the banking sector in all three economies. The relative growth of both bond and equity markets points to a changing disintermediation on both the asset and liability side of banks. As corporations turn to the capital market for financing, consumer credit has become an increasingly important type of business for banks in all three economies so much so that rapid growth in this area has led to market instability in both Korea and Thailand (Turner 2007). Not only has there been a gradual shift towards greater capital market financing but the growth of asset management companies (AMCs) in Thailand in recent years suggests that savers also appear to be turning to the capital market, and thus away from bank deposits, for greater returns (Disyatat and Nakornthab 2003; IMF 2009b).

Finally, we should note the unique form of diversification that has emerged in the Malaysian financial sector in the form of Islamic finance. Assets in the Islamic financial sector more than doubled between 1999 and 2007 and this segment of the market now forms an integral part of the overall Malaysian financial system, operating in parallel with the conventional system. Financial services provided under Islamic principles cover the range of banking, insurance, money market and capital market. Islamic financial assets, financing and deposits now comprise about 15 per cent of the total banking system equivalents (see Table 4.4). This development, largely the result of a government policy initiative, is another element of diversification in the country's financial market that contributes to market competition, especially given the significant foreign participation in this segment. However, given its recent emergence, there have so far been few studies of the actual impact of the growth of Islamic finance on the Malaysian financial system and wider economy. The results of early studies are however not encouraging as they suggested that Islamic banks in Malaysia were less efficient than conventional ones (Mokhtar, Abdullah and Alhabshi 2008), as well as more sensitive to monetary policy shocks (Kassim, Majid and Yusof 2009). Given the relative immaturity of the market, these results are perhaps unsurprising.

To summarise, the financial sectors in all three economies have become more diversified since the Asian financial crisis. However, much of this diversification has been the result of government initiatives and activity. As we noted in the previous empirical chapters, state influence in the diversification of the financial sector is not negligible.

Rise in foreign participation

Increased foreign participation in the financial sectors of East Asia was seen as a desirable development on two grounds (Levine 1996; Mathieson and Roldos 2001). First, foreign actors were expected to help modernise the financial sector through the introduction of better systems, managerial expertise, best practices and new products and services. Second, increasing foreign participation would lead to greater market dynamics while simultaneously reducing the influence of the state.

In the period since the Asian financial crisis of 1997–8, foreign participation has increased in the financial sectors of Korea, Malaysia and Thailand. On one level, this was inevitable. Given the devastation wrecked by the crisis on domestic economies, in particular in Korea and Thailand, foreign actors were, apart from their respective governments, a major source of capital to fund the restructuring and recapitalisation of domestic financial institutions. Thus, in both Korea and Thailand, most of the change in ownership took place in the period immediately following the crisis. The exception to this is Malaysia where the effect of the crisis was more modest and therefore the need for recapitalisation lower. Nevertheless, even in Malaysia, the level of foreign participation in the financial sector has also increased in the last decade although for different reasons as I shall discuss shortly.

In Korea, foreigners' total share in commercial banks has risen from 12.3 per cent in 1998 to more than 70 per cent in 2006 (Kang 2009b). Foreigners' share of every bank except Woori Bank and Jeonbuk Bank was over 50 per cent as of February 2007 (Kim and Lee 2008). Considering the miniscule equity stakes held by foreigners in the period before the crisis, this is significant. In the Korea Stock Exchange, the share of foreign investors in Korean capital markets, when measured by trading value, has also increased substantially in the post-crisis period from 5.2 per cent in 1999 to 26.9 per cent in 2008 (see Figure 3.2). Foreign-ownership and participation have also similarly increased in the Thai banking sector. The need to recapitalise several former domestic commercial banks has resulted in 'hybrid' banks that have large domestic-networks but are foreign-owned. This is in contrast to the period before the crisis when banks with large domestic networks were all domestically owned. Even among the remaining nominally Thai private banks, foreign ownership has also increased significantly (Nakornthab 2007, Table 1). This development, together with the increased state-ownership as a result of the recapitalisation of Thai banks, meant that only 9 out of 29 commercial banks in Thailand remain privately owned by Thais, compared to 14 out of 15 before the crisis (Nakornthab 2007). The

Sino-Thai banking families presence in the banking sector has consequently been significantly reduced (Hewison 2001a; Wailerdsak 2008).

The change in foreign participation in Malaysia in the last decade has not been as stark as in Korea and Thailand but it is nonetheless notable. The number of foreign commercial banks and their share of total assets have remained roughly the same (see Table 4.3). However, restrictions on foreign participation have been considerably liberalised in the capital market and significantly greater participation has been observed in the new market segment of Islamic finance. Ownership restrictions have been lifted in the former and are relatively liberal in the latter. Full ownership is now permitted in a range of financial institutions across the capital market and Islamic finance, though crucially not in conventional commercial banking although this began to change in 2009 when the government committed to issuing up to five new commercial banking licences in the 'conventional' sector subject to certain criterion. This is in addition to the three new Islamic banking licences that have been issued since 2004 with two more Islamic banking licences announced in 2009. All this stands in stark contrast to the previous freeze on new banking licences since 1973 and is the result of two primary factors: first, the government's commitment to liberalise the financial sector in international agreements; and second, the government's desire to promote the development of sub-sectors within the financial system such as investment banking and Islamic finance. As foreign participation in the Malaysian financial sector had already been significant, in terms of market share, even before the crisis, changes in foreign liberalisation have generally been incremental in the last decade and is largely the result of selective and targeted measures.

What have been the effects of increased foreign participation in these financial sectors? With the limited and selective changes in foreign participation in Malaysia in the last decade, the authorities have been able to manage, and to an extent harness, the effects of foreign liberalisation. For instance, the relatively extensive foreign liberalisation in the Islamic financial sector has contributed to its rapid expansion and internationalisation in contrast with the continued restrictions placed in the 'conventional' banking sector. The selective and controlled approach to liberalisation in Malaysia helps to mitigate the potential negative repercussions of market liberalisation. In Thailand, the entry of foreign banks appeared to have contributed to the improvement in cost efficiency of domestic banks (Chantapong and Menkhoff 2005), while the effects of foreign liberalisation appear to have been more mixed in Korea. Although the presence of foreign banks has contributed to greater cost efficiency on the part of private domestic banks in Korea, there is no evidence to suggest that foreign bank entry has improved local banks' profits (H E Kim and B-Y Lee 2004). This may be the result of greater competition leading to declining margins. It is also plausible that domestic banks have had to deal with less creditworthy customers as foreign banks tended to 'cherry-pick' their clients. Of more concern to observers of the Korean economy is the increasing 'separation' of finance from real productive activities as commercial banks shift their focus from corporate lending to retail banking, a trend led largely by foreign-owned banks (Ahn, Hahm and Kim 2008; Kang 2009b).

Regulation and supervision

During the debates about the Asian financial crisis, some observers such as Frederic Mishkin (2001), Professor of Banking and Financial Institutions at the Columbia Business School, argued that the introduction and adoption of internationally recognised financial standards and codes would help eradicate excessive state intervention of a discretionary kind that created problems of moral hazard and chronic regulatory failure, while simultaneously propelling the Asian financial sectors into becoming more like the LME ideal type. How have the economies in this study responded on this score in the last decade?

In Korea, the previously fragmented regulatory structure has now been considerably streamlined with the introduction of new legislation at the end of 1997 to consolidate supervisory authority into the Financial Supervisory Commission (later morphed into the Financial Services Commission) that was empowered to oversee effectively all financial institutions. In Thailand, consolidated supervision of all types of financial institutions under the purview of the BOT was made possible when the new *Bank of Thailand Act* was finally approved by Parliament in 2007 although the capital market is still overseen by the Securities and Exchange Commission. Supervision in Malaysia is also split between the central bank and the Securities Commission with the power of the latter strengthened post-crisis with revisions to the *Securities Commission Act*. While there are both advantages and disadvantages to different models of regulatory structures, the recent trend towards the consolidation of financial institutions and their activities; the increasingly blurred distinctions between different types of financial services; and the growing links between market segments and products suggest that consolidated supervision might be the better option to mitigate regulatory arbitrage and oversee systemic risks.[5]

[5] For a more detailed discussion, see Ghosh (2006, p.170 ff).

All three economies have gradually moved towards instituting regulations that are principle-based, as opposed to rule-based, and more sensitive to market developments following the current global norm. New forward-looking risk management mechanisms were introduced in all three economies, with prompt corrective action systems put in place. All three economies have also adopted the Basel II framework although Thailand lags behind having only introduced the system in late-2007 whereas both Korean and Malaysian banks have been 'more enthusiastic' with preparations made much earlier (Parreñas 2006). In fact, the Basel I framework was already adopted in Malaysia in 1989, well before the 1997 crisis reflective of the country's better and stronger regulatory framework (Hamilton-Hart 2002; Zamani 2006, p.269); while in Korea, the BIS capital ratios were adopted only for guidance purposes in 1992, becoming mandatory at the end of 1995. All three economies now have formal disclosure policies for banks and audit standards are required to materially conform to the International Standards on Auditing with compulsory external audit exercises of their financial statements and accounts. Corporate governance codes have also been introduced in all three countries in an attempt to instil better practices in the banking institutions, and the corporate sector more generally.

While these developments help to instil and strengthen a more market-sensitive or -oriented approach of regulation, the level of public disclosure of risk exposure is uneven and this prevents effective market monitoring.[6] A detailed survey of risk-management practices revealed that while most banks in all three countries have formal disclosure policies, with banks in Malaysia being the most compliant, they differ in terms of their levels and frequency of disclosure (Parreñas 2006). Malaysian banks appeared to fare better in their levels of disclosure of market and credit risks, while Korean and Thai banks demonstrated low levels of disclosure. Thai banks however scored relatively higher in the *frequency* of public disclosures, that is how often information is disclosed as opposed to the substance of the disclosure, as compared with their Korean and Malaysian counterparts. Banks in all three countries however have performed well in the disclosure of balance sheet items (see Ghosh 2006, Table 3.2).

---

[6] Although it appears that even with the availability of more information on the quality of governance, market actors may not use it for decisions on investment, see Walter (2008, pp.174–6).

While Korea, Malaysia and Thailand may be in the process of moving towards more significant *formal* adoption of international 'best practices', it is difficult to assess whether the authorities and market actors in these economies are actually complying with the *substance* of these practices. Andrew Walter (2007, p.41) differentiated between 'implementation' and 'compliance' where the latter occurs 'when countries' actual behaviour conforms to the prescriptions of a specific rule or standard' and a gap between implementation and compliance arises when actors behave in ways that are inconsistent with implemented regulations or when domestic enforcement is weak. Plummer and Trivellato (2001, p.97) made a similar distinction between policy convergence and 'real' convergence. In the cases of Korea, Malaysia and Thailand, there are reasons to suspect that this gap between implementation and compliance, or policy and 'real' convergence, is significant, leading us to doubt that market norms have taken root following the adoption of the international standards and codes.[7]

First, although all three countries have adopted the Basel Core Principles and now have reported capital adequacy ratios that exceed the minimum 8 per cent requirement, these ratios are not comparable across countries and do not necessarily reflect the 'true' strength of the banking sectors as a result of differences in country classification of debt and loan accounting standards. Thailand, for instance, has a less conservative standard for reclassifying and upgrading 'sub-standard' debt than the United States, thus masking potential problems behind the appearance of meeting Basel capital adequacy ratios (Walter 2007, p.53). Similarly, a liberal approach to the valuation of collateral in Thailand means that banks make lower provisions against NPLs.

Second, the rapid rise of consumer credit in the period after the crisis and the consequent destabilisation of financial systems in Korea and Thailand in 2002–3 and 2002 respectively raise questions as to the ability of the respective regulators to monitor and enforce prudential regulation. While the shift in the banks' focus from corporate lending to consumer credit might be welcome from one perspective given the role of 'connected lending' in the crisis, this new segment of business has also brought with it new market risks. However, this was not just a matter of 'sins of omission' by regulators and supervisors, as 'sins of commission' were also important as both the Korean and Thai

[7] For a longer and more detailed discussion, see Walter (2007).

governments had encouraged the proliferation of credit card usage and other forms of consumer credit (Ghosh 2006, Box 4.1).

Third, until recently, the BOT did not have the legal power to take prompt corrective action to address weaknesses in troubled banks, unlike its counterparts in Korea and Malaysia. This changed with the new *Bank of Thailand Act* that was passed in December 2007. Nevertheless, while the legal power to take action is important, so is the capacity to do so. A study on the banking systems in the region indicated that the number of officers in charge of supervising banks varied from 50 in Thailand to 345 in Malaysia (Nam and Lum 2006). Korea had about 180 professional bank supervisors and examiners. This in part explained why regular on-site inspections were much more frequent in Malaysia than in the other countries. Given this varying capacity to monitor banking activity, it is reasonable to question whether regulators, especially those in Thailand, are able to enforce the standards and codes that they have adopted.

Finally, the phenomenon of regulatory forbearance has not altogether disappeared. The Malaysian central bank for instance was unable to enforce limits on individual holdings of bank stocks in 2002 as a result of government policy preferences (Walter 2008, p.104). Politically connected firms and individuals also occasionally find themselves being dispensed from having to comply with regulations in the Malaysian capital market (Walter 2008, p.117). Regulatory forbearance in asset classification and poor enforcement of provisioning rates have also been reported in Korea (IMF 2003a).

To summarise, there are doubts as to whether convergence on liberal market norms is occurring with respect to regulation and supervision. While there has certainly been progress in the adoption and implementation of 'best practices', that is formal implementation, the question of normative or substantive compliance remains open. Some market actors certainly concur with this observation. Moody's evaluation of the financial strength of banks in Korea, Malaysia and Thailand is lower than that given to Australia even though the average capital adequacy ratio in Australia is lower than in Malaysia and Thailand (Moody's Investors Service 2006). A recent study found that while major credit rating agencies have given an improved evaluation to banks in Korea since the crisis, ratings for banks in Malaysia and Thailand have not shown much improvement (Adams 2008, Table 6). On the other hand, share prices of banks in both Korea and Thailand have underperformed their respective markets up until 2005, while the converse was true for banks in Malaysia (Adams 2008, Table 7). The reluctance of Malaysia to submit itself to the IMF's FSAP review process also does not encourage confidence in the progress that might have been made in the regulation and supervision of its financial system.

The observations that have been made in this section should not be surprising. Although international financial institutions and private financial markets were expected to become two of the main mechanisms promoting compliance with 'voluntary' Western-style standards and 'best practices', domestic factors ultimately condition how regulations are adopted and implemented. Whether legislative revisions are made to comply with international 'best practices', sufficient resources are allocated to regulatory authorities, or enforcement is appropriately and uniformly applied are to a large extent the result of the interaction between domestic actors and their institutions. As we saw in an earlier chapter, historical cultural and institutional factors explain the existing concerns over the capacity of the Korean financial regulators to enforce compliance with formally adopted rules and policies, as well as the difficulty encountered in transforming the regulatory culture to comply more with market-driven norms. Although Malaysia fared much better than either Korea or Thailand in terms of compliance with market norms in regulation, variation in enforcement is nevertheless observed when the discriminatory principles embodied in the institutional context of the NEP/NDP came in contact with the relatively more open and rules-based regulatory framework. In Thailand, government ownership of financial institutions and the government's policy to direct credit to selected social groups have created a conflict of interest as well as led to regulatory forbearance on the part of financial regulators and supervisors.

Convergence onto the LME model?

The review thus far suggests that while the banks are still dominant players in the financial sectors of Korea, Malaysia and Thailand, growth in the capital markets of all three economies point to increasing market diversification, and consequently improving market competition in the broader financial sector. The rise in foreign participation in all three economies, in particular in Korea and Thailand, also contributes towards greater market competition and the promotion of international standards and practices. Regulatory institutions and systems have also been updated to conform more closely to current international 'best practices' although there are doubts as to the nature of 'real' compliance. While state ownership of financial institutions has increased in Thailand, it has remained largely the same in Malaysia. In Korea, the state continues to find indirect means of intervening in the operations of financial institutions.

The picture is therefore mixed when we attempt to arrive at a simple conclusion about the nature of institutional change in the financial sectors of these economies. Of the three economies, Korea has clearly moved closer towards a liberal market model from where it first began in the late-1990s as a result of significant foreign liberalisation, growth in the capital markets and an improved regulatory framework. Malaysia, on the other hand, appears to have more of the same mix of state and market features in its financial sector albeit with selective foreign liberalisation and the persistence of what was already a very large equity market even before the crisis. The most significant changes in the Malaysian financial sector since the crisis have been the growth of the bond market and the emergence of Islamic finance and this has undoubtedly been welcome developments from a liberal market model perspective in terms of its contribution towards market diversity and competitive dynamics, although the state's significant role in these developments run counter to the LME ideal type. The situation in Thailand is somewhat more ambiguous. While there has been observed diversification in the financial sector, greater foreign participation in the banking sector, and improvement in its regulatory framework, state ownership and influence have also increased substantially from its previous relatively more hands-off approach.

Thus, whether the financial sectors of Korea, Malaysia and Thailand have acquired greater characteristics of the LME model in the decade since the Asian financial crisis, the short answers on the basis of the previous discussion appear to be 'yes', 'not really' and 'difficult to conclude' respectively. However, as I noted in this discussion and in the previous chapters, even as these financial sectors began to adopt greater aspects of a liberal market model, state intervention and influence have not been far. The state in each country continued to shape and influence the evolution of their financial sectors in ways that went beyond merely enhancing the market, and as such, these economies cannot be considered to be in the process of conforming to the LME ideal type. If anything, they still reflect significant aspects of the SiME ideal type. I discuss more systematically how the state still influences the financial sectors of these economies in the following section.

The state still influences?

Drawing on the detailed accounts of developments in the financial sectors of Korea, Malaysia and Thailand in the previous chapters, I set out in this section how the state still influences, if not intervenes, in the financial sectors of these three economies. While it is debatable whether the 'developmental state' exists or still exists, at least as it is understood in the literature as a coordinated socio-institutional arrangement having positive economic growth-enhancing effects, there is no doubt, as the case study chapters have demonstrated, that the state still significantly shapes and influences the way that the financial sector evolves as well as the way in which it functions. The nature of state influence in the financial sectors of these economies as recounted in detail in the preceding chapters can be conceptually differentiated into three categories: shaping the nature of the market, directing the path of development and responding to demands of specific interest groups. These forms of state influence, if not interference, were made evident when we analysed state action in key issue areas using the framework of the three P's: policy, 'polity', and politics. This section lays out more systematically the different types of state influence, drawing on material already presented in the previous chapters.

Shaping the market

In all three economies, the state has attempted to shape the market by creating new sub-sectors within the financial sector. In order to develop the market in a specific fashion or encourage its growth, the state has offered incentives for market actors to act in particular ways. Changes in government policies for the financial sector in the last decade have contributed to changes in market structures. In all cases, state action has contributed to a change in the nature of the market, in terms of size, competition, diversification and ownership structures. State action has therefore shaped the market, for better or worse.

For instance, in all three economies, new forms of legal institutions were made possible in the banking sector. In Korea, 'financial holding companies' were introduced in the midst of resolving the financial crisis in order to facilitate the consolidation of unviable financial institutions. This led to a significant reduction in the number of institutions as well as the emergence of large, consolidated banks or financial groups under the holding company structure. In Malaysia, the central bank initially corralled the financial industry to consolidate the commercial banks, finance companies and merchant banks around an 'anchor bank' before introducing legislative changes in 2003 that brought in a new entity called the 'Banking and Finance Company' or Bafin to facilitate further consolidation. By the end of 2005, when all domestic banking groups completed their rationalisation exercises, finance companies ceased to exist as a category in the Malaysian financial system. Similarly in Thailand, the licensing of financial institutions was rationalised into only four different types, two each for domestic and foreign institutions. A 'one presence' policy was also introduced to eliminate the duplication of functions as well as regulatory arbitrage. This contributed to the reduction in the number of financial institutions in Thailand from 83 in 2003 to 44 in 2005 and IBF licensees, the weak link in the Thai financial system prior to the 1997–8 crisis, disappeared altogether. The market consolidation resulting from these state-induced exercises in all three financial sectors has potentially reduced market competition as well as increased the relevance of the 'too big to fail' argument, as noted earlier in this chapter.

While the process of institutional consolidation might have impaired competitive dynamics in the market, changes in state policy in the last decade have also had clearer positive effects on competition in the market. In Korea, permission was granted to financial investment companies (FICs) to participate in retail payment and settlement services, once the preserve only of banks. This gave the FICs access to new customers and enabled former brokerages and securities firms to compete with banks in attracting deposits. In the commercial banking sector of Malaysia, greater competitive dynamics were generated through selective market liberalisation. After over two decades of tight restrictions, existing foreign commercial banks were given permission to open new branches, albeit with conditions imposed on the areas in which the new branches could be established. While new licences for financial institutions were issued to foreigners in Malaysia, they were limited to certain types of activities, largely in areas where domestic incumbents were few and only emergent. Nevertheless, these changes were a welcome improvement after decades of restrictive policies. In all three economies, government liberalisation of the range of activities that market players could undertake, and fiscal incentives offered to market actors, contributed to the expansion of market segments and the improvement of market dynamics, in particular in the capital market (as detailed in the individual case study chapters).

However, state policies and action, or the lack thereof, also had less benign effects. The Thai authorities tolerated the proliferation of non-deposit taking financial intermediaries in the early-2000s because they offered consumer credit services to low income groups and provided additional competition to the banking sector. The rapid growth of such credit however undermined systemic risk and stability, and the central bank had to react by introducing additional regulations. Similarly in Korea, the government deregulated cardholder requirements and card issuing processes and provided tax benefits for card users in order to encourage the expansion of consumer credit. The Korean government had hoped that this would help boost economic activity, which it did, but it also led to a consumer credit bubble and insolvencies among credit card companies in early 2003.

The state still developmental?

Discussions on the developmental nature of East Asian economies tend to see the phenomenon in a holistic manner, in that both public and private actors were either tacitly or explicitly parties to a 'social contract' that involved a distribution of labour, or coordinated activity, to achieve the primary objectives of economic growth and development.[8] For instance, the World Bank's *East Asian Miracle* report described the East Asian development model as a 'functional growth framework'. Robert Wade (2004) used the notion of a 'governed market', while Linda Weiss (1998) thought of the phenomenon as 'governed interdependence'. Underlying these various concepts is an understanding of a complex interaction of macroeconomic policies and 'micro' foundations or supporting institutions, exhibiting pervasive state intervention, which girded the Asian development process and explains their success (Amsden 1994; Yusuf 2001). Hence the frequent use of the term 'developmental states' to refer to the East Asian 'miracle' economies, although it is frequently recognised that they can be grouped into two variants – one comprising the Northeast Asian economies of Japan, Korea and Taiwan; and one the Southeast Asian economies of Indonesia, Malaysia, Thailand and perhaps the Philippines where economic achievement in the Southeast Asian economies has been inferior when compared to their Northeastern neighbours.

In this discussion on the nature of state influence in the post-crisis period, I wish to make a distinction between a 'developmental state' and state policies that have a 'developmental' aspect. With the latter, I refer to policies that are intended to contribute to and direct the growth

---

[8] Peter Evans (1998) attempted to extract the key elements of the East Asian developmental states as lessons for other countries.

of, or upgrade, aspects of the society or economy without prejudging the outcomes of such policies. Referring to similar phenomena, Dani Rodrik (2007, p.100) employs the term 'industrial policy' which he defined as 'restructuring policies in favour of more dynamic activities'. The distinction I make between a state policy being 'developmental' and a 'developmental state' is that the former does not necessarily have to, although it could, reside within a holistic 'framework' or form part of a 'governed market'. Thus, when I use the term 'developmental' in this discussion, I do so in a broader and looser sense than the manner in which it is employed in the literature on the 'developmental state'. I use the term here as more an adjective of the noun 'development' rather than as a socio-scientific concept that carries with it a broader set of ideas and arguments, although admittedly the distinction is relative rather than absolute.[9]

With this in mind, one of the ways in which the state in Korea, Malaysia and Thailand has influenced the financial sector post-crisis is through policies that have been developmental in that the respective governments have attempted to enhance the nature of their respective financial sectors by influencing the direction of its evolution or expediting the rate of its growth. They have attempted to do so by proposing and implementing strategies for development as well as supporting their intentions with material resources. Following the financial crisis in 1997–8, the governments in all three economies adopted various strategic 'master' plans to further develop their respective financial sectors. Korea, for instance, introduced a Financial Hub Strategy at the end of 2003 as part of a broader plan to shape Korea into a major business centre for Northeast Asia. Malaysia had two ten-year financial sector and capital market master plans designed to strengthen the domestic financial system in the face of external pressures for greater liberalisation and economic competitiveness. For Thailand, it was the desire to improve access to financial services for a wider segment of the population that formed the foundation for its financial sector master plan. A similar motivation to develop basic infrastructural issues underlined the Thai capital market master plan.

---

[9] I should note that unlike the conventional use of the term 'developmental states', I am not suggesting that the use of 'developmental' policies are restricted only to East Asian states, or developing countries more generally. Industrialised countries also adopt such policies even if they choose not to use the term 'development', see Weiss (2005); Block (2008).

In all three economies, the master plans were developed amid challenging economic conditions. Poor returns on deposit investments and the shortage of credit, as banks were more cautious in their lending, led many in Thailand to turn to the capital market. In Malaysia, the capital market master plan was meant to address the lacklustre activity that had not returned to the levels that were in the market prior to the crisis. The master plans in Malaysia were also responses to the 'crisis of confidence' that resulted from the imposition of capital controls during the financial crisis. In Korea, the financial hub strategy identified the financial sector as an alternative source of economic growth in the face of the then poor performance of the manufacturing industry. Malaysia too viewed the financial sector as an alternative route to economic development in its own right, in particular with the Islamic finance sector.

The strategies for the financial sectors are developmental in that they were viewed as critical contributions to general economic growth. For Korea and Malaysia, financial services were seen as new sources of potential export earnings and specialisations within the financial sector were identified to serve this goal: Korea aspired to be an asset management centre and Malaysia focussed on Islamic finance. Although the Thai master plans harboured no ambitious goal of becoming a regional or global financial centre, nor did it really strive to improve the competitiveness of the Thai financial sector at the global level, it nevertheless strove to address sectoral weaknesses; improve the market dynamics of the financial system; and address an identified gap in the demand for financial services among low-income groups and the SME sector. In this limited sense, it is also an effort at market development.[10] A key strategy adopted by the Thai authorities was the consolidation of the banking sector in order to lift the game of industry players, a strategy that was similarly employed by both Korea and Malaysia. The imposition of consolidation in all three economies was seen as a way of developing capacity, efficiency and market stability. In Korea, the introduction of such developmental policies marked a form of influence, if not interference, in the financial sector that was different from the past, in that the financial sector is now viewed as an instrument for economic growth in its own right rather than just as a hand-maiden to the real sector.

---

[10] Developmental policies in Thailand in the post-crisis period were stronger in the food, fashion, automobiles, tourism, computer graphics, medical care and logistics sectors that the Thaksin government sought to nurture and promote as sources of export earnings.

Of course, intent alone does not lead to outcome, let alone success. Many governments make various claims about their intent but nevertheless fail in their endeavour. However, to define 'developmental policies' by their outcome is also problematic as it falls perilously close to a tautological exercise, as has sometimes been the case with the 'developmental state' literature: only those governments that are successful in enforcing their visions of development are 'developmental' whereas those that are less successful or fail are considered 'ersatz capitalism' or non-'developmental states', and by implication employed no 'developmental' policies.[11] One way around this circular logic would be to look at the resources directed at implementing stated goals without prejudging the outcome of state action and to consider state policies that demonstrate 'commitment' in this form as 'developmental'.[12]

In all three countries, public funds were employed to develop aspects of their financial sectors. The Korea Investment Corporation (KIC) was established in July 2005 with an initial fund of about USD20 billion to act as a catalyst for growth in the capital market industry and help realise the vision of a financial hub more quickly. The Thai government established the Thai Opportunity Fund in 2002 and Equity Thailand Fund in 2001 with a total of about THB40 billion, representing about 10 per cent of the value of total outstanding securities in the capital market at the time, to achieve similar objectives. Malaysia also made use of public funds to support the capital market, although ethnic-political considerations were an important part of the process. In all three economies, governments committed to regularly issue a variety of bonds, even though there was no fiscal need to do so, in order to facilitate the establishment of benchmark yields and the development of the bond market.

Governments did not just pour money into the markets to realise their developmental goals but they also made legislative changes to facilitate the development of their financial sectors. Malaysia's *Banking and Financial Institutions Act 1989* was amended in 2003 to introduce a new legal entity, the 'Banking and Finance Company' or 'Bafin', to

[11] For instance, in discussing the 'developmental state', Clapham (1996) argued that an autonomous and powerful state alone is not enough but that it is also important for 'developmental' states to do the 'right thing' with a commitment to an 'appropriate' division of labour between the state and market institutions.

[12] One could of course debate the quantity and quality or resources devoted to developmental projects in demonstrating 'commitment'.

enable further consolidation to take place within the banking groups. The cornerstone of the Korean government's vision of establishing a financial hub came in the form of the new *Financial Investment Services and Capital Market Act* (FISCMA) that introduced greater liberalisation in the market and changed the regulatory and supervisory structures and systems. Thailand amended their *Bank of Thailand Act* and introduced a new *Financial Institutions Business Act* in 2007 that accorded greater independence to the central bank, strengthened its supervisory powers and liberalised various aspects of the financial sector.

In at least the Korean and Malaysian cases, these various measures amounted to more than just mere market liberalisation as they also embodied a developmental dimension. In creating markets and promoting market activity, government policies and actions did not just enhance the market but were also influential in shaping or directing the nature of the evolution of the financial system by directing attention and initiatives to selected aspects and dimensions of the system. The governments also hastened the growth and expansion of the financial sector through the use of various fiscal incentives and the liberalisation of policies. This is most clear in the Malaysian case. Although the Malaysian authorities were committed to further liberalising the financial sector to foreign participation, this was done in both a selective and controlled manner seen to be consistent with policy makers' developmental goals. Foreign liberalisation was targeted and took place in sub-sectors in which the state believed it could leverage on foreign expertise to contribute to the development of nascent segments of the financial sector. Admittedly, private domestic interests rendered foreign liberalisation measures more difficult in the established segments of the market, however even in the well-established conventional commercial banking sector, foreign liberalisation took place albeit circumscribed by criterion that would channel foreign banks into underserved areas. In Islamic finance, the state promoted exponential growth through aggressive liberalisation measures and by courting international organisations to issue Islamic bonds in the Malaysian market. As discussed in an earlier chapter, the government of Korea has taken similarly developmental approaches to the capital market, in particular in investment banking. The case of Thailand is somewhat more circumspect with the stated aims of the master plans being more modest. This is attributable to the less developed nature of the Thai financial system; and to the country's earlier experience with developing an international banking facility that was perceived to have contributed to financial instability leading to the crisis.

State capture

While the positive effects of state influence and intervention in the economy is highly contested, as any cursory survey of the literature on the East Asian 'developmental states' will attest, few would dispute the potential negative outcomes – in the form of corruption, cronyism and patronage – of state interference. These features, that is the phenomenon of state capture, also persisted in the economies that are the focus of this study in the decade since the crisis.

In Korea, the modus operandi of the FSC did not make a complete break from the administrative procedures and organisational culture of preceding agencies and a great deal of discretion still constituted a significant part of the FSC's regulatory operations. There were questions as to the opaque way in which some regulations have been introduced and interpreted (IMF 2003a). There was also a perception in the market that violations of applicable regulations were often overlooked or weakly sanctioned while officials may interpret and apply regulations more strictly for foreign firms (Klingner 2006). The IMF also voiced concern over the regulator's ability to keep abreast of the role of connected lending and cross ownership (IMF 2003a). Regulatory forbearance also persisted in that asset classification was, at times, not implemented properly while provisioning rates were low and non-bank deposit taking institutions seemed inadequately supervised. Foreign financial services suppliers also remain concerned about the systemic problem of administrative guidance and were put off by the requirement to submit what they considered to be an excessive amount of documentation to the regulators (Y-m Kim 2008). Kim and Lee (2004) argued that reforms that had been undertaken were mostly in formal institutions of financial supervision while 'informal institutions', such as supervisory culture, had barely changed.

In Malaysia, two institutions that were set up during the crisis to resolve NPLs and recapitalise financial institutions, Danaharta and Danamodal, were actively used as vehicles to secure discreet bailout arrangements (Hilley 2001), in particular of individuals who were recipients of state largesse in the late-1980s and early-1990s when the government was actively promoting the rise of *bumiputera* 'enterpreneurs' (Gomez and Jomo 1999, Chapters 4 and 5). The use of political connection for private gains appears to persist in the period post-crisis as exemplified by the case of the son-in-law of the then Prime Minister who was appointed a director of a boutique investment bank in July 2004, and then subsequently given the opportunity in December 2005 to acquire a stake in the bank at what was perceived to be a rather favourable price (for details, see the chapter on Malaysia). The post-crisis period also saw capture of the policy making process in Malaysia when the exercise of financial sector consolidation, initiated by the central bank, was modified in response to ethnic and political concerns. The then Prime Minister, Mahathir, had to interject and address some of these claims by modifying aspects of the policy before consolidation could proceed. Similarly, when the Malaysian government modified the ethnically biased listing requirement for the stock market in June 2009, it also created an investment fund with public money tasked with nurturing *bumiputera* business individuals, precisely the ethnic group that would be disadvantaged by the change in listing requirements.

Similar forms of state capture were also observed in Thailand. The rise to power of Thaksin Shinawatra brought with it increased availability of credit to low-income groups as well as SMEs to which state finance institutions were put to task, including two new ones established for this very purpose. While there might well be an economic rationale for these policies, it was also designed to shore up popular political support for Thaksin. Politics was also significant in complicating and delaying the restructuring of troubled financial institutions during the crisis. Public funds were injected into institutions with close ties to politicians in the ruling coalition; state-owned institutions were used to buy low-quality assets rather than sell them to foreigners at 'bargain basement' prices; and the resolution of NPLs was protracted reflecting the close ties of not just the financial institutions but also the indebted family-owned corporations with the Thai political system (see chapter on Thailand for details).

The persistence of state capture by special interest groups, in particular by business groups, in all three economies can in large part be explained by the institutional setting of local politics and policy making, that is 'polity'. Political clientelism has long existed in Thai politics, as noted in our historical review of the evolution of the Thai financial sector in Chapter 5. During the era of military rule, the owners of large local banks invested in their relationships with military leaders in return for protection of their business interests (Crone 1988; Overholt 1999). The cultivation of links between the business sector and politicians became more prevalent with increasing democratisation in the 1990s as politicians needed to fund campaigns and bankroll support; while owners of private businesses sought to influence the policy making process to promote specific interests (Handley 1997; Phongpaichit and Baker 1998b, Chapter 10).

In Malaysia, the racial dimension of policy making has been institutionalised since the introduction of the New Economic Policy (NEP) in 1970. While there were arguably legitimate social and economic justifications for the discriminatory policies introduced under the NEP, its implementation over the course of time has been criticised for favouring selected individuals rather than the targeted social group for which the policies were designed (Gomez and Jomo 1999). This derogation from a more rules-based approach became particularly prevalent when Mahathir, as Prime Minister, decided to promote specific *bumiputera* entrepreneurs in the late-1980s and early-1990s as a strategy to expedite the achievement of NEP goals, or at least the spirit thereof. Since then, patronage politics has become a significant feature of the Malaysian political system that coloured policy formulation and implementation.

Although Korea is usually held up as a prime example of a 'developmental state' that successfully harnessed domestic resources in the promotion of economic growth, it was also not immune to corruption or rent seeking. As David Kang (2002) persuasively demonstrated, since the beginning of Korea's developmental trajectory in the 1960s under the regime of Park Chung Hee, decisions concerning bailouts, loans and the benefits of policy have been influenced by personal connections rather than just economic merit. Corruption however did not spin out of control as the competitors for rents, that is the *chaebol*, were both small in number and yet large in size, so their relationship with the state evolved into a 'mutual hostage' situation.

Despite these long-standing rent seeking and corrupt behaviour, economic growth in all three economies has been widely acknowledged to have been impressive, not least in the World Bank's *East Asian Miracle* report. While the capture of the policy making and implementation processes might not yield positive benefits to the economy, they are not necessarily incompatible with economic growth. The latter refers to the absolute measurement of a societal-wide effect, whereas the former relates to how the benefits derived from economic growth is to be distributed within society. Kang (2002) argued that corruption was partially a function of economic growth in that rapid increases in wealth facilitate the exploitation of superior access to information, personal connections and influence. The converse, that economic growth is partially a function of corruption can also be true. In Malaysia, the widening circle of individuals seeking rents in the country's politics of patronage served as a further incentive for politicians to ensure continuing economic growth in order to avoid the limits and constraints posed by the policies on economic distribution. While rent seeking and corruption can have negative consequences, such as reducing the efficiency and effectiveness of economic policies, the most averse effects of such behaviour were kept at bay in all three economies through institutional arrangements. Competent bureaucrats and technocrats were given sufficient autonomy to manage the economy, albeit with different degrees of success in different issue areas relative to the varying degrees of penetration by interest groups, as well as the capability of staffing, with Korea historically performing the best among the three on this score.

In summary, this discussion of the state's influence and interference in the financial sectors of all three economies in the last decade suggests that despite the significant structural changes enumerated earlier, we should be cautious in drawing conclusions about the nature of these changes. We cannot unequivocally conclude that the financial sectors of all three economies have been moving towards the ideal type of the liberal market model, with the exception of perhaps Korea. Even then, the changes in the financial sector of Korea have not materialised as we would expect from the perspective of a liberal market model, as it is generally understood in its ideal typical form, given that the state still maintains a significant role in influencing, if not interfering, in the nature of its evolution and operation. Changes in the financial sectors of Korea, Malaysia and Thailand in the last decade appear to have been more evolutionary rather than revolutionary, and as such, the financial sectors have become, at best, more hybrid systems in which there are elements of SiMEs 'layered' over elements of LMEs, or vice versa.

Epilogue: the East Asian financial sectors and the global financial crisis

Thus far, we have looked at the financial sectors of Korea, Malaysia and Thailand from the perspective of 1997–8 and analysed how they have evolved as well as explained some of the key changes. In closing this book, it is perhaps useful to also take a brief look at the financial sectors from the perspective of 2011 and ask how the changes that we have seen in this book have affected or influenced the experience of these economies through the more recent global financial crisis (GFC) of 2007–9.

As it is now widely known, the GFC had its genesis in the sub-prime mortgage business in the US, in which banks extended loans to individuals who were unable to qualify under traditional, more stringent criteria due to limited or poor credit histories. When interest rates rose in the US from 1 per cent in 2004 to 5.35 per cent in 2006, mortgage defaults began to emerge in the sub-prime market carrying with it global repercussions due to a phenomenon in the financial markets called 'securitisation' that was designed to spread risks in the market and which linked the American financial market with global ones (Rajan 2005).

The global dimension of the crisis became apparent in August 2007 when investors in the French investment bank, BNP Paribas, were informed that they would not be able to withdraw from two of its funds as a result of vanishing liquidity in the market. Soon after, governments in Europe and the US began to nationalise or take significant equity stakes in key financial institutions in order to prevent large-scale market failures. The first of these was Northern Rock in the UK, a financial institution that had earlier relied heavily on the markets, rather than savers' deposits, to fund its mortgage lending. When National Rock's sources of funding dried up in February 2008, it was nationalised by the British government. In September 2008, global attention turned to Fannie Mae and Freddie Mac, which together accounted for nearly half of the outstanding mortgages in the US. They were rescued by the US government in one of the largest bailouts in US history. Shortly after, the US Federal Reserve announced an USD85 billion rescue package for AIG, the country's biggest insurance company, in return for an 80 per cent stake in the firm. Other institutions that were (partly) nationalised included Europe's Fortis, the UK's Bradford & Bingley and the Icelandic Glitnir. Not all financial institutions were saved by their governments as some were 'allowed' to fail and close, the most spectacular of which were Lehman Brothers and Washington Mutual. The cost of this series of financial collapse has been astounding. It was estimated that US taxpayers would bear upwards of USD23.7 trillion to bolster the economy and bail out financial companies – in comparison, US GDP in 2007 was just over USD14 trillion (Kopecki and Dodge 2009). In the UK, support for the banking system had risen to GBP1.4 trillion by July 2009, about half of annual GDP (MacAskill 2009). In Iceland, where the economy was very dependent on the financial sector, the government had to turn to the IMF for a USD2.1 billion loan when its banking system virtually collapsed.

By late-2008, it became clear that the US economy was on the verge of a recession and slow growth, a development that was also expected in a number of European economies. Comparisons of the economic affects of the GFC with those of the Great Depression of the 1930s were made. The integration of global trade and financial links suggested that the repercussions would spread further afield, including Asia. There were general concerns in the more open economies about their financial sectors' exposure to the mortgage-backed financial derivatives that had lost value in the course of the crisis. However, as it became clearer that financial markets in East Asia had minimal exposure, they were spared the worst of the economic fallout. In Thailand, for example, banks held collateralised debt obligations (CDOs) representing just 0.04 per cent of their balance sheets (Filardo et al. 2010). Kawai et al. (2008) calculated that subprime losses amounted to 1.0 per cent, 0.5 per cent and 0.3 per cent for China, Korea and Malaysia respectively. The IMF (2009a) estimated that Asia's (excluding Japan) exposure to subprime and related assets to be at 5 to 10 per cent of bank capital.

The fortunes of the East Asian economies however changed in mid-September 2008 when Lehman Brothers went bankrupt and AIG had to be rescued triggering a global crisis of market confidence. Risk appetites began to collapse and emerging markets suffered the consequence of a 'flight to quality' that had no necessary correspondence to any economic 'fundamentals'. According to a study written by staff at the BIS Representative Office for Asia and the Pacific (Filardo et al. 2010), portfolio outflows in the region were largest in Korea and New Zealand, which have liquid and open equity markets, and Malaysia, which has a large domestic bond market with significant foreign participation. More than USD50 billion of investment left the Korean market in 2008, although outflows of portfolio investment and FDI had already begun in 2005 in 2006 respectively (Kang 2009a). Similarly in Malaysia, portfolio flows recorded a net outflow of MYR84.4 billion in 2008, in contrast with a net inflow of MYR18.4 billion in 2007 (Goh and Lim 2010). Although this massive withdrawal occurred in every type of foreign investment, the decline in net private capital flows in emerging Asia's economies was driven primarily by private portfolio flows (Goldstein and Xie 2009). The rapid outflow of portfolio investments and the fall in investor confidence sent stock markets down across the region (see Table 6.7). It also became very costly, if not impossible, for Asian borrowers to access international capital markets as foreign banks chose to scale back lending to the region (Filardo et al. 2010). These outflows were mirrored in the movement of external reserves as well as exchange rates. Currencies tumbled against the US dollar, with the Korean won falling the most among currencies in the region (see Table 6.7).

The outflow of capital from the East Asian financial markets was one of two key channels through which the GFC had significant impact on the East Asian economies, the other being the trade channel. As the

Table 6.7 Comparing the impact of the Asian and global financial crises

	Exchange Rate Changes (in %)		**Stock Market Changes (in %)**		**Changes in GDP Growth (in percentage points)**	
	AFC	**GFC**	**AFC**	**GFC**	**AFC**	**GFC**
China	0	12	–12	–71	–3.5	–6.5
Japan	–21	36	–35	–58	–4.6	–11
Indonesia	–83	–24	–62	–55	–23.5	–2.2
Korea	–47	–37	–60	–49	–14.1	–9.9
Malaysia	–43	–14	–72	–40	–19.6	–13.6
Philippines	–40	–17	–58	–51	–8.4	–7.9
Singapore	–19	–11	–56	–58	–13.6	–19.6
Thailand	–53	–12	–68	–56	–13.3	–13.1

Source: Filardo et al. 2010, Table I.2.

American and European economies slowed down, demand for Asian exports also fell, in particular for consumer electronics, IT hardware and automobiles (Guimaraes-Filho et al. 2008; Grimes 2009). The contraction of Asian exports was swift and sharp, tumbling by about 35 per cent from peak to trough (July 2008 to February 2009), far sharper than the 16 per cent fall experienced during the Asian financial crisis (Heng 2009). Intra-Asian exports fell by 48 per cent against a 29 per cent decline in exports to the US and the EU-15 over the same period. Malaysia was particularly affected given that it is one of the most open economies in the region, at least where trade was concerned. Manufactured products accounted for more than 80 per cent of the country's total gross exports, of which more than 65 per cent were electronics and electrical components (Goh and Lim 2010). Furthermore, Malaysia's exports were heavily reliant on the US and EU markets. Exports from Malaysia fell 28 per cent year-on-year in January 2009, the biggest decline experienced since 1982.

While the East Asian economies did not escape the impact of the GFC, they weathered this much better than they did during the crisis 1997–8. On the whole, even though economic growth decelerated, the crisis did not cause an overall decline in GDP in East Asia (Chhibber, Ghosh and Palanivel 2009). The five Asian emerging economies most affected during the Asia financial crisis of 1997–8 (Indonesia, Korea, Malaysia, the Philippines and Thailand) had growth declines in 2008–9 that were about half as large as those encountered during the earlier crisis (Goldstein and Xie 2009) – see Table 6.7.

A number of factors explain why these economies fared better in 2008–9 than in 1997–8. First, as noted earlier, they had limited exposure to the subprime-related financial derivatives. Most of the East Asian financial sectors were at an early stage of involvement in the overall process of securitisation and there was little pressure to search for higher yields due to the continued profitability of bank lending. Second, their dependence on foreign borrowing has declined since 1997 and this had minimised their exposure to financial stress emanating from the advanced economies during the GFC (Balakrishnan et al. 2009). Third, currency mismatches have been reduced over the past decade and these economies have built up their foreign reserves as insurance for precisely such occasions (Goldstein and Xie 2009). In Korea, foreign currency reserves were used not just to smooth volatility in the foreign exchange market but also to provide foreign currency liquidity to domestic banks and exporters, partially mitigating the effects of the capital withdrawal and foreign currency liquidity pressures (Filardo et al. 2010). Fourth, the financial sectors and its institutions were in a much better shape than they had been a decade earlier during the Asian financial crisis – see Table 6.8. Income and balance sheet data of banks suggest that banking systems are generally much healthier (Turner 2007). NPL ratios, provisioning ratios, profitability and risk-weighted capital ratios have also improved according to the Asian Development Bank (2009).[13] Marked improvements have also been observed in asset quality and in capital adequacy with reported capital adequacy exceeding 10 per cent of total risk-weighted assets in most economies, and non-performing loan ratios low and declining across the region (Pomerleano 2009). In fact, BIS capital adequacy ratios in Korea increased during the crisis and reached 14.6 per cent in December 2009, the highest level since 2002 (Tsutsumi, Jones and Cargill 2010). A final important factor that contributed to the resilience of the banking institutions in the region is their 'conventional' business model (Filardo et al. 2010). On the liability side, wholesale funding played a limited role in the banks' balance sheet, while deposits were the main source of funding. On the asset side, bank lending has typically been 'originate-to-hold', and investments in complex innovative financial instruments were kept at a low level. As credit risks were retained within institutions' balance sheets, there was greater incentive to act prudently with regard to risk-tasking and to vigilantly assess and monitor borrowers.

---

[13] See also Ibrahim (2010) for the case of Malaysia.

Table 6.8 Financial soundness indicators

	Non-Performing Loans (% of total loans)				Risk Weighted Capital Adequacy Ratio				Bank Return on Assets			
	1999	2001	2007	2009	1999	2001	2007	2009	1999	2001	2007	2009
East Asia												
China	n/a	29.8	6.2	1.6	12.8	n/a	8.4	11.4	0.1	n/a	0.9	0.8
Indonesia	32.9	31.9	4.1	3.3	-6.7	18.2	19.2	17.6	-8.7	0.6	2.8	2.6
Japan	5.8	8.4	1.4	1.7	11.9	10.8	12.3	15.8	-0.9	-0.6	0.3	0.2
Korea	8.3	3.4	0.7	1.2	10.8	11.7	12.3	14.4	-1.3	0.7	1.1	0.4
Malaysia	16.6	17.8	6.5	3.7	12.5	13.0	13.2	15.4	0.7	1.0	1.5	1.2
Philippines	14.6	27.7	5.8	4.1	17.5	15.6	15.7	15.8	0.4	0.4	1.0	1.2
Singapore	5.3	8.0	1.5	2.3	20.6	18.2	13.5	16.5	1.2	1.0	1.3	1.1
Thailand	38.6	11.5	7.9	5.3	12.4	13.3	14.8	15.8	-5.7	1.5	0.1	1.0
Other												
Australia	0.6	0.6	0.2	1.2	10.1	10.4	10.2	12.0	1.2	1.3	1.0	0.6
France	5.7	5.0	2.7	3.6	12.7	12.1	10.2	12.4	0.4	0.5	0.4	0.4
Germany	4.6	4.6	2.6	3.3	11.5	12.0	12.9	14.8	0.2	0.2	0.3	n/a
UK	3.0	2.6	0.9	3.5	14.0	13.2	12.6	14.8	0.8	0.5	0.4	0.1
US	1.0	1.3	1.4	5.4	12.2	12.9	12.8	14.3	1.3	1.1	0.8	0.1

Source: IMF's Global Financial Stability Report (various issues).

In summary, the East Asian economies in general, and Korea, Malaysia and Thailand in particular, had more room to manoeuvre during the GFC as the fundamentals of their macroeconomy and financial sector institutions were more robust when the global crisis struck in 2008, relative to 1997–8. It is however difficult, if not impossible, to conclude that the reform efforts of the past decade have directly contributed to these economies' ability to avoid the worst excesses of the GFC. This is in part due to the difficulties of causal arguments in a complex and multi-faceted issue. More importantly, the key reason these financial sectors were not directly embroiled in the sub-prime crisis was because they were not exposed to the 'toxic' financial derivatives. This in turn was a function of the state of development of these economies as well as the state of liberalisation in their financial sectors. Insufficient liberalisation, or conversely, the persistence of existing forms of state regulation prevented financial institutions from offering such products in their domestic markets, and as such it was what the state did not do rather than reforms introduced in the last decade that shielded these economies from recent innovations in the global financial industry.

Policies adopted at the turn of the century did however affect how these economies experienced the GFC. Korea and Malaysia were much more susceptible to the reversal of capital flows. In the years prior to the crisis, short-term foreign debt increased in Korea, especially from 2006 when amendments to the Foreign Exchange Transaction Act went into effect, with banks borrowing in excess of USD75 billion within a period of two years (Kang 2009a; Tsutsumi, Jones and Cargill 2010). The branches of foreign banks played a significant role in channeling these short-term foreign borrowings and were also key factors in the volatility of the capital account during the crisis (Kang 2009a).[14] Although the funding structure of the Malaysian banking system was predominantly deposit-based (about 70 per cent of total funding) and denominated largely in domestic currency that was used to fund ringgit-denominated assets (Ibrahim 2010), there was significant foreign participation in its large domestic bond market. Thailand in contrast had a relatively

[14] The latter is attributable to the fact that the external borrowing of the branches of foreign banks was more closely linked to 'carry trade', that is borrowing short-term from abroad to invest in domestic bonds and equities while hedging the exchange rate risk by arbitraging between forward and spot market rates, see Tsutsumi, Jones and Cargill (2010). For the domestic banks, a large portion of foreign debt is attributable to loans extended against future foreign currency revenues, also known as bridge financing, see Kang (2009a).

low reliance on foreign sources of funding prior to the GFC. Foreign funding accounted for only 3.5 per cent of the total liabilities of the banking system, with stable domestic deposits forming the core of the Thai banking system's funding source, at around 77 per cent of total liabilities (Bank of Thailand 2010). The differences in prior conditions across these economies can in large part be attributed to the fact that the Korean financial sector has been more 'aggressively' liberalised since 1997–8 which included measures such as internationalising the won, easing restrictions on capital transactions, developing the foreign currency market and relaxing the obligation to prove external credits. Furthermore, unlike Malaysia, where foreign banks were obliged to incorporate their businesses locally and thus be subjected to local regulation, foreign institutions in Korea were not subjected to the same liquidity regulations imposed by the local authorities on domestic institutions (Tsutsumi, Jones and Cargill 2010). As such, there were no specific rules or regulations that could have been used to better monitor and supervise the capital flows managed by domestic branches of foreign banks in Korea. While the Malaysian banks were much more strongly regulated than the Korean ones where foreign capital flows were concerned, the Malaysian government had been encouraging foreign participation in its bond market, thus exposing its financial sector to external disturbances on this front. Thailand, on the other hand, had in the years since the 1997–8 crisis become more inward-focussed in developing its financial sector and this has indirectly contributed to insulating its economy from the more destabilising elements of international financial flows in the last decade, when compared with Korea and Malaysia.

Finally, it has become clear from the experience of the GFC that increasing integration with the global economy, through both trade and financial links, had exposed the East Asian economies to the risk of global systemic shocks. These greater international linkages were promoted as part of broader developmental strategies. International financial links were meant to increase domestic investment while exports helped to increase their national incomes. While the Asian financial crisis of the late-1990s exposed the weakness of international financial integration, the experience of the GFC in 2008–9 for the East Asian economies made clear the weakness of a developmental strategy reliant on global exports.

Bibliography

Adams, Charles (2008). *Emerging East Asian Banking Systems Ten Years After the 1997/98 Crisis*. Working Paper Series on Regional Economic Integration, No. 16. Tokyo: Asian Development Bank (May).

Ahmad, R and Mei Ling Sieh-Lee (2000). 'Financial Sector.' In *Taking on the World: Globalization Strategies in Malaysia*, (ed.) Mei Ling Sieh-Lee. Kuala Lumpur: McGraw-Hill, 235–64.

Ahmad, Rubi (2007). 'A Note on the 1999–2002 Malaysian Banking Consolidation.' *Banker's Journal Malaysia* No. 131, 4–9.

Ahn, Choong-yong (2001). 'Policy Decision Making in Restructuring South Korea's Economy.' *Korea's Economy* Vol. 17, 13–22.

Ahn, Sanghoon, Joon-Ho Hahm and Joon-Kyung Kim (2008). 'External Finance and Productivity Growth in Korea: Firm Level Evidence before and after the Financial Crisis.' *Korea Development Review* Vol. 30, No. 2, 29–59.

Albert, Michel (1993). *Capitalism vs. Capitalism*. New York: Four Wall Eight Windows.

Allen, Franklin and Douglas Gale (2000). *Comparing Financial Systems*. Cambridge, Massachusetts: MIT Press.

Amable, Bruno (2003). *The Diversity of Modern Capitalism*. Oxford: Oxford University Press.

Amsden, Alice H (1989). *Asia's Next Giant: South Korea and Late Industrialization*. New York: Oxford University Press.

—— (1994). 'Why Isn't the Whole World Experimenting with the East Asian Model to Develop?: Review of the East Asian Miracle.' *World Development* Vol. 22, No. 4, 627–33.

Anderson, Sarah (2009). *Policy Handcuffs in the Financial Crisis: How U.S. Trade and Investment Policies Limit Government Power to Control Capital Flows*. Washington, D.C.: Institute for Policy Studies (February).

Andrews, Edmund L (2008). 'Greenspan Concedes Error on Regulation.' *New York Times* (New York), 23 October.

Anwar, Sajid and Desh Gupta (2006). 'Financial Restructuring and Economic Growth in Thailand.' *Global Economic Review* Vol. 35, No. 1 (March), 113–27.

Arestis, Philip, Machiko Nissanke and Howard Stein (2005). 'Finance and Development: Institutional and Policy Alternatives to Financial Liberalization Theory.' *Eastern Economic Journal* Vol. 31, No. 2 (Spring), 245–63.

Armijo, Leslie Elliott (1999). *Financial Globalization and Democracy in Emerging Markets*. Basingstoke: Palgrave Macmillan.

Asami, Tadahiro (2000). 'Non-Performing Loans in East Asia.' *Institute for International Monetary Affairs Newsletter*, No. 8, 1–8 (02 November).

Asia Pulse (2001). 'S Korea to Simplify Financial Regulations.' *Asia Pulse* (Seoul), 30 August.

—— (2007). 'Shift of Funds to Cash Management Accounts Accelerates.' *Asia Pulse* (Seoul), 05 August.

Asian Development Bank (2009). *Asia Economic Monitor*. Manila: Asian Development Bank (July).
Athukorala, Prema-Chandra (2001). 'The Macroeconomy up to 1997.' In *Modern Malaysia in the Global Economy*, (ed.) Colin Barlow. Cheltenham, UK: Edward Elgar, 13–27.
Baker, Chris (2005). 'Pluto-Populism: Thaksin and Thai Politics.' In *Thailand Beyond the Crisis*, (ed.) Peter G Warr. New York: Routledge Curzon.
Balakrishnan, Ravi, Stephan Danninger, Selim Elekdag and Irina Tytell (2009). *The Transmission of Financial Stress from Advanced to Emerging Economies*. IMF Working Paper, No. 09/133. Washington, D.C.: International Monetary Fund (June).
Banchongduang, Somruedi (2009). 'CIMB Thai Seeks 15% Loan Growth.' *Bangkok Post* (Bangkok), 07 May.
Banerjee, Abhijit, Angus Deaton, Nora Lustig and Kenneth S Rogoff (2006). *An Evaluation of World Bank Research, 1998 – 2005*. 24 September. Washington, D.C.: World Bank.
Bangkok Post (2003). 'Stock Market – SET Improves in Line with Plan.' *Bangkok Post* (Bangkok), 01 August.
—— (2006). 'Thailand-US FTA Talks: Approach Financial Liberalisation with Caution, Central Bank Advises.' *Bangkok Post* (Bangkok), 14 January.
Bank Negara Malaysia (1999a). 'Merger Programme for Domestic Banking Institutions.' Press Release. Kuala Lumpur (29 July).
—— (1999b). 'Tax Incentives for Consolidation of Domestic Banking Institutions.' Press Release. Kuala Lumpur (10 August).
—— (2001). *Financial Sector Masterplan: Building a Secure Future*. Kuala Lumpur: Bank Negara Malaysia.
—— (2004). *Annual Report 2003*. Kuala Lumpur: Bank Negara Malaysia.
—— (2005a). *Annual Report 2004*. Kuala Lumpur: Bank Negara Malaysia.
—— (2005b). 'Operational Flexibilities to the Locally-Incorporated Foreign Banking Institutions Operating in Malaysia.' Press Release. Kuala Lumpur: Bank Negara Malaysia (28 December).
—— (2009a). 'Issuance of New Commercial Banking Licences.' Press Release. Kuala Lumpur: Bank Negara Malaysia (27 April).
—— (2009b). 'Issuance of New Islamic Banking and Family Takaful Licences.' Press Release. Kuala Lumpur: Bank Negara Malaysia (27 April).
Bank of Thailand (1992). *Annual Economic Report*. Bangkok: Bank of Thailand.
—— (1993). *Annual Economic Report*. Bangkok: Bank of Thailand.
—— (1998). *Annual Economic Report*. Bangkok: Bank of Thailand.
—— (2005). *Supervision Report 2004*. Bangkok: Bank of Thailand.
—— (2006). *Thailand's Financial Sector Master Plan Handbook*. Bangkok: Bank of Thailand.
—— (2009). *The Financial Sector Master Plan Phase II*. Press Release, No. 54/2552. Bangkok: Bank of Thailand (04 November).
—— (2010). 'The International Banking Crisis: Impact on Thailand's Financial System and Policy Responses.' In *The Global Crisis and Financial Intermediation in Emerging Market Economies*, Vol. 54, (ed.) Bank for International Settlements. Basel: Bank for International Settlements.
Banoo, Sreerema (1999). 'PM – Banks Can Work out Mergers Themselves.' *Business Times* (Kuala Lumpur), 13 October.

Beck, Thorsten, and Asli Demirgüç-Kunt (2009). *Financial Institutions and Markets Across Countries and over Time: Data and Analysis*. World Bank Policy Research Working Paper, No. 4943. Washington, D.C.: World Bank (May).

Beck, Thorsten, and Ross Levine (2002). 'Industry Growth and Capital Allocation: Does Having a Market- or Bank-Based System Matter?' *Journal of Financial Economics* Vol. 64, 147–80.

Beddoes, Zanny Minton (2008). 'A Special Report on the World Economy: When Fortune Frowned.' *The Economist* (London), 11 October.

Beeson, Mark, and Richard Robison (2000). 'Introduction: Interpreting the Crisis.' In *Politics and Markets in the Wake of the Asian Crisis*, (eds) Richard Robison, Mark Beeson, Jayasuriya Kanishka and Hyuk-Rae Kim. London: Routledge, 3–24.

Beh, Lih Yi (2006). 'ECM-Avenue Merger a Conflict of Interest?' *MalaysiaKini.com* (Kuala Lumpur), 10 August.

Berger, Suzanne and Ronald Dore (1996). *National Diversity and Global Capitalism*. Ithaca, New York: Cornell University Press.

Bernama (2009a). 'Equity Limit for Investment, Islamic Banks and Takaful Firms Raised to 70 Pct.' *Bernama* (Kuala Lumpur), 27 April.

—— (2009b). 'Malaysia Received Rm4.2 Billion in FDI from Jan-May This Year.' *Bernama* (Kuala Lumpur), 02 July.

Bhagwati, Jagdish (1989). *Protectionism*. Cambridge, Massachusetts: MIT Press.

Bianco, Magda, Andrea Gerali and Riccardo Massaro (1997). 'Financial Systems across "Developed Economies": Convergence or Path Dependence.' *Research in Economics* Vol. 51, 303–31.

Bird, Graham and Ramkishen S Rajan (2002). *The Evolving Asian Financial Architecture*. Essays in International Economics, No. 226. Princeton, New Jersey: International Economics Section, Department of Economics, Princeton University (February).

Block, Fred L (2008). 'Swimming Against the Current: The Rise of a Hidden Developmental State in the United States.' *Politics & Society* Vol. 36, 169–206.

Blustein, Paul (2001). *The Chastening: Inside the Crisis That Rocked the Global Financial System and Humbled the IMF*. New York: Public Affairs.

Blyth, Mark (2003). 'Structures Do Not Come with an Instruction Sheet: Interests, Ideas, and Progress in Political Science.' *Perspectives on Politics* Vol. 1, No. 4 (December), 695–706.

Blyth, Mark M (1997). '"Any More Bright Ideas?" The Ideational Turn of Comparative Political Economy.' *Comparative Politics* Vol. 29, No. 2 (January), 229–50.

Brown, Gordon (2009). 'London Summit Press Conference.' Transcript of the press conference given by the Prime Minister Gordon Brown at the end of the London Summit. London: London Summit (02 April).

Byrne, Joseph P, and E Philip Davis (2002). 'A Comparison of Balance Sheet Structures in Major EU Countries.' *National Institute Economic Review*, No. 180, 83–95.

Byrne, Thomas (2004). 'The Korean Banking System Six Years after the Crisis.' *Korea's Economy* Vol. 20, 15–9.

—— (2005). 'Post-Crisis Transformation of Korea's Banking System.' *Korea's Economy* Vol. 21, 9–12.

Case, William (2005). 'Malaysia: New Reforms, Old Continuities, Tense Ambiguities.' *Journal of Development Studies* Vol. 41, No. 2 (February), 284–309.

Cerulli Associates (2008). *Shariah Investing: Market Sizing & Analysis*. Boston: Cerulli Associates (December).

Chaiwat, Thanee and Pasuk Phongpaichit (2008). 'Rents and Rent-Seeking in the Thaksin Era.' In *Thai Capital after the 1997 Crisis*, (eds) Pasuk Phongpaichit and Chris Baker. Singapore: Institute of Southeast Asian Studies, 249–66.

Chan, Cathy (2009). 'HSBC, Bank of Nova Scotia Said to Bid for Siam Bank.' *Bloomberg* (Hong Kong), 16 December.

Chang, Ha-Joon, Hong-Jae Park and Chul Gyue Yoo (1998). 'Interpreting the Korean Crisis: Financial Liberalisation, Industrial Policy and Corporate Governance.' *Cambridge Journal of Economics* Vol. 22, 735–46.

Chantapong, Saovanee and Lukas Menkhoff (2005). 'Cost Efficiency of Domestic and Foreign Banks in Thailand: Evidence from Panel Data.'Paper presented at the Xth Spring Meeting of Young Economists at HEI. Geneva.

Chapra, M Umer (2008). 'The Global Financial Crisis: Can Islamic Finance Help Minimize the Severity and Frequency of Such a Crisis in the Future?' Paper presented at the 'Forum on the Global Financial Crisis' held at the Islamic Development Bank. (25 October).

Charumilind, Chutatong, Raka Kali and Yupana Wiwattanakantang (2006). 'Connected Lending: Thailand before the Financial Crisis.' *Journal of Business* Vol. 79, 181–217.

Checkel, Jeffrey T (2003). 'Going Native in Europe? Theorizing Social Interaction in European Institutions.' *Comparative Political Studies* Vol. 36, 209–31.

—— (2004). 'Social Constructivisms in Global and European Politics: A Review Essay.' *Review of International Studies* Vol. 30, 229–44.

Chee, Adrian and Hwee Hoon Tan (2006). 'Bank Industry Risk Analysia: Malaysia.' In *Malaysian Banking Outlook*, (ed.). New York: Standard & Poor's, 18–29.

Chhibber, Ajay, Jayati Ghosh and Thangavel Palanivel (2009). *The Global Financial Crisis and the Asia-Pacific Region: A Synthesis Study Incorporating Evidence from Country Case Studies*. Colombo: UNDP Regional Centre for Asia and the Pacific.

Chin, Kok Fay (2004). 'Malaysia's Post-Crisis Bank Restructuring.' In *After the Storm: Crisis, Recovery, and Sustaining Development in Four Asian Economies*, (ed.) K S Jomo. Singapore: Singapore University Press, 204–29.

—— (2005). 'Bank Restructuring in Malaysia.' In *Malaysian 'Bail Outs'? Capital Controls, Restructuring and Recovery*, (eds) Sook Ching Wong, K S Jomo and Kok Fay Chin. Singapore: Singapore University Press, 112–38.

Chin, Kok Fay and K S Jomo (2000). 'Financial Sector Rents in Malaysia.' In *Rents, Rent-Seeking and Economic Development: Theory and Evidence in Asia*, (eds) Mushtaq H Khan and K S Jomo. Cambridge: Cambridge University Press.

—— (2001). 'Financial Liberalisation and System Vulnerabilities.' In *Malaysian Eclipse: Economic Crisis and Recovery*, (ed.) K S Jomo. London: Zed Books.

—— (2003). 'From Financial Liberalization to Crisis in Malaysia.' In *Financial Liberalization and the Economic Crisis in Asia*, (ed.) Chung H Lee. London: Routledge Curzon.

Chin, Kok Fay and Kristen Nordhaug (2002). 'Why Are There Differences in the Resilience of Malaysia and Taiwan to Financial Crisis?' *European Journal of Development Research* Vol. 14, No. 1 (June), 77–100.

Cho, Sung-hoon (2007). '"Big Bang" on Korea's Capital Markets: Reform Legislation and Its Impact.' *Korea's Economy* Vol. 23, 19–23.

Cho, Yoon Je (1997). 'Government Intervention, Rent Distribution, and Economic Development in Korea.' In *The Role of Government in East Asian Economic Development: Comparative Institutional Analysis,* (eds) Masahiko Aoki, Hyung-Ki Kim and Masahiro Okuno-Fujiwara. Oxford: Clarendon Press, 208–32.

Cho, Yoon Je and Joon-Kyung Kim (1995). *Credit Policies and the Industrialization of Korea.* Discussion Papers, No. 286. Washington, D.C.: World Bank.

—— (1997). *Credit Policies and the Industrialization of Korea.* Seoul: Korea Development Institute.

Choi, Byung-Sun (1993). 'Financial Policy and Big Business in Korea: The Perils of Financial Regulation.' In *The Politics of Finance in Developing Countries,* (eds) Stephan Haggard, Chung H Lee and Sylvia Maxfield. Ithaca, New York: Cornell University, 23–54.

Choi, Jin-Wook (2002). 'Regulatory Forbearance and Financial Crisis in South Korea.' *Asian Survey* Vol. 42, No. 2 (March–April), 251–75.

Christensen, Scott, David Dollar, Ammar Siamwalla and Pakorn Vichyanond (1993). *Thailand: The Institutional and Political Underpinnings of Growth.* Washington, D.C.: World Bank.

Claessens, Stijn, Simeon Djankov and Daniela Klingebiel (1999). *Financial Restructuring in East Asia: Halfway There?* Financial Sector Discussion Paper, No. 3. Washington, D.C.: World Bank (September).

Claessens, Stijn and Tom Glaessner (1997). *Are Financial Sector Weaknesses Undermining the East Asian Miracle?* Washington, D.C.: World Bank.

—— (1998). *The Internationalization of Financial Services in Asia.* Policy Research Working Paper, No. 1911. Washington, D.C.: World Bank (April).

Clapham, Christopher (1996). 'Liberalisation, Regionalism and Statehood in the New Development Agenda.' *Third World Quarterly* Vol. 17, No. 4, 593–602.

Cole, David C and Yung Chul Park (1983). *Financial Development in Korea, 1945–1978.* Cambridge, Massachusetts: Council on East Asian Studies, Harvard University.

Cook, Malcolm (2008). Banking Reform in Southeast Asia: The Region's Decisive Decade. London: Routledge.

Cooper, Helene and Charlie Savage (2008). 'A Bit of "I Told You So" Outside World Bank Talks.' *New York Times* (Washington, D.C.), 11 October.

Corbett, Jenny (2007). 'Financial Institutions and Structures for Growth in East Asia.' Paper presented at the ANU-MOF Conference on Advancing East Asian Economic Integration. Bangkok (22–23 February).

Corbett, Jenny and Tim Jenkinson (1996). 'The Financing of Industry, 1970–1989: An International Comparison.' *Journal of the Japanese and International Economies* Vol. 10, No. 1 (March), 71–96.

Crone, Donald K (1988). 'State, Social Elites, and Government Capacity in Southeast Asia.' *World Politics* Vol. 40, No. 2 (January), 252–68.

Crouch, Colin (2005). *Capitalist Diversity and Change: Recombinant Governance and Institutional Entrepreneurs.* Oxford: Oxford University Press.

Crouch, Colin and Henry Farrell (2004). 'Breaking the Path of Institutional Development? Alternatives to the New Determinism.' *Rationality and Society* Vol. 16, No. 1, 5–43.

Culpepper, Pepper D (2005). 'Institutional Change in Contemporary Capitalism: Coordinated Financial Systems since 1990.' *World Politics* Vol. 57, No. 2 (January), 173–99.

—— (2008). 'The Politics of Common Knowledge: Ideas and Institutional Change in Wage Bargaining.' *International Organization* Vol. 62 (Winter), 1–33.

Deeg, Richard (2005). 'Path Dependency, Institutional Complementarity, and Change in National Business Systems.' In *Changing Capitalisms? Internationalism, Institutional Change, and Systems of Economic Organization,* (eds) Glenn Morgan, Richard Whitley and Eli Moen. Oxford: Oxford University Press, 21–52.

Demirgüç-Kunt, Asli and Enrica Detragiache (1999). 'Financial Liberalization and Financial Fragility.' In *Proceedings of the 1998 World Bank Conference on Development Economics,* (eds) B Pleskovic and Joseph E Stiglitz. Washington, D.C.: World Bank.

Demirgüç-Kunt, Asli, and Ross Levine (1996). 'Stock Market Development and Financial Intermediaries: Stylized Facts.' *World Bank Economic Review* Vol. 10, No. 2, 291–321.

—— (2001). Financial Structure and Economic Growth: A Cross-Country Comparison of Banks, Markets, and Development. Cambridge, Massachusetts: MIT Press.

Disyatat, Piti and Don Nakornthab (2003). *The Changing Nature of Financial Structure in Thailand and Implications for Policy.* Discussion paper, No. DP/06/2003. Bangkok: Bank of Thailand (November).

Dixon, Chris (2004). 'Post-Crisis Restructuring: Foreign Ownership, Corporate Resistance and Economic Nationalism in Thailand.' *Contemporary Southeast Asia* Vol. 26, No. 1 (April), 45–72.

Dobson, Wendy and Pierre Jacquet (1998). *Financial Services Liberalization in the WTO.* Washington, D.C.: Institute for International Economics.

Dolar, Veronika and Cesaire Meh (2002). *Financial Structure and Economic Growth: A Non-Technical Survey.* Working Paper, No. 2002–24. Ottawa: Bank of Canada.

Domac, Ilker, Giovanni Ferri and Tae Soo Kang (2005). *The Credit Crunch in East Asia: Evidence from Field Findings on Bank Behavior and Policy Issues.* Working Paper, No. 34090. Washington, D.C.: World Bank.

Doner, Richard F and Ansil Ramsay (2003). 'The Challenges of Economic Upgrading in Liberalising Thailand.' In *States in the Global Economy: Bringing Domestic Institutions Back In,* (ed.) Linda Weiss. Cambridge: Cambridge University Press, 121–41.

Doner, Richard F and Daniel Unger (1993). 'The Politics of Finance in Thai Economic Development.' In *The Politics of Finance in Developing Countries,* (eds) Stephan Haggard, Chung H Lee and Sylvia Maxfield. Ithaca, New York: Cornell University, 93–122.

Doraisami, Anita (2005). 'The Political Economy of Capital Flows and Capital Controls in Malaysia.' *Journal of Contemporary Asia* Vol. 35, No. 2, 249–63.

Dore, Ronald (1973). *British Factory-Japanese Factory: The Origins of National Diversity in Industrial Relations.* Berkeley: University of California Press.

—— (1996). 'Convergence in Whose Interest?' In *National Diversity and Global Capitalism*, (eds) Suzanne Berger and Ronald Dore. Ithaca, New York: Cornell University, 366–74.

Dumez, Hervé and Alain Jeunemaître (1996). 'The Convergence of Competition Policies in Europe: Internal Dynamics and External Imposition.' In *National Diversity and Global Capitalism*, (eds) Suzanne Berger and Ronald Dore. Ithaca, New York: Cornell University, 216–38.

Economic Analytical Unit (2002). *Changing Corporate Asia: What Business Needs to Know.* Canberra: Department of Foreign Affairs and Trade.

Eichengreen, Barry (1999). *Toward a New International Financial Architecture.* Washington, D.C.: Institute for International Economics.

—— (2003). 'Governing Global Financial Markets: International Responses to the Hedge-Fund Problem.' In *Governance in a Global Economy*, (eds) Miles Kahler and David A Lake. Princeton, New Jersey: Princeton University Press, 168–98.

—— (2008). 'Reforming the International Financial Architecture after Ten Years: The View from Emerging Markets.' Paper presented in *Meeting of the Tokyo Club.* Tokyo (11–12 November).

Eichengreen, Barry and Michael D Bordo (2002). *Crises Now and Then: What Lessons from the Last Era of Financial Globalization?* NBER Working Paper, No. 8716. Cambridge, Massachusetts: National Bureau of Economic Research (January).

El - Hawary, Dahlia, Wafik Grais and Zamir Iqbal (2007). 'Diversity in the Regulation of Islamic Financial Institutions.' *The Quarterly Review of Economics and Finance* Vol. 46, No. 5 (February), 778–800.

Evans, Peter (1998). 'Transferable Lessons? Re-Examining the Institutional Prerequisites of East Asian Economic Policies.' *Journal of Development Studies* Vol. 34, No. 6, 66–86.

Evans, Peter B (1995). *Embedded Autonomy: States and Industrial Transformation.* Princeton, New Jersey: Princeton University Press.

Fan, Joseph P H and Yupana Wiwattanakantang (2006). 'Bank Ownership and Governance Quality in Four Post-Crisis Asian Economies.' In *Corporate Governance of Banks in Asia: A Study of Indonesia, Republic of Korea, Malaysia, and Thailand*, Vol. 2, (eds) Sang-Woo Nam and Chee Soon Lum. Tokyo: Asian Development Bank Institute, 75–105.

Filardo, Andrew, Jason George, Mico Loretan, Guonan Ma, Anella Munro, Ilhyock Shim, Philip Wooldridge, James Yetman and Haibin Zhu (2010). 'The International Financial Crisis: Timeline, Impact and Policy Responses in Asia and the Pacific.' In *The International Financial Crisis and Policy Challenges in Asia and the Pacific*, Vol. 52, (ed.) Bank for International Settlements. Basel: Bank for International Settlements, 52–82.

Financial Services Commission (2009). 'The Financial Investment Services and Capital Markets Act (FSCMA) & Common Concerns in the Market.' Seoul: Financial Services Commission (16 February).

Fine, Ben, Costa Lapavitsas and Jonathan Pincus, (eds) (2001). *Development Policy in the Twenty-First Century: Beyond the Post-Washington Consensus.* London: Routledge Studies in Development Economics.

Forbes (2007). 'Korea Capital Market Consolidation Act Brings Opportunities, Challenges – Fitch.' *Forbes.com*, 10 July.

Fratzscher, Oliver (2002). *Thailand Financial Sector Strategy: Current Status and Future Priorities*. Washington, D.C.: World Bank.

Friedman, Thomas L (1999). *The Lexus and the Olive Tree: Understanding Globalization*. London: Harper Collins.

Gan, Wee Beng and Lee Ying Soon (2001). 'Credit Crunch During a Currency Crisis: The Malaysian Experience.' *ASEAN Economic Bulletin* Vol. 18, No. 2, 176–92.

Garrett, Geoffrey and Barry R Weingast (1993). 'Ideas, Interests, and Institutions: Constructing the European Community's Internal Market.' In *Ideas and Foreign Policy: Beliefs, Institutions, and Political Change*, (eds) Judith Goldstein and Robert O Keohane. Ithaca, New York: Cornell University Press, 173–206.

Gearen, Sarah (2009). *Islamic Finance: Malaysia's Growing Role*. Asia Focus. San Francisco: Federal Reserve Bank of San Francisco (July).

Ghosh, Jayati (2008). 'Global Inequity Must End.' *Guardian* (London), 24 October.

Ghosh, Swati R (2006). *East Asian Finance: The Road to Robust Markets*. Washington, D.C.: World Bank.

Goh, Soo Khoon' and Michael Mah-Hui Lim (2010). *The Impact of the Global Financial Crisis: The Case of Malaysia*. TWN Global Economy Series, No. 26. Penang: Third World Network.

Goldstein, Morris (1998). *The Asian Financial Crisis*. Policy Briefs, No. 98–1. Washington, D.C.: Institute for International Economics (March).

—— (2008). 'Addressing the Financial Crisis.' Speech presented at a Peterson Institute event, 'Addressing the Current Financial Crisis'. Washington, D.C. (07 October).

Goldstein, Morris and Daniel Xie (2009). 'The Impact of the Financial Crisis on Emerging Asia.' In *Asia and the Global Financial Crisis (Proceedings of Asia Economic Policy Conference, 19–20 October 2009)*, (eds) Reuven Glick and Mark M Spiegel. San Francisco: Federal Reserve Bank of San Francisco, 27–80.

Goldthorpe, John H (ed.) (1984). *Order and Conflict in Contemporary Capitalism*. Oxford: Oxford University Press.

Gomez, Edmund Terence (1994). *Political Business: Corporate Involvement of Malaysian Political Parties*. Townsville: Centre for Southeast Asian Studies, James Cook University of North Queensland.

—— (2004). 'Paradoxes of Governance: Ownership and Control of Corporate Malaysia.' In *The Governance of East Asian Corporations: Post Asian Financial Crisis*, (eds) A Gul Ferdinand and Judy S L Tsui. Houndmills, Basingstoke, Hampshire: Palgrave Macmillan, 117–37.

—— (2005). 'The Perils of Pro-Malay Politics.' *Far Eastern Economic Review* Vol. 168, No. 8 (September), 36–9.

Gomez, Edmund Terence and K S Jomo (1999). *Malaysia's Political Economy: Politics, Patronage and Profits*. Cambridge: Cambridge University Press.

Goodin, Robert E (2003). 'Choose Your Capitalism?' *Comparative European Politics* Vol. 1, 203–13.

Gore, Charles (2000). 'The Rise and Fall of the Washington Consensus as a Paradigm for Developing Countries.' *World Development* Vol. 28, No. 5, 789–804.

Graham, Edward M (2003). *Reforming Korea's Industrial Conglomerates*. Washington, D.C.: Institute for International Economics.

Greenspan, Alan (1997). 'Growth and Flexibility: Lessons from Asia.' Remarks delivered at the Economic Club of New York. New York (02 December).

Grenville, Stephen (2006). *Regional and Global Responses to the Asian Crisis*. Sydney: Lowy Institute (October).

—— (2007). 'Regional and Global Responses to the Asian Crisis.' *Asian Economic Policy Review* Vol. 2, No. 1, 54–70.

Griffith-Jones, Stephany and Jose Antonio Ocampo (2003). *What Progress on International Financial Reform? Why So Limited?* Study, No. 2003:1. Stockholm: Expert Group on Development Issues.

Grimes, William W (2009). *The Global Financial Crisis and East Asia: Testing the Regional Financial Architecture*. EAI Fellows Program Working Paper Series, No. 20. Seoul: The East Asia Institute.

Gu, Bon-sung (2008). 'The 1997 Crisis: Learning from Hindsight.' *Korea Herald* (Seoul), 02 April.

Guimaraes-Filho, Masahiro Hori, Jacques Miniane and Papa N'Diaye (2008). 'Can Asia Decouple? Investigating Spillovers from the United States to Asia.' In *Regional Economic Outlook: Asia and the Pacific (April)*, (ed.) IMF. Washington, D.C.: International Monetary Fund.

Haggard, Stephan (1990). *Pathways from the Periphery: The Politics of Growth in the Newly Industrializing Countries*. Ithaca, New York: Cornell University Press.

—— (2000). *The Political Economy of the Asian Financial Crisis*. Washington, D.C.: Institute for International Economics.

Haggard, Stephan and Chung-in Moon (1990). 'Institutions and Economic Policy: Theory and a Korean Case Study.' *World Politics* Vol. 42 (January), 210–37.

Hahm, Joon-Ho (1999). 'Financial System Restructuring in Korea: The Crisis and Its Resolution.' In *East Asia's Financial Systems: Evolution & Crisis*, (eds) Seiichi Masuyama, Donna Vandenbrink and Siow Yue Chia. Singapore: Institute of Southeast Asian Studies, 109–43.

—— (2001). The Financial Structure in Transition: Financial Liberalization and Economic Crisis in Korea. CIS Working Paper Series. Seoul: Yonsei University (July).

—— (2003). 'The Government, the Chaebol and Financial Institutions before the Economic Crisis.' In *Economic Crisis and Corporate Restructuring in Korea*, (eds) Stephan Haggard, Wonhyuk Lim and Euysung Kim. Cambridge: Cambridge University Press, 79–101.

—— (2004). 'Financial Restructuring.' In *The Korean Economy Beyond the Crisis*, (eds) Duck-Koo Chung and Barry J Eichengreen. Cheltenham, UK: Edward Elgar, 172–93.

—— (2005). 'The Resurgence of Banking Institutions in Post-Crisis Korea.' *Journal of Contemporary Asia* Vol. 35, No. 3, 386–403.

—— (2007). 'Ten Years after the Crisis: Financial System Transition in Korea.' Paper presented in *Ten Years after the Korean Crisis*. Seoul: International Monetary Fund and Korean Institute for International Economy Policy (September).

Hall, Peter A and Daniel W Gingerich (2006). *Varieties of Capitalism and Institutional Complementarities in the Macroeconomy: An Empirical Analysis*. Discussion Paper, No. 04/5. Max Planck Institute for the Study of Societies.

Hall, Peter A and David Soskice (2001a). 'An Introduction to Varieties of Capitalism.' In *Varieties of Capitalism: The Institutional Foundations of Comparative Advantage*, (eds) Peter A Hall and David Soskice. Oxford: Oxford University Press, 1–68.

—— (2003). 'Varieties of Capitalism and Institutional Change: A Response to Three Critics.' *Comparative European Politics* Vol. 1, 241–50.

—— (eds) (2001b). *Varieties of Capitalism: The Institutional Foundations of Comparative Advantage*. Oxford: Oxford University Press.

Hall, Peter A and Rosemary C R Taylor (1996). 'Political Science and the Three New Institutionalisms.' *Political Studies* Vol. 44, 936–57.

Hall, Peter A and Kathleen Thelen (2009). 'Institutional Change in Varieties of Capitalism.' *Socio-Economic Review* Vol. 7, 7–34.

Hamilton-Hart, Natasha (2002). *Asian States, Asian Bankers: Central Banking in Southeast Asia*. Ithaca, New York: Cornell University Press.

Hancke, Bob, Martin Rhodes and Mark Thatcher (2007). 'Introduction: Beyond Varieties of Capitalism.' In *Beyond Varieties of Capitalism: Conflict, Contradictions, and Complementarities in the European Economy* (eds) Bob Hancke, Martin Rhodes and Mark Thatcher. Oxford: Oxford University Press, 3–38.

Handley, Paul (1997). 'More of the Same? Politics and Business, 1987–96.' In *Political Change in Thailand: Democracy and Participation*, (ed.) Kevin Hewison. London: Routledge, 94–113.

Hay, Colin (2004). 'Ideas, Interests and Institutions in the Comparative Political Economy of Great Transformations.' *Review of International Political Economy* Vol. 11, No. 1 (February), 204–26.

Hay, Colin and Daniel Wincott (1998). 'Structure, Agency and Historical Institutionalism.' *Political Studies* Vol. 44, 951–7.

Heng, Swee Keat (2009). 'The Global Financial Crisis: Impact on Asia and Policy Challenges Ahead.' In *Asia and the Global Financial Crisis (Proceedings of Asia Economic Policy Conference, 19–20 October 2009)*, (eds) Reuven Glick and Mark M Spiegel. San Francisco: Federal Reserve Bank of San Francisco, 267–74.

Heo, Uk and Sunwoong Kim (2000). 'Financial Crisis in South Korea: Failure of the Government-Led Development Paradigm.' *Asian Survey* Vol. 40, No. 3 (May–June), 492–507.

Hewison, Kevin (1996). 'Emerging Social Forces in Thailand: New Political and Economic Roles.' In *The New Rich in Asia: Mobile Phones, McDonald's and Middle-Class Revolution*, (eds) Richard Robison and David S G Goodman. London: Routledge.

—— (2000). 'Thailand's Capitalism before and after the Economic Crisis.' In *Politics and Markets in the Wake of the Asian Crisis*, (eds) Richard Robison, Mark Beeson, Kanishka Jayasuriya and Hyuk-Rae Kim. London: Routledge, 192–211.

—— (2001a). *Pathways to Recovery: Bankers, Business and Nationalism in Thailand*. Southeast Asia Research Centre Working Papers Series, No. 1. Hong Kong: City University of Hong Kong (April).

—— (2001b). 'Thailand's Capitalism: Development through Boom and Bust.' In *The Political Economy of South-East Asia: Conflict, Crises, and Change*, 2nd ed., (eds) Garry Rodan, Kevin Hewison and Richard Robison. Melbourne: Oxford University Press.

—— (2005). 'Neo-Liberalism and Domestic Capital: The Political Outcomes of the Economic Crisis in Thailand.' *Journal of Development Studies* Vol. 41, No. 2 (February), 310–30.

Hicken, Allen (2006). 'Party Fabrication: Constitutional Reform and the Rise of Thai Rak Thai.' *Journal of East Asian Studies* Vol. 6, No. 3 (December), 381–407.

—— (2008). 'Politics of Economic Recovery in Thailand and the Philippines.' In *Crisis as Catalyst: Asia's Dynamic Political Economy,* (eds) Andrew J MacIntyre, T J Pempel and John Ravenhill. Ithaca, New York: Cornell University Press.

Hilley, J (2001). Malaysia: Mahathirism, Hegemony and the New Opposition. London: Zed Books.

Hollingsworth, Roger, Philippe Schmitter and Wolfgang Streeck (eds) (1994). *Governing Capitalist Economies.* Oxford: Oxford University Press.

Höpner, Martin (2001). *Corporate Governance in Transition: Ten Empirical Findings on Shareholder Value and Industrial Relations in Germany.* MPIfG Discussion Paper, No. 01/5. Cologne: Max Planck Institute for the Study of Societies.

Horn, Robert (2000). 'Collision Course.' *Time Asia* Vol. 156, No. 19 (15 May).

Hosono, Kaoru (2005). 'Market Discipline to Banks in Indonesia, the Republic of Korea, Malaysia and Thailand.' Paper presented in *Corporate Governance of Banks in Asia – Second Seminar.* Tokyo, Japan (20–21 January).

Hudson, Michael and Jeffrey Sommers (2008). 'The End of the Washington Consensus.' *Counter Punch,* 12/14 December.

Hussein, Awang Adek (1994). 'Financial System.' In *Malaysia's Economy in the Nineties,* (ed.) K S Jomo. Petaling Jaya: Pelanduk Publications, 137–69.

Ibrahim, Muhammad bin (2010). 'Impact of the Global Crisis on Malaysia's Financial System.' In *The Global Crisis and Financial Intermediation in Emerging Market Economies,* Vol. 54, (ed.) Bank for International Settlements. Basel: Bank for International Settlements.

Ibrahim, Muhammad bin and Adrian Wong (2006). 'The Corporate Bond Market in Malaysia.' In *Developing Corporate Bond Markets in Asia,* Vol. 26, (ed.) Bank for International Settlements. BIS Papers. Basel: Bank for International Settlements, 114–28.

IMF (2001). *International Capital Markets Report.* Washington, D.C.: International Monetary Fund.

—— (2003a). *Financial Sector Assessment Korea.* Washington, D.C.: International Monetary Fund (June).

—— (2003b). *Republic of Korea: Financial System Stability Assessment.* IMF Country Report, No. 03/81. Washington, D.C.: International Monetary Fund (March).

—— (2009a). *Global Crisis: The Asian Context.* Regional Economic Outlook: Asia and Pacific. Washington, D.C.: International Monetary Fund (May).

—— (2009b). *Thailand: Financial System Stability Assessment.* IMF Country Report, No. 09/147. Washington, D.C.: International Monetary Fund (May).

Irwin, Douglas A and Randall S Kroszner (1999). 'Interests, Institutions, and Ideology in Securing Policy Change: The Republican Conversion to Trade Liberalization after Smoot-Hawley.' *Journal of Law and Economics* Vol. 42, No. 2 (October), 643–73.

Ito, Takatoshi (2001). 'Growth, Crisis, and the Future of Economic Recovery in East Asia.' In *Rethinking the East Asian Miracle*, (eds) Joseph E Stiglitz and Shahid Yusuf. New York: A co-publication of the World Bank and Oxford University Press, 55–94.

—— (2007). 'Asian Currency Crisis and the International Monetary Fund, 10 Years Later: Overview.' *Asian Economic Policy Review* Vol. 2, No. 1, 16–49.

Ito, Takatoshi and Yuko Hashimoto (2007a). Bank Restructuring in Asia: Crisis Management in the Aftermath of the Asian Financial Crisis and Prospects for Crisis Prevention, Korea. RIETI Discussion Paper Series, No. 07-E-038. Tokyo: (16 April).

—— (2007b). Bank Restructuring in Asia: Crisis Management in the Aftermath of the Asian Financial Crisis and Prospects for Crisis Prevention, Malaysia. RIETI Discussion Paper Series, No. 07-E-039. Tokyo: (16 April).

Jansen, Karel (2001). 'Thailand: The Making of a Miracle?' *Development and Change* Vol. 32, 343–70.

Jayasankaran, S (1995). 'Demands of Freedom.' *Far Eastern Economic Review* (28 September).

—— (1997). 'Pooling Power.' *Far Eastern Economic Review* (09 January).

—— (1999). 'Merger by Decree.' *Far Eastern Economic Review* Vol. 162, No. 36, 10–14.

—— (2001a). 'Come Back!' *Far Eastern Economic Review* Vol. 164, No. 9 (17 May), 56.

—— (2001b). 'The Curious Tale of RHB Bank.' *Far Eastern Economic Review* Vol. 164, No. 7 (22 February), 51–3.

—— (2001c). 'National Burden.' *Far Eastern Economic Review* Vol. 164, No. 3 (25 January), 53–4.

—— (2001d). 'Not Much Fun.' *Far Eastern Economic Review* Vol. 164, No. 8 (01 March), 36.

—— (2002a). 'Mahathir's Troubleshooter.' *Far Eastern Economic Review* Vol. 165, No. 10 (14 March), 42–4.

—— (2002b). 'We Are About in the Middle.' *Far Eastern Economic Review* Vol. 165, No. 20 (23 May), 42.

—— (2003a). 'Balancing Act.' *Far Eastern Economic Review* Vol. 166, No. 12 (27 March), 47.

—— (2003b). 'In the Dock.' *Far Eastern Economic Review* (23 January).

—— (2003c). 'The Right Price.' *Far Eastern Economic Review* Vol. 166, No. 4 (30 January), 43.

Jeon, Jong-kyou (2004). 'A Macroeconomic Overview of the Korean Economy.' *Korea's Economy* Vol. 20, 1–6.

—— (2005). 'Prospects for Developing Korea's Financial Market in 2005.' *Korea's Economy* Vol. 21, 13–6.

Jesudason, J V (1989). *Ethnicity and the Economy: The State, Chinese Business and, Multinationals in Malaysia*. Singapore: Oxford University Press.

Jin, Hyun-joo (2008). 'New Agency to Aid Lee's Deregulation Plan.' *Korea Herald* (Seoul), 17 January.

Johnson, Simon (2009). 'The Economic Crisis and the Crisis in Economics.' Revised version of speech prepared for the Presendential Address to the Association for Comparative Economics. San Francisco (04 January).

Johnston, Alasdair Iain (2001). 'Treating International Institutions as Social Environments.' *International Studies Quarterly* Vol. 45, 487–516.

Jomo, K S (2001). *What's Different About Southeast Asian Capitalism?* PROSEA East Asia Research paper, No. 44. Taipei: Academia Sinica, Program for Southeast Asian Area Studies (April).

—— (2004). 'Were Malaysia's Capital Controls Effective?' In *After the Storm: Crisis, Recovery, and Sustaining Development in Four Asian Economies,* (ed.) K S Jomo. Singapore: Singapore University Press, 173–203.

—— (2006). 'Pathways through Financial Crisis: Malaysia.' *Global Governance,* No. 12, 489–505.

—— (2007). 'What Did We Really Learn from the 1997–98 Asian Debacle?' In *Ten Years After: Revisiting the Asian Financial Crisis,* (ed.) Bhumika Muchhala. Washington, D.C.: Woodrow Wilson International Center for Scholars, 21–38.

Jomo, K S and Yun-Chung Ch'en (1997). Southeast Asia's Misunderstood Miracle: Industrial Policy and Economic Development in Thailand, Malaysia and Indonesia. Boulder, Colorado: Westview Press.

Joo, Sangyong (1998). 'Opening Capital Markets.' *Korea's Economy* Vol. 14, 33–7.

Jung, Ha-won (2007). 'Finance Minister Vows to Improve Banking Climate.' *JoongAng Daily* (Seoul), 28 June.

Kahler, Miles (1996). 'Trade and Domestic Differences.' In *National Diversity and Global Capitalism,* (eds) Suzanne Berger and Ronald Dore. Ithaca, New York: Cornell University, 298–332.

Kalinowski, Thomas and Hyekyung Cho (2009). 'The Political Economy of Financial Liberalization in South Korea: State, Big Business, and Foreign Investors.' *Asian Survey* Vol. 49, No. 2 (March/April), 221–42.

Kang, David C (2002). *Crony Capitalism: Corruption and Development in South Korea and the Philippines.* Cambridge: Cambridge University Press.

Kang, Kenneth, Geena Kim and Changyong Rhee (2006). 'Developing the Government Bond Market in South Korea: History, Challenges, and Implications for Asian Countries.' *Asian Economic Papers* Vol. 4, No. 2, 91–113.

Kang, Myung-koo (2009a). *Global Financial Crisis and Systemic Risks in the Korean Banking Sector.* Academic Paper Series. Seoul: Korea Economic Institute (May).

—— (2009b). 'The Sequence and Consequences of Bank Restructuring in South Korea, 1998–2006.' *Asian Survey* Vol. 49, No. 2 (March/April), 243–67.

Kang, Nahee (2006). *A Critique of the 'Varieties of Capitalism' Approach.* ICCSR Research Paper Series, No. 45–2006. Nottingham: International Centre for Corporate Social Responsibility, Nottingham University Business School.

Kang, Sammo (2003). 'Macroeconomic Developments and Structuring.' *Korea's Economy* Vol. 19, 1–7.

Kasikorn Research Center (2005). 'Retail Investors: Their Increasing Role in Thailand's Capital Market.' *Thai News Service* (Bangkok), 06 October.

Kassim, Salina H, M Shabri Abd Majid and Rosylin Mohd Yusof (2009). 'Impact of Monetary Policy Shocks on the Conventional and Islamic Banks in a Dual Banking System: Evidence from Malaysia.' *Journal of Economic Cooperation and Development* Vol. 30, No. 1, 41–58.

Kaur, Pavanjit (2003). *Merging of Finance Companies and Commercial Banks: For Better or Worse?* Kuala Lumpur: RAM Holdings (April).

Kawai, Masahiro, M Lamberte and D Y Yang (2008). *Global Shocks, Capital Flows, and Asian Regional Economic Cooperation.* Tokyo: Asian Development Bank Insitute.

Kawai, Masahiro, Yuzuru Ozeki and Hiroshi Tokumaru (2002). 'Banking on East Asia: Expansion and Retrenchment of Japanese Firms.' In *Winning in Asia, Japanese Style: Market and Non-Market Strategies for Success,* (eds) Vinod K Aggarwal and Shujiro Urata. Houndmills, Basingstoke, Hampshire: Palgrave Macmillan, 61–97.

Kawai, Masahiro and Ken-ichi Takayasu (1999). 'The Economic Crisis and Financial Sector Restructuring in Thailand.' In *Rising to the Challenge in Asia: A Study of Financial Markets,* Vol. 11, (ed.) Asian Development Bank. Manila: Asian Development Bank, 37–104.

Kester, W Carl (1996). 'American and Japanese Corporate Governance: Convergence to Best Practice?' In *National Diversity and Global Capitalism,* (eds) Suzanne Berger and Ronald Dore. Ithaca, New York: Cornell University Press, 107–37.

Kettle, Martin (2008). 'In Times Like These.' *Guardian* (London), 23 October.

Khor, Kok Peng (1987). *Malaysia's Economy in Decline: What Happened? Why? What to Do?* Penang: Consumers' Association of Penang.

Khor, Martin (2005). The Malaysian Experience in Financial-Economic Crisis Management: An Alternative to the IMF-Style Approach. TWN Global Economy Series, No. 6. Penang: Third World Network.

Kim, Byoung-yun (2008). 'Restructuring Financial and Corporate Sectors.' *Korea Herald* (Seoul), 07 April.

Kim, Dong Won and Inn Won Park (2001). 'Financial Reform in the Republic of Korea: Past and Present.' In *Financial Big Bang in Asia,* (ed.) Masayoshi Tsurumi. Aldershot: Ashgate, 63–88.

Kim, Dong-hwan (2008). 'The Capital Market Consolidation Act and the Korean Financial Market.' *Korea's Economy* Vol. 24, 39–44.

Kim, Dong-hwan and Soon-ho Lee (2008). 'Caution Urged in Easing Bank Ownership Rules.' *Korea Herald* (Seoul), 12 May.

Kim, Han-soo (2008). 'Korea as International Financial Center in Asia.' *Korea Herald* (Seoul), 15 May.

Kim, Hong-Bum and Chung H Lee (2004). *Post-Crisis Financial Reform in Korea: A Critical Appraisal.* Working Paper, No. 04–10. Honolulu: Department of Economics, University of Hawaii at Manoa.

Kim, Hyun E and Byung-Yoon Lee (2004). *The Effects of Foreign Bank Entry on the Performance of Private Domestic Banks in Korea.* Committee on the Global Financial System Working Group, No. 22. Basel: Bank for International Settlements (March).

Kim, Joon-Kyung (2000). *Chaebols and Financial Sector Restructuring in Korea.* Seoul: Korea Development Institute.

Kim, Mi-hui (2002). 'Blueprint Proposed for Making Korea Financial Hub.' *Korea Herald* (Seoul), 20 November.

—— (2003). 'Korea's Rating as Financial Hub Poor.' *Korea Herald* (Seoul), 06 June.

Kim, Soo-Myung, Ji-Young Kim and Hoon-Tae Ryoo (2006). 'Restructuring and Reforms in the Korean Banking Industry.' In *The Banking System in Emerging Economies: How Much Progress Has Been Made?,* Vol. 28, (ed.) Bank for International Settlements. BIS Papers. Basel: Bank for International Settlements, 259–68.

Kim, Tae-Gyu (2009a). 'KEB Likely to Face Closer Scrutiny.' *Korea Times* (Seoul), 24 April.

—— (2009b). 'New Capital Market Act Breaks Down Barriers.' *Korea Times* (Seoul), 26 February.

Kim, Wangsik (2005). 'Policy Reforms in Japan and South Korea (1997 – 2002).' *International Review of Public Administration* Vol. 9, No. 2, 81–95.

Kim, Yoon-mi (2008). 'Hurdles That Impede FDI in Financial Sector.' *Korea Herald* (Seoul), 22 August.

King, Desmond and Stewart Wood (1999). 'The Political Economy of Neoliberalism: Britain and the United States in the 1980s.' In *Continuity and Change in Contemporary Capitalism*, (eds) Peter Lange, Gary Marks and John D Stephens. Cambridge: Cambridge University Press, 371–97.

Klingner, Bruce (2006). 'Long Road Ahead for Korean Financial Sector.' *Asia Times Online*, 02 May.

Knight, Malcolm (2004). 'Banking and Insurance Regulation and Supervision: Greater Convergence, Common Challenges.' Speech delivered at the International Conference of Banking Supervisors. Madrid (22–23 September).

Ko, Kyoung-tae (2008a). 'Financial Regulator Releases Deregulatory Plan.' *Korea Herald* (Seoul), 25 April.

—— (2008b). 'Tension Mounts among Financial Regulators.' *Korea Herald* (Seoul), 18 January.

Kohli, Atul (2004). *State-Directed Development: Political Power and Industrialization in the Global Periphery*. Cambridge: Cambridge University Press.

Kopecki, Dawn and Catherine Dodge (2009). 'U.S. Rescue May Reach $23.7 Trillion, Barofsky Says.' *Bloomberg*, 20 July.

Korea Times (2005). 'Finance Minister Promises to Overhaul Regulatory System.' *Korea Times* (Seoul), 07 October.

—— (2007). 'Allowing New Brokerages: Bold Measures Needed to Speed up Financial Big Bang.' *Korea Times* (Seoul), 10 October.

Korea.net (2005). 'Roh Calls for Speedily Developing Korea as a Financial Hub.' *Korea.net* (Seoul).

Kosai, Yutaka (1996). 'Competition and Competition Policy in Japan: Foreign Pressures and Domestic Institutions.' In *National Diversity and Global Capitalism*, (eds) Suzanne Berger and Ronald Dore. Ithaca, New York: Cornell University, 197–215.

Krugman, Paul (1998). 'Will Asia Bounce Back?' Speech given to Credit Suisse First Boston, Hong Kong. (March).

Kubo, Koji (2006). 'The Degree of Competition in the Thai Banking Industry Before and After the East Asian Crisis.' *ASEAN Economic Bulletin* Vol. 23, No. 3 (December), 325–40.

Kwon, Tae-shin (2006). 'The Korean Government's Financial Hub Strategy.' Speech given at the 'Financial Centres Summit' organised by Financial Times Asia. Seoul (13 April).

La Porta, Rafael, Florencio Lopez-de-Silanes, Andrei Shleifer and Robert W Vishny (1998). 'Law and Finance.' *Journal of Political Economy* Vol. 106, 1113–55.

—— (2000). 'Investor Protection and Corporate Governance.' *Journal of Financial Economics* Vol. 58, 3–27.

Laeven, Luc (2005). 'Banking Sector Performance in East Asian Countries: The Effects of Competition, Diversification, and Ownership.' Washington, D.C.: World Bank.

Laothamatas, Anek (1996). 'A Tale of Two Democracies: Conflicting Perceptions of Elections and Democracy in Thailand.' In *The Politics of Elections in Southeast Asia*, (ed.) R H Taylor. Cambridge: Cambridge University Press.

Lauridsen, Laurids (2000). Industrial Policies, Political Institutions and Industrial Development in Thailand, 1959–91. Working Paper, No. 21. Roskilde: Roskilde University.

Lee, Chung H (1992). 'The Government, Financial System, and Large Private Enterprises in the Economic Development of South Korea.' *World Development* Vol. 20, No. 2, 187–97.

Lee, Hock Lock (1981). Public Policies, Commercial Banks, and Other Deposit Instittions in Malaysia: A Study in Resource Mobilization and Utilization. Kuala Lumpur: UMBC Publications.

—— (1987). *Central Banking in Malaysia: A Study of the Development of the Financial System and Monetary Management*. Singapore: Butterworths.

Lee, Hyo-sik (2008). '"Less Talk, More Action" Approach Needed.' *Korea Times* (Seoul), 26 November.

Lee, Jae-youn (2008). 'Reform: Korea's Way out of Financial Crisis.' *Korea Herald* (Seoul), 04 April.

Lee, Jong-Wha and Changyong Rhee (2007). 'Crisis and Recovery: What We Have Learned from the South Korean Experience?' *Asian Economic Policy Review* Vol. 2, No. 1, 146–64.

Lee, Sohan (1998). 'Korea's Financial Sector under Reform.' *Korea's Economy* Vol. 14, 22–7.

Levine, Ross (1996). 'Foreign Banks, Financial Development, and Economic Growth.' In *International Financial Markets: Harmonization Versus Competition*, (ed.) Claude E Barfield. Washington, D.C.: AEI Press, 224–54.

—— (1997). 'Financial Development and Economic Growth: Views and Agenda.' *Journal of Economic Literature* Vol. 35, No. 2 (June), 688–726.

—— (2002). 'Bank-Based or Market-Based Financial Systems: Which Is Better?' *Journal of Financial Intermediation* Vol. 11, 398–428.

Li, John Shuhe (2003). 'Relation-Based Versus Rule-Based Governance: An Explanation of the East Asian Miracle and Asian Crisis.' *Review of International Economics* Vol. 11, No. 4, 651–73.

Liau, Y-Sing (2008). 'Malaysia to Hand out More Islamic Fund Licences.' *Reuters* (Kuala Lumpur), 13 August.

Lim, Bomi (2008). '"KIKO" Hedges Slay Korean Exporters, Threaten Banks.' *Bloomberg*, 17 October.

Lim, Kit Siang (1985). 'Untitled.' Speech by the Parliamentary Opposition Leader, DAP Secretary-General and MP for Kota Melaka, Lim Kit Siang, at the National DAP Publicity Secretaries' meeting. Petaling Jaya (08 December).

Lim, Wonhyuk and Joon-Ho Hahm (2006). 'Turning a Crisis into an Opportunity: The Political Economy of Korea's Financial Sector Reform.' In *From Crisis to Opportunity: Financial Globalization and East Asian Capitalism*, (eds) Jongryn

Mo and Daniel I Okimoto. Washington, D.C.: Brookings Institution Press, 85–121.

Lin, See-Yan (1994). 'The Current State of the Malaysian Financial System, with Special Reference to the Capital Market Developments.' *Pacific-Basin Finance Journal* Vol. 2, 113–38.

Lindgren, Carl-Johan, Tomás J T Baliño, Charles Enoch, Anne-Marie Gulde, Marc Quintyn and Leslie Teo (1999). *Financial Sector Crisis and Restructuring: Lessons from Asia*. IMF Occassional Paper, No. 188. Washington, D.C.: International Monetary Fund.

Linklaters (2004). *Thai Financial Sector Master Plan*. Bangkok: Linklaters (February).

Lopez, Leslie (1999). 'Malaysia's Plan to Merge Banks Causes Concern.' *Wall Street Journal*, 02 August.

Lum, Chee Soon and Philip T N Koh (2006). 'Corporate Governance of Banks in Malaysia.' In *Corporate Governance of Banks in Asia: A Study of Indonesia, Republic of Korea, Malaysia, and Thailand*, Vol. 1, (eds) Sang-Woo Nam and Chee Soon Lum. Tokyo: Asian Development Bank Institute, 243–314.

—— (2007). 'Corporate Governance of Banks in Malaysia.' *Banker's Journal Malaysia*, No. 131, 10–48.

Lütz, Susanne (2000). 'From Managed to Market Capitalism? German Finance in Transition.' *German Politics* Vol. 9, No. 2, 149–70.

MacAskill, Andrew (2009). 'U.K Financial Bailout Reaches 1.4 Trillion Pounds.' *Bloomberg*, 23 April.

Mackie, J A C (1988). 'Economic Growth in the ASEAN Region: The Political Underpinnings.' In *Achieving Industrialization in East Asia*, (ed.) Helen Hughes. Cambridge ; Melbourne: Cambridge University Press, 283–326.

Mann, Catherine L (1998). 'Korea and the International Financial System.' *Korea's Economy* Vol. 14, 42–6.

Mansor, Lokman (1999). 'Govt Flexibility on Bank Merger Issue Hailed.' *Business Times* (Kuala Lumpur), 13 October.

Marashdeh, Omar (1994). 'Foreign Banks Activities and Factors Affecting Their Presence in Malaysia.' *Asia Pacific Journal of Management* Vol. 11, No. 1, 113–23.

Martin, Cathie Jo and Kathleen Thelen (2007). 'Varieties of Coordination and Trajectories of Change: Social Policy and Economic Adjustment in Coordinated Market Economies.' Paper presented in *Annual Meeting of the American Political Science Association*. Chicago (30 August).

Mathews, John A (2001). 'Fashioning a New Korean Model out of the Crisis: The Rebuilding of Institutional Capabilities.' In *Financial Liberalization and the Asian Crisis*, (eds) Ha-Joon Chang, J Gabriel Palma and D H Whittaker. Houndmills, Basingstoke, Hampshire: Palgrave Macmillan, 156–74.

Mathieson, Donald J and Jorge Roldos (2001). 'Foreign Banks in Emerging Markets.' In *Open Doors: Foreign Participation in Financial Systems in Developing Countries*, (eds) Robert E Litan, Paul Masson and Michael Pomerleano. Washington, D.C.: Brookings Institute, 15–55.

Maxfield, Sylvia (1994). 'Financial Incentives and Central Bank Authority in Industrializing Nations.' *World Politics* Vol. 46, No. 4 (July), 556–88.

Mayer, Colin (1988). 'New Issues in Corporate Finance.' *European Economic Review* Vol. 32, No. 5 (June), 1183–6.

—— (1990). 'Financial Systems, Corporate Finance, and Economic Development.' In *Asymmetric Information, Corporate Finance, and Investment,* (ed.) R Glenn Hubbard. Chicago: Chicago University Press, 307–32.

McKinnon, Ronald I (1973). *Money and Capital in Economic Development.* Washington, D.C.: Brookings Institution.

Md Khalid, Khadijah (2004). 'Malaysia's Growing Economic Relations with the Muslim World.' *Kyoto Review,* No. 4 (March).

Menon, Jayant (2001). 'Openness to Trade, Capital and Labour Flows up to the Currency Crisis: Degree and Impacts.' In *Modern Malaysia in the Global Economy,* (ed.) Colin Barlow. Cheltenham, UK: Edward Elgar, 28–44.

Merton, R C and Z Bodie (1995). 'A Conceptual Framework for Analyzing the Financial Environment.' In *The Global Financial System: A Functional Perspective,* (eds) D B Crane, K A Froot, S P Mason, A F Perold, R C Merton, E R Sirri and Tufano P Boston, Massachusetts: Harvard Business School Press, 3–32.

Mihaljek, D (2006). 'Privatisation, Consolidation and the Increased Role in Foreign Banks.' In *The Banking System in Emerging Economies: How Much Progress Has Been Made?,* Vol. 28, (ed.) Bank for International Settlements. BIS Papers. Basel: Bank for International Settlements, 41–65.

Milner, Helen V and B Peter Rosendorff (1997). 'Democratic Politics and International Trade Negotiations: Elections and Divided Government as Constraints on Trade Liberalization.' *Journal of Conflict Resolution* Vol. 41, No. 1 (February), 117–46.

Mishkin, Frederic S (2001). *Financial Policies and the Prevention of Financial Crises in Emerging Market Economies.* NBER Working Paper, No. 8087. Washington, D.C.: National Bureau of Economic Research (January).

Mokhtar, Hamim S Ahmad, Naziruddin Abdullah and Syed M Alhabshi (2008). 'Efficiency and Competition of Islamic Banking in Malaysia.' *Humanomics* Vol. 24, No. 1, 28–48.

Molina, Oscar and Martin Rhodes (2007). 'The Political Economy of Adjustment in Mixed Market Economies: A Study of Spain and Italy.' In *Beyond Varieties of Capitalism: Conflict, Contradictions, and Complementarities in the European Economy* (eds) Bob Hancke, Martin Rhodes and Mark Thatcher. Oxford: Oxford University Press, 223–52.

Monnet, Cyril and Erwan Quintin (2007). 'Why Do Financial Systems Differ? History Matters.' *Journal of Monetary Economics* Vol. 54, 1002–17.

Montreevat, Sakulrat and Ramkishen S Rajan (2001). *Financial Crisis, Bank Restructuring and Foreign Bank Entry: An Analytic Case Study of Thailand.* Discussion Paper, No. 131. Adelaide: Adelaide University (June).

Moody's Investors Service (2006). *Asia Banking Outlook 2006.* Moody's Special Comment.

Moran, Michael (2003). *The British Regulatory State: High Modernism and Hyper-Innovation.* Oxford: Oxford University Press.

Morgan, Glenn (2005). 'Introduction: Changing Capitalisms? Internationalization, Institutional Change, and Systems of Economic Organization.' In *Changing Capitalisms? Internationalization, Institutional Change, and Systems of Economic Organization,* (eds) Glenn Morgan, Richard Whitley and Eli Moen. Oxford: Oxford University Press, 1–18.

Muscat, Robert J (1995). 'Thailand.' In *Financial Systems and Economic Policy in Developing Countries*, (eds) Stephan Haggard and Chung H Lee. Ithaca, New York: Cornell University Press, 113–39.

Na, Jeong-Ju (2008). 'Privatization of State Firms to Gather Steam.' *Korea Times* (Seoul), 25 February.

Naim, Moises (2000). 'Fads and Fasion in Economic Reforms: Washington Consensus or Washington Confusion?' *Third World Quarterly* Vol. 21, No. 3, 505–28.

Nakornthab, Don (2007). Thai Commercial Banks One Decade after the Crisis: Assessment of Risk to Financial Stability. Discussion Paper. Bangkok: Bank of Thailand.

Nam, Sang-Woo and Chung H Lee (1995). 'Korea.' In *Financial Systems and Economic Policy in Developing Countries*, (eds) Stephan Haggard and Chung H Lee. Ithaca, New York: Cornell University Press, 31–55.

Nam, Sang-Woo and Chee Soon Lum (2006). 'Survey of Banks' Corporate Governance in Indonesia, Republic of Korea, Malaysia, and Thailand.' In *Corporate Governance of Banks in Asia: A Study of Indonesia, Republic of Korea, Malaysia, and Thailand*, Vol. 1, (eds) Sang-Woo Nam and Chee Soon Lum. Tokyo: Asian Development Bank Institute, 11–83.

Nidhiprabha, Bhanupong (2003). 'Premature Liberalization and Economic Crisis in Thailand.' In *Financial Liberalization and the Economic Crisis in Asia*, (ed.) Chung H Lee. London: Routledge Curzon, 27–46.

Nijathaworn, Bandid (2009). 'Financial Developments and the Thai Banking Sector.' Keynote address given at the Third Euromoney Thailand Investment Forum. Bangkok (10 June).

Njie, Matarr (2007). 'Impact of Financial Liberalisation on the Productive Efficiency of the Banking Industry in Malaysia.' *Banker's Journal Malaysia*, No. 131, 49–67.

Noland, Marcus (1998). 'The Financial Crisis in Asia.' Testimony before the House International Relations Committee, Subcommittees on Asian and Pacific Affairs, and International Economic Policy and Trade. Washington, D.C. (03 February).

—— (2005). *South Korea's Experience with International Capital Flows*. Working Paper, No. WP 05–4. Washington, D.C.: Institute for International Economics (June).

Obstfeld, Maurice and Alan M Taylor (2004). *Global Capital Markets: Integration, Crisis, and Growth*. Cambridge: Cambridge University Press.

OECD (2004). *Economic Survey – Korea 2004: Reform of the Corporate and Financial Sectors*. Paris: Organisation for Economic Co-Operation and Development.

—— (2007). *Korea: Progress in Implementing Regulatory Reform*. Policy Brief. Paris: Organisation for Economic Co-Operation and Development (March).

Office of the United States Trade Representative (2008). *National Trade Estimate Report on Foreign Trade Barriers: Korea*. Washington, D.C.: Office of the United States Trade Representative.

—— (2009). *National Trade Estimate Report on Foreign Trade Barriers: Korea*. Washington, D.C.: Office of the United States Trade Representative.

Ohmae, Kenichi (1990). *The Borderless World: Power and Strategy in the Interlinked Economy*. London: Collins.

Okuda, Hidenobu and Fumiharu Mieno (1996). *The Impact of Financial Liberalization Policy on ASEAN Commercial Banks: A Case Study of Thai Commercial Banks*. APEC Study Center Series. Tokyo: APEC Study Center, Hitotsubashi University and Institute of Developing Economies.

Omar, Tamimi (2006). 'Malaysia Slips Four Places to 6th in ASEAN FDI Ranking.' *The Edge Financial Daily* (Kuala Lumpur), 17 October.

Ong, Hong Cheong (1999). 'Evolution of the Malaysian Financial System Beyond the Financial Crisis.' In *East Asia's Financial Systems: Evolution & Crisis*, (eds) Seiichi Masuyama, Donna Vandenbrink and Siow Yue Chia. Singapore and Tokyo: Institute of Southeast Asian Studies and Nomura Research Institute, 144–65.

Ostry, Sylvia (1996). 'Policy Approaches to System Friction: Convergence Plus.' In *National Diversity and Global Capitalism*, (eds) Suzanne Berger and Ronald Dore. Ithaca, Nwe York: Cornell University, 333–52.

Overholt, William H (1999). 'Thailand's Financial and Political Systems: Crisis and Rejuvenation.' *Asian Survey* Vol. 39, No. 6 (November–December), 1009–35.

Pandey, Umesh (2006). 'GE Arm Said to Be Buying into BAY; Talks "Not Expected to Drag on Much Longer".' *Bangkok Post* (Bangkok), 20 January.

Papanek, Gustav (1988). 'The New Asian Capitalism: An Economic Portrait.' In *In Search of an East Asian Development Model*, (eds) Peter L Berger and Hsin-Huang Michael Hsiao. New Brunswick: Transaction Books.

Park, Hun Joo (2001). 'Small Business in Korea, Japan, and Taiwan.' *Asian Survey* Vol. 41, No. 5 (September/October), 846–64.

Park, Jae-Ha (2006). 'Corporate Governance of Banks in Republic of Korea.' In *Corporate Governance of Banks in Asia: A Study of Indonesia, Republic of Korea, Malaysia, and Thailand*, Vol. 1, (eds) Sang-Woo Nam and Chee Soon Lum. Tokyo: Asian Development Bank Institute, 167–241.

—— (2008). 'Bond Market Development: The Experience of the Republic of Korea.' Paper presented in *Capacity Building for Development of Bond Markets in ESCAP Member States* United Nations Economic and Social Commission for Asia and the Pacific.

Park, Yung Chul (1994). 'Korea: Development and Structural Change of the Financial System.' In *The Financial Development of Japan, Korea, and Taiwan*, (eds) Hugh T Patrick and Yung Chul Park. New York: Oxford University Press, 129–87.

Parreñas, Julius Caesar (2006). 'Banks' Risk Management Practices: A Survey of Four Asian Emerging Markets.' In *Corporate Governance of Banks in Asia: A Study of Indonesia, Republic of Korea, Malaysia, and Thailand*, Vol. 2, (eds) Sang-Woo Nam and Chee Soon Lum. Tokyo: Asian Development Bank Institute, 171–223.

Pattnapong, Chantranontwong (1999). 'Time to Chuan to Train the Tigers.' *Bangkok Post* (Bangkok), 14 April.

Pettifor, Ann (2008). 'Economies of Scale.' *Guardian* (London), 21 October.

Phongpaichit, Pasuk, and Chris Baker (1995). *Thailand: Economy and Politics*. Kuala Lumpur: Oxford University Press.

—— (1998a). 'The Political Economy of the Thai Crisis.' *Journal of the Asia Pacific Economy* Vol. 4, No. 1 (February), 193–208.

—— (1998b). *Thailand's Boom and Bust*. Chiang Mai: Silkworm Books.

—— (2001). 'Thailand's Crisis: Neo-Liberal Agenda and Local Reaction.' In *Financial Liberalization and the Asian Crisis*, (eds) Ha-Joon Chang, Gabriel Palma and D Hugh Whittaker. Houndmills, Basingstoke, Hampshire: Palgrave Macmillan, 82–101.

Pirie, Iain (2008). The Korean Developmental State: From Dirigisme to Neo-Liberalism. Abingdon: Routledge.

Plummer, Michael G and Benedetta Trivellato (2001). 'Economic and Policy Convergence in ASEAN: Malaysia and Thailand Compared.' In *Reforming Economic Systems in Asia: A Comparative Analysis of China, Japan, South Korea, Malaysia and Thailand*, (ed.) Maria Weber. Cheltenham, UK: Edward Elgar, 95–126.

Polkuamdee, Nuntawan (1999). 'Some Gain after All the Pain.' *Bangkok Post* (Bangkok), Year-End Edition.

—— (2002). 'Challenges for the Market.' *Bangkok Post* (Bangkok), 08 January.

—— (2003). '"Tough Job Romancing the Masses.' *Bangkok Post* (Bangkok), 29 May.

Pomerleano, Michael (2009). What Is the Impact of the Global Financial Crisis on the Banking System in East Asia? 146, August ADBI Working Paper, No. 146. Tokyo: ADB Institute (August).

Prasirtsuk, Kitti (2007). 'From Political Reform and Economic Crisis to Coup D'etat in Thailand.' *Asian Survey* Vol. 47, No. 6, 872–93.

Price, Richard (1998). 'Reversing the Gun Sights: Transnational Civil Society Targets Land Mines.' *International Organization* Vol. 52, 613–44.

Purcell, Susan Kaufman (2003). 'The Washington Consensus Is Not Dead.' Americas Society-Council of the Americas (21 February).

Radelet, Steven and Jeffrey Sachs (1998). 'The East Asian Financial Crisis: Diagnosis, Remedies, Prospects.' *Brookings Papers on Economic Activity*, No. 1, 1–74.

Rajan, Raghuram G (2005). *Has Financial Development Made the World Riskier?* NBER Working Paper, No. 11728. Cambridge, Massachusetts: National Bureau of Economic Research.

Rajan, Raghuram G and Luigi Zingales (2003). 'The Great Reversals: The Politics of Financial Development in the Twentieth Century.' *Journal of Financial Economics* Vol. 69, 5–50.

Rasiah, Rajah (1995). *Foreign Capital and Industrialization in Malaysia*. London: Palgrave Macmillan.

—— (1998). 'The Malaysian Financial Crisis: Capital Expansion, Cronyism and Contraction.' *Journal of the Asia Pacific Economy* Vol. 3, No. 3, 358–78.

Rethel, Lena (2010a). 'Financialisation and the Malaysian Political Economy.' *Globalizations* Vol. 7, No. 4, 489–506.

—— (2010b). 'The New Financial Development Paradigm and Asian Bond Markets.' *New Political Economy* Vol. 15, No. 4, 493–517.

—— (2011). 'Whose Legitimacy? Islamic Finance and the Global Financial Order.' *Review of International Political Economy* Vol. 18, No. 1, 75–98.

Risse, Thomas (2000). '"Let's Argue!": Communicative Action in World Politics.' *International Organization* Vol. 54, No. 1 (Winter), 1–39.

Roche, David (2000). 'The "Global" World Is Anglo-Saxon.' *Wall Street Journal (Europe)*, 05 January.

Rodrik, Dani (2007). *One Economics, Many Recipes: Globalization, Institutions, and Economic Growth*. Princeton: Princeton University Press.

Rogowski, Ronald (2003). 'International Capital Mobility and National Policy Divergence.' In *Governance in a Global Economy,* (eds) Miles Kahler and David A Lake. Princeton, New Jersey: Princeton University Press, 255–74.

Ruengvirayudh, Pongpen and Sakkapop Panyanukul (2006). 'The Corporate Bond Market in Thailand.' In *Developing Corporate Bond Markets in Asia,* Vol. 26, (ed.) Bank for International Settlements. BIS Papers. Basel: Bank for International Settlements, 152–60.

Salleh, Ismail Mohd. and Saha Dhevan Meyanathan (1993). *Malaysia: Growth, Equity, and Structural Transformation*. Washington, D.C.: World Bank.

Sarawuth, Sinfah (2007). 'Giving Farang the Cold Shoulder.' *Far Eastern Economic Review* Vol.170, No. 2 (March), 24–6.

Satsanguan, Plearnpit and Sukanda Lewis (2009). 'Thailand's Financial and Banking Systems.' Paper presented in *Economic Transition and Social Changes of Countries in Asian Sub-region*. Bangkok: Thailand Research Fund (28 May).

Schimmelfennig, Frank (2003). *The EU, Nato and the Integration of Europe: Rules and Rhetoric*. Cambridge: Cambridge University Press.

Schmidt, Reinhard H (1999). 'Differences between Financial Systems in European Countries: Consequences for EMU.' Paper presented in *The Monetary Transmission Process*. Frankfurt am Main: Deutsche Bundesbank (26 – 27 March).

Schmidt, Vivien A (2002). *The Futures of European Capitalism*. Oxford: Oxford University Press.

—— (2006a). 'Bringing the State Back into the Varieties of Capitalism and Discourse Back into the Explanation of Change.' Paper presented in *Annual Meetings of the American Political Science Association*. Philadelphia, PA (31 August – 03 September).

—— (2006b). 'Institutionalism.' In *The State: Theories and Issues,* (eds) Colin Hay, Michael Lister and David Marsh. Houndmills, Basingstoke, Hampshire: Palgrave Macmillan, 98–117.

—— (2009). 'Putting the Political Back into Political Economy by Bringing the State Back in yet Again.' *World Politics* Vol. 61, No. 3 (July), 516–46

Securities Commission of Malaysia (2001). *Capital Market Masterplan Malaysia*. Kuala Lumpur: Securities Commission of Malaysia.

—— (2002). SC Relaxes Conditions for Injection of Foreign Assets and Multinational Companies into Malaysian Listed Companies to Further Facilitate Corporate Restructuring. Press Release. Kuala Lumpur: (08 May).

Semblat, Romuald (2006). 'The Development of the Financial Sector in Korea.' In *Republic of Korea: Selected Issues,* (ed). International Monetary Fund. Washington, D.C.: International Monetary Fund, 19–35.

Sender, Henry (1997). 'The Devil to Pay.' *Far Eastern Economic Review* Vol.160, No. 23 (05 June), 50–6.

Sender, Henry, and Charles Lee (1998). "Rotten to the Core." *Far Eastern Economic Review* (02 April), 14–6.

Seoul Financial Forum (2003). *Korea as an International Financial Center.* Seoul: Seoul Financial Forum (January).

Shari, Ishak (2003). 'Economic Growth and Social Development in Malaysia, 1971–98: Does the State Still Matter in an Era of Economic Globalisation?' In

Development and Structural Change in Asia-Pacific: Globalising Miracles or End of a Model?, (eds) Martin Andersson and Christer Gunnarsson. London: Routledge Curzon, 108–24.

Sharma, Shalendra (2003). *The Asian Financial Crisis: Crisis, Reform and Recovery.* Manchester: Manchester University Press.

Shaw, Edward Stone (1973). *Financial Deepening in Economic Development.* New York: Oxford University Press.

Sheng, Andrew (1989). *Bank Restructuring in Malaysia, 1985–88.* Policy, Planning and Research Working Paper, No. WPS54. Washington, D.C.: World Bank.

Shin, Inseok (2002). 'Evolution of the KOSDAQ Stock Market: Evaluation and Policy Issues.' Paper presented in *The Role of Capital Markets in Asian Economic Development.* Tokyo: Tokyo Club Foundation for Global Studies (7–8 March).

Shin, Inseok and Joon-Ho Hahm (1999). 'The Korean Financial Crisis: Causes and Resolution.' In *Restructuring the Korean Financial Market in a Global Economy,* (eds) Lee-Jay Cho, Yoon Hyung Kim and Inseok Shin. Seoul: Korea Development Institute, 91–141.

Shin, Inseok and Hongkyu Park (2001). *Historical Perspective on Korea's Bond Market: 1980 – 2000.* Working Paper, No. 2001–02. Seoul: Korea Development Institute (March).

Siamwalla, Ammar (2007). 'Thailand: The Financial System Ten Years after the Crisis.' *IDS Bulletin* Vol. 38, No. 4 (July), 40–4.

Sila-On, Amaret (1998). 'Thailand: Path of Financial Restructuring.' In *Regulatory and Supervisory Challenges in a New Era of Global Finance,* (ed.) Jan Joost Teunissen. The Hague: Forum on Debt and Development (FONDAD), 223–8.

Simmons, Beth A and Zachary Elkins (2003). 'Globalization and Policy Diffusion: Explaining Three Decades of Liberalization.' In *Governance in a Global Economy,* (eds) Miles Kahler and David A Lake. Princeton, New Jersey: Princeton University Press, 275–304.

Singh, Ranjit Ajit and Zainal Aznam Yusof (2002). 'Development of the Capital Market in Malaysia.' Paper presented in *The Role of Capital Markets in Asian Economic Development.* Tokyo: Tokyo Club Foundation for Global Studies (07–08 March).

Singh, Supriya (1984). *Bank Negara Malaysia: The First Twenty-Five Years, 1959–1984.* Kuala Lumpur: Bank Negara Malaysia.

Smith, Dwight (2008). *Asian Asset Management Companies in Retrospect.* Asia Focus. San Francisco: Federal Reserve Bank of San Francisco (September).

Streeck, Wolfgang and Kathleen Thelen (2005). 'Introduction: Institutional Change in Advanced Political Economies.' In *Beyond Continuity: Institutional Change in Advanced Political Economies,* (ed.) Wolfgang Streeck and Kathleen Thelen. 1–39.

Streeten, Paul (1996). 'Free and Managed Trade.' In *National Diversity and Global Capitalism,* (eds) Suzanne Berger and Ronald Dore. Ithaca, New York: Cornell University, 353–65.

Suehiro, Akira (1998). 'Mismatched Systems and Organizations: The Domestic Origins of the Thai Economic Crisis.' *Social Science Japan Newsletter* Vol. 13 (August), 20–2.

Sussangkarn, Chalongphob and Pakorn Vichyanond (2007). 'Ten Years after the Financial Crisis in Thailand: What Has Been Learned or Not Learned?' *Asian Economic Policy Review* Vol. 2, 100–18.

Tarullo, Daniel K (2009). 'Financial Regulation in the Wake of the Crisis.' Remarks presented at the Peterson Institute event, 'Global Financial Regulation Reform in the Wake of the Crisis'. (08 June).

Thai News Service (2001a). 'Committee Set up to Carry out Capital Market Master Plan.' *Thai News Service* (Bangkok), 04 September.

—— (2001b). 'Somkit Orders Team to Work out Capital Market Master Plan.' *Thai News Service* (Bangkok), 16 October.

—— (2004). 'Finance Minister, Capital Market-Related Organizations, and Business Sector Unit in Grand Workshop June 11–13.' *Thai News Service* (Bangkok), 09 June.

—— (2006a). 'Increasing Free Float Another Key Factor to Boosting Liquidity.' *Thai News Service* (Bangkok), 12 October.

—— (2006b). 'Thai Bourse and Others Implement 2nd Capital Market Master Plan.' *Thai News Service* (Bangkok), 24 April.

—— (2006c). 'Trading on Thai Bond Exchange Boosted by Real-Time Trading System.' *Thai News Service* (Bangkok), 04 July.

Thatcher, Mark (2002). 'Analysing Regulatory Reform in Europe.' *Journal of European Public Policy* Vol. 9, No. 6 (December), 859–72.

The Economist (1993). 'Islam and Economics in Malaysia.' *The Economist* (London), 07 August.

—— (1998). 'Thailand's Asset Sale.' *The Economist* (London), 19 December.

—— (2008). 'A Special Report on the World Economy: Shifting the Balance.' *The Economist* (London), 11 October.

—— (2009). 'Britain: More to Do.' *The Economist* (London), 25 July.

The Edge (2002). 'Roundtable on Islamic Banking – Going Forward, Going Global.' *The Edge* (Kuala Lumpur), 21 October.

The Hankyoreh (2008). 'S. Korea's Commercial Banks See Their Investment Banking Dreams Deferred.' *The Hankyoreh* (Seoul), 18 September.

The Nation (2002). 'Fund Aimed at Stoking Demand.' *The Nation* (Bangkok), 06 January.

—— (2004a). 'Bank of Asia: Comlink Considering Joint Bid.' *The Nation* (Bangkok), 13 February.

—— (2004b). 'Master Plan Aimed at Opening up Credit Channels.' *The Nation* (Bangkok), 21 May.

—— (2009). 'A Demise of the Washington Consensus.' *The Nation* (Bangkok), 09 February.

The Star (2009). 'Malaysia Liberalises Financial Sector.' *The Star* (Kuala Lumpur), 28 April.

Thelen, Kathleen (2004). *How Institutions Evolve: The Political Economy of Skills in Germany, Britain, the United States, and Japan*. Cambridge: Cambridge University Press.

Thillainathan, R (2003). 'Malaysia and the Asian Crisis: Lessons and Challenges.' In *Malaysian Economics and Politics in the New Century*, (eds) Colin Barlow and Francis Kok Wah Loh. Cheltenham, UK: Edward Elgar, 13–28.

Thomas, Abdulkader (2007). 'Islamic Finance Goes Global.' *Far Eastern Economic Review* (March).

Tsutsumi, Masahiko, Randall S Jones and Thomas F Cargill (2010). *The Korean Financial System: Overcoming the Global Financial Crisis and Addressing the Remaining Problems*. Working Papers, No. 796. Paris: OECD Economics Department.

Turner, Philip (2007). 'Are Banking Systems in East Asia Stronger?' *Asian Economic Policy Review* Vol. 2, 75–95.

Unger, Danny (1998). *Building Social Capital in Thailand: Fibers, Finance and Infrastructure*. Cambridge: Cambridge University Press.

Vajragupta, Yos and Pakorn Vichyanond (1999). 'Thailand's Financial Evolution and the 1997 Crisis.' In *East Asia's Financial Systems: Evolution and Crisis*, (eds) Seiichi Masuyama, Donna Vandenbrink and Siow Yue Chia. Singapore: Institute of Southeast Asian Studies, 34–73.

Varshney, Ashutosh (1989). 'Ideas, Interest and Institutions in Policy Change: Transformation of India's Agricultural Strategy in the Mid-1960s.' *Policy Sciences* Vol. 22, No. 3/4, 289–323.

Vestergaard, Jakob (2004). 'The Asian Crisis and the Shaping of 'Proper' Economies.' *Cambridge Journal of Economics* Vol. 28, No. 6, 809–27.

Vichyanond, Pakorn (1995). 'The Evolution of Thailand's Financial System: Future Trends.' *TDRI Quarterly Review* Vol. 10, No. 3 (September), 16–20.

—— (2007). 'Crucial Transitions in Thailand's Financial System after the 1997 Crisis.' Paper presented in *Asian Economic Panel 2007*. Brookings Institution (April).

Vitols, Sigurt (1997). 'The German Industrial Strategy: An Overview.' *Industry and Innovation* Vol. 4, No. 1, 15–36.

Volmer, Philipp B, Werner Richard Jörg and Jochen Zimmermann (2007). 'New Governance Modes for Germany's Financial Reporting System: Another Retreat of the Nation State?' *Socio-Economic Review* Vol. 5, 437–65.

Wade, Robert (2004). *Governing the Market: Economic Theory and the Role of Government in East Asian Industrialization*. Princeton, New Jersey: Princeton University Press.

—— (2007). 'A New Global Financial Architecture?' *New Left Review* Vol. 46 (July/August), 113–29.

Wade, Robert and Frank Veneroso (1998). 'The Asian Crisis: The High Debt Model Versus the Wall Street-Treasury-IMF Complex.' *New Left Review*, No. 228, 3–23.

Wailerdsak, Natenapha (2008). 'Companies in Crisis.' In *Thai Capital after the 1997 Crisis*, (eds) Pasuk Phongpaichit and Chris Baker. Singapore: Institute of Southeast Asian Studies, 17–57.

Walker, Andrew (2009). 'Will Tough New G20 Measures Work?' *BBC News* (Pittsburgh), 26 September.

Walker, Rupert (2008). 'Korea's "Big Bang" Could Turn into a Whimper.' *Business Week*, 29 September.

Wall Street Journal (1999). 'Malaysia's Mergers.' *Wall Street Journal*, 11 August.

Walter, Andrew (2007). 'Do Voluntary Standards Work among Governments? The Experience of International Financial Standards in East Asia.' In *Making Global Self-Regulation Effective in Developing Countries*, (eds) Dana Brown and Ngaire Woods. Oxford: Oxford University Press, 32–61.

—— (2008). *Governing Finance: East Asia's Adoption of International Standards*. Ithaca, New York: Cornell University Press.

Warde, Ibrahim (2000). *Islamic Finance in the Global Economy*. Edinburgh: Edinburgh University Press.

Watanagase, Tarisa and Financial Institutions Policy Group (2006). 'Maintaining Financial Stability: The Experience of Thailand.' In *The Banking System in Emerging Economies: How Much Progress Has Been Made?*, Vol. 28, (ed.) Bank for International Settlements. BIS Papers. Basel: Bank for International Settlements, 347–61.

Weisman, Jonathan and Alistair Macdonald (2009). 'Obama, Brown Strike Similar Notes on Economy.' *Wall Street Journal* (London), 03 April.

Weiss, Linda (1998). *The Myth of the Powerless State: Governing the Economy in a Global Era*. Cambridge: Polity Press in association with Blackwell.

—— (2003). 'Guiding Globalisation in East Asia: New Roles for Old Developmental States.' In *States in the Global Economy: Bringing Domestic Institutions Back In*, (ed.) Linda Weiss. Cambridge: Cambridge University Press, 245–70.

—— (2005). 'Global Governance, National Strategies: How Industrialized States Make Room to Move under the WTO.' *Review of International Political Economy* Vol. 12, No. 5 (December), 723–49.

—— (2010). 'The State in the Economy: Neoliberal or Neoactivist.' In *Oxford Handbook of Comparative Institutional Analysis*, (eds) Glenn Morgan, John L Campbell, Colin Crouch, Ove Kai Pedersen and Richard Whitley. Oxford: Oxford University Press.

Weiss, Linda and John M Hobson (2000). 'State Power and Economic Strength Revisited: What's So Special About the Asian Crisis?' In *Politics and Markets in the Wake of the Asian Crisis*, (eds) Richard Robison, Mark Beeson, Jayasuriya Kanishka and Hyuk-Rae Kim. London: Routledge, 53–74.

Westrup, Jonathan (2007). 'The Politics of Financial Regulatory Reform in Britain and Germany.' *West European Politics* Vol. 30, No. 5 (November), 1096–119.

Whitley, Richard (2005). 'How National Are Business Systems? The Role of Different State Types and Complemntary Institutions in Constructing Homogeneous Systems of Economic Coordination and Control.' In *Changing Capitalisms? Internationalization, Institutional Change, and Systems of Economic Organization*, (eds) Glenn Morgan, Richard Whitley and Eli Moen. Oxford: Oxford University Press, 190–231.

Williamson, John (1990). 'What Washington Means by Policy Reform.' In *Latin American Adjustment: How Much Has Happened*, (ed.) John Williamson. Washington, D.C.: Institute of International Economics, 5–20.

—— (2000). 'What Should the World Bank Think About the Washington Consensus?' *World Bank Research Observer* Vol. 15, No. 2 (August), 251–64.

—— (2009). *The 'Washington Consensus': Another near-Death Experience?* Realtime Economic Issues Watch. Washington, D.C.: Peterson Institute.

Womack, James P and Daniel T Jones (1990). *The Machine That Changed the World: The Story of Lean Production*. New York: Palgrave Macmillan.

Woo, Jung-En (1991). *Race to the Swift: State and Finance in Korean Industrialization*. New York: Columbia University Press.

Woo-Cumings, Meredith (1997). 'Slouching toward the Market: The Politics of Financial Liberalization in South Korea.' In *Capital Ungoverned: Liberalizing Finance in Interventionist States*, (eds) Michael Maurice Loriaux, Meredith Woo-Cumings, Kent E Calder, Sylvia Maxfield and Sofia A Perez. Ithaca, New York: Cornell University Press, 57–91.

World Bank (1993). *The East Asian Miracle: Economic Growth and Public Policy*. Oxford: Oxford University Press.

—— (2004). *East Asia Update – Malaysia Country Brief*. Washington, D.C.: World Bank (November).

World Trade Organization (2005). *Trade Policy Review: Malaysia*. No. WT/TPR/S/156. Geneva: World Trade Organization (12 December).

Yap, Michael Meow-Chung (2001). 'The 1997 Currency Crisis and Subsequent Policy Response.' In *Modern Malaysia in the Global Economy*, (ed.) Colin Barlow. Cheltenham, UK: Edward Elgar, 45–58.

Yeap, Cindy (2009). 'Bumiputera Equity Rule Redundant.' *The Edge* (Kuala Lumpur), 24 February.

Yeoh, Oon (2009). 'Najib's 100 Days, Pt 2.' *The Edge* (Kuala Lumpur), 12 July.

Yoon, Il-Hyun (2005). 'The Changing Role of the IMF: Evidence from Korea's Crisis.' *Asian Perspective* Vol. 29, No. 2, 179–201.

Yoon, Ja-young (2008). 'Language Barrier Stifles Financial Hub Plan.' *Korea Times* (Seoul), 01 June.

Yoshihara, Kunio (1988). *The Rise of Ersatz Capitalism in Southeast Asia*. Singapore: Oxford University Press.

Yun, Hing Ai (1987). 'The Financial System and Industrial Investment in West Malaysia.' *Journal of Contemporary Asia* Vol. 17, No. 4, 409–35.

Yusof, Zainal Aznam, Awang Adek Hussin, Ismail Alowi, Chee Sing Lim and Sukhdave Singh (1994). 'Financial Reform in Malaysia.' In *Financial Reform: Theory and Experience*, (eds) Gerard Caprio, Izak Atiyas and James A Hanson. Cambridge: Cambridge University Press, 276–320.

Yusuf, Shahid (2001). 'The East Asian Miracle at the Millenium.' In *Rethinking the East Asian Miracle*, (eds) Joseph E Stiglitz and Shahid Yusuf. New York: A co-publication of the World Bank and Oxford University Press, 1–53.

Yuthamanop, Parista (2008). 'CIMB Cleared for Majority Share in BT.' *Bangkok Post* (Bangkok), 10 October.

Zamani, Abdul Ghani (2006). 'Re-Engineering the Malaysian Financial System to Promote Sustainable Growth.' In *The Banking System in Emerging Economies: How Much Progress Has Been Made?*, Vol. 28, (ed.) Bank for International Settlements. BIS Papers. Basel: Bank for International Settlements, 269–75.

Zeti, Akhtar Aziz (2002). 'The Malaysian Banking Industry: Gearing up for Excellence.' Keynote address presented at the Malaysian Banking and Financial Services Summit 2002. Kuala Lumpur (20 May).

—— (2003). 'Governor's Keynote Address.' Keynote address given at the Asian Banker Summit 2003, 'Post-Asian Financial Crisis: Securing Financial Stability'. Kuala Lumpur (16 September).

—— (2004). 'Towards World-Class Banking – Efficient, Effective and Resilient Banking System.' Keynote address presented at the Malaysian Banking and Financial Services Summit 2004. Kuala Lumpur (14 May).

—— (2006). 'Extending the Boundaries in the New Financial Landscape.' Governor's Speech at the 10th Malaysian Banking, Finance and Insurance Summit: 'Liberalisation and Consolidation of Malaysian Banking and Finance Sector: Enhancing Competitiveness and Resilience of Our Economy'. Kuala Lumpur: Bank Negara Malaysia (09 June).

Zhang, Xiaoke (2003). The Changing Politics of Finance in Korea and Thailand: From Deregulation to Debacle. London: Routledge.

—— (2007). 'Political Parties and Financial Development: Evidence from Malaysia and Thailand.' *Journal of Public Policy* Vol. 27, No. 3, 341–74.

Zysman, John (1983). *Governments, Markets, and Growth: Financial Systems and the Politics of Industrial Change*. Ithaca, New York: Cornell University Press.

Index